Religious Freedom in America

D1607515

Studies in American Constitutional Heritage
Justin Wert and Kyle Harper, Series Editors

Religious Freedom in America

Constitutional Roots and Contemporary Challenges

Edited by
Allen D. Hertzke

Preface by
Kyle Harper

University of Oklahoma Press : Norman

Library of Congress Cataloging-in-Publication Data

Religious freedom in America : constitutional roots and contemporary
challenges / edited by Allen D. Hertzke ; preface by Kyle Harper.
    pages cm. — (Studies in American constitutional heritage ; volume 1)
  Includes index.
    ISBN 978-0-8061-4672-0 (hardcover : alk. paper)
    ISBN 978-0-8061-4707-9 (pbk. : alk. paper)   1. Freedom of religion—
United States.   2. Church and state—United States.   3. Religion and state—
United States.   I. Hertzke, Allen D., 1950–
    BR516.R375 2015
    323.44'20973—dc23   2014025253

Religious Freedom in America: Constitutional Roots and Contemporary Challenges
is Volume 1 in the Studies in American Constitutional Heritage series.

The paper in this book meets the guidelines for permanence and durability of
the Committee on Production Guidelines for Book Longevity of the Council
on Library Resources, Inc. ∞

1 2 3 4 5 6 7 8 9 10

To Barbara, always. . .

Contents

Illustrations

FIGURES

Preface

In March of 2014, Emily Bazelon, an editor for *Slate* magazine, wrote a column entitled "In Defense of Religious Liberty." The occasion for the piece was perhaps more interesting than its substance. With legal battles over the contraceptive coverage mandate and same-sex marriage looming in the courts, Bazelon worried that religious liberty itself was getting a bad name: "Religious liberty looks like a shield fundamentalists are throwing up against, well, sexual modernity." Even if the author's social and geographic horizons are not representative of a vast and deeply fragmented America, her observation says something important about the fragility of a constitutional value that is always more controversial and uncomfortable in application than in theory. Religious liberty is a central feature of the American constitutional regime, and as the United States becomes in decisive ways a more secular nation, the constitutional guarantees of disestablishment and free exercise are likely to become more, rather than less, significant. Hence, a thorough and clear-eyed understanding of the meaning, history, and value of religious liberty is an imperative for scholars and citizens alike.

The essays in this volume are meant to contribute to our understanding of the richness of the American constitutional heritage of religious liberty. At one level, the theme of religious freedom is a constitutional one, embedded in the jurisprudence of, principally, the First Amendment to the U.S. Constitution. But, as these essays make clear, if judicial interpretation of the First Amendment is the fuse box, the wiring of religious freedom extends throughout the entire structure of American society. What makes this set of essays unique, then, is the collective effort by a group of historians, social scientists, legal scholars, and advocates to hold a meaningful dialogue about the place of religious freedom in America, past and present. In the academy, "interdisciplinary" has been a buzzword for decades, more an ideal than a reality. These essays are hard proof that inter-disciplinary conversation is not only possible but highly valuable, encouraging us to make explicit our terms of inquiry and reminding us of the real-world implications of our scholarship.

An approach that includes history, theory, and doctrine, and an engagement between scholarship and practice, are at the heart of the mission of the Institute for the American Constitutional Heritage (IACH) at the University of Oklahoma, a program started in 2009 by University President David Boren to foster interdisci-plinary teaching and scholarship on American constitutionalism. The essays in this volume come out of the programming of the Institute's Religious Freedom Project, chaired by Allen Hertzke, which makes religious freedom a major theme of focus for the Institute. This volume is fittingly the first in a new series at the University of Oklahoma Press that will seek to bring fresh and genuinely interdisciplinary inquiry into the foundations of the American constitutional order.

As the essays attest, the theme of religious freedom demands multiple perspectives. The historians in this volume help us trace the contested legacy of religious freedom from the American found-ing to the nineteenth-century rise of public education to the succes-sive waves of immigration, each adding new layers of diversity to American society. All of these contributions insist on going beyond "law-office history" to achieve a more genuine grasp of the evolution of religious freedom and the persistently controversial character of its meaning. The social scientists call attention to the striking and swift effects of judicial decision-making, and open our eyes to the wide and diffuse battleground over free exercise in a complex, bureaucratic society. The advocates remind us that tensions abide in the most familiar institutional domains, such as schools, and that religious minorities have played, and still play, a major role in shap-ing the meaning of free exercise in the constitutional regime. The jurists make one thing clear: here is an exceedingly messy area of constitutional law. The interpretation of the First Amendment is messy, in part because of a tension at its very core between free exercise and disestablishment. It is messy in part because of political tensions between legislative and judicial branches of government. Ultimately, it is messy because the boundaries of religion, state, and society are complex and ever shifting.

This complexity is revealed in two undercurrents that course throughout this book. Religious freedom has been, and remains, an instrument of protection for vulnerable religious minorities, as the stories of American Sikhs and Muslims in this volume reveal. At the same time, religious freedom is ever more frequently invoked by those holding once-mainstream views, especially regarding marriage and reproductive issues, for accommodation within an increasingly secular culture. This paradox explains the contradiction that Bazelon recently found herself trying to understand within contemporary constitutional politics. But as the essays in this volume remind us, religious liberty is so essential to America's civic fabric that, whatever the outcome of various contests, we can only hope it never earns a "bad name."

Kyle Harper

Acknowledgments

This volume grew out of the inaugural symposium of the "Religious Freedom Project" of the Institute for the American Constitutional Heritage (IACH) at the University of Oklahoma. I am profoundly indebted to the founding director of IACH, Kyle Harper, for his interdisciplinary vision and support in bringing together this top-flight group of scholars to plumb the constitutional roots and contemporary horizons of religious liberty in America. The superlative staff at IACH also played a crucial role in making the symposium a success and in bringing this volume to fruition.

I am deeply grateful to the President of the University of Oklahoma, David Boren. In creating the IACH, he has elevated America's constitutional heritage to a central place in this university's research, teaching, and outreach. But I am especially thankful for his personal support of the Religious Freedom Project I direct under the auspices of IACH.

Thanks go to my departmental home, the Political Science Department, and the many colleagues who inspire my endeavors. I am also indebted to my students, whose questions and insights have informed my explorations of religious liberty as a fundamental constitutional value. Special thanks go to my longtime undergraduate research assistant, Gabriella Skillings, who adroitly kept me on track as I navigated this project and competing tasks.

I am particularly obliged to the University of Oklahoma Press,
and to its energetic Editor-in-Chief, Charles Rankin, for the superb
work in publishing this book. I am also thankful for the two
anonymous readers for the Press, whose suggestions turned out to
be pivotal in expanding the coverage and enhancing the clarity of
the volume.

Finally, there is one person without whose support I literally
would not be where I am today or doing projects like this one. She
is my married partner of thirty-six years, Barbara Norton—sage coun-
selor, muse, sounding board, coach, inspiration, and more. Since
there is no way to adequately credit Barbara's influence, I am left
simply to express my undying love—and dedicate this book to her.

Allen D. Hertzke
May 2014
Norman, Oklahoma

Religious Freedom in America

Introduction

A Madisonian Framework for Applying Constitutional Principles on Religion

Allen D. Hertzke

Religious liberty in America is much in the news today, a major flashpoint of political battles, court challenges, public mobilization, lobby campaigns, and sermons from a host of pulpits. Most visibly we see this in the clash between religious interests and the Obama administration over the so-called contraceptive mandate in the Affordable Care Act, as well as in emerging tensions between gay marriage and religious rights.

But these high-profile struggles mask a deeper, more widespread set of challenges to religious freedom in the United States, the very cradle of religious liberty. Consider:

- 2006: Boston Catholic Charities shuts down an historic adoption program after the State of Massachusetts refuses conscience accommodation in license requirement.[1]
- 2006: Morristown, New York, begins prosecuting Amish home-builders for code violations.[2]
- 2007: In order to maximize tax revenue, the city of Leon Valley, Texas, changed its zoning laws to ban churches entirely from its large retail corridor (overturned in circuit court in 2012).[3]
- 2007: A request by the Christian Science Church to demolish an ugly and dysfunctional building in downtown Washington, D.C., is denied when historical preservationists have the structure declared a landmark example of "Brutalist" architecture (overturned after two-year legal battle).[4]

- 2009: The U.S. Equal Opportunity Employment Commission rules that Belmont Abbey College in North Carolina violated discrimination laws by not offering birth control in its health plan coverage.[5]
- 2009: A federal court of appeals affirms a school district's veto of a public school student ensemble's musical selection, Franz Biebl's "Ave Maria," for a graduation program, even though it was an entirely instrumental piece.[6]
- 2009: A family court in Laconia, New Hampshire, orders a Christian mother to stop home schooling her daughter, who was excelling in a curriculum approved by the school district, because she "appeared to reflect her mother's rigidity on questions of faith."[7]
- 2010: Directors at a senior citizen center near Savannah, Georgia, ban residents from praying aloud before meals.[8]
- 2010: Faced with mandates that violate church teaching on marriage, Catholic Charities of Washington, D.C., shuts down its foster care program.[9]
- 2011: Three Illinois diocese adoption and foster care programs shut down for the same reason.[10]
- 2010–14: After the Supreme Court upholds a University of California Law School policy denying the right of religious clubs to select leaders according to faith tenets, numerous colleges bar Christian student groups from campus recognition.[11]
- 2011: The U.S. Department of Health and Human Services (HHS) ends its contract with the U.S. Conference of Catholic Bishops for services to human trafficking victims after insisting that such services include abortion referral and contraceptives.[12]
- 2011: Alabama law makes it illegal for churches to serve undocumented immigrants, including providing baptisms, hearing confessions, anointing the sick, giving marriage counseling, and providing Sunday school, Bible studies, or Alcoholics Anonymous (AA) meetings at church.[13]
- 2012: The New York City Board of Education orders the end of church rental of school buildings on weekends.[14]
- 2012: A local judge in Murfreesboro, Tennessee, blocks Muslims from using their new mosque on the eve of Ramadan (overturned after lawsuit).[15]

- 2012: A Pew Research Center report finds significant rise in restrictions on religion in the United States, both from government actions and social hostilities.[16]
- 2012–14: Facing huge fines for violating religious principles, over three hundred religious institutions and businesses file lawsuits against the HHS contraceptive mandate.[17]

At first glance there seems to be no pattern here. These vignettes cover local actions and national policies; administrative edicts and legislative acts; major precedents and idiosyncratic decrees; temporary setbacks and permanent outcomes. What unites these disparate examples, I would submit, is the lack of weight given to religious claims or needs, and a corresponding ignorance about the contributions of religious communities to a vibrant civil society.

Why is this so? Why now? The explanation lies, in part, in the erosion of the intellectual appreciation of the pivotal role of religious liberty in the American constitutional heritage. Combined with the innate hegemonic impulse of the modern regulatory state, this amnesia erodes the legal protections for the autonomy of religious communities, institutions, and individuals in America.

We see this amnesia among some statist conservatives, such as Justice Antonin Scalia, who conjure visions of chaos if religious conscience rights are accorded significant weight in law. We see it among certain secularists who would strip religion of its privileged status in our constitutional order. Brian Leiter's book, *Why Tolerate Religion*, is but the most extreme example of the skepticism, indifference, or outright hostility toward religion (and, by implication, religious freedom) we sometimes see in academic, media, and cultural circles.[18] Less polemical thinkers merely contend that religious liberty is redundant, that protections for freedom of speech, association, and assembly are sufficient in a modern pluralist society.

Other legal scholars see the need to balance religious freedom against competing claims, such as gender equality, and often draw inspiration from the influential work of John Rawls.[19] Rawls argued that comprehensive religious ideas are incompatible with liberal political norms and therefore must not be the basis for public policy and law. As such, his formulation provides leverage to those who would privilege other social goals against religious freedom claims. Professor Leslie Griffin provides the most systematic treatment of this view.[20] She is particularly concerned with the capacity of patriarchal religious institutions to stifle women's rights. To her, the Rawlsian formulation provides a justification to limit such religious institutional autonomy.[21]

While understandable in light of particular policy preferences, the Rawlsian formulation actually provides a limiting principle versus a real framework for grounding religious freedom. Rawls' argument about illegitimacy of religious arguments in the public square indeed produces a chilling climate for religious expression, and provides reasons to allow a plethora of other political claims to trump religious rights.

This limiting principle even reaches beyond our shores, impeding the promotion of religious rights around the world, as Thomas Farr discovered when he served as the first director of the State Department Office of International Religious Freedom.[22] As Farr recounts, colleagues at the State Department often employed Rawlsian arguments to justify their resistance to the congressional law mandating the promotion of religious freedom as a "basic aim" of American foreign policy.

In sum, if there is nothing special about religious claims, or if they are viewed as retrograde or nettlesome to orderly law, then we should not be surprised by the erosion of religious freedom. Indeed, without a solid grounding for the defense of religious rights, just about any public aim—even historical preservation—can potentially trump religious exercise. But if modern "innovations" are more limiting principles than serious philosophical and constitutional grounds to guarantee religious liberty, what is the best grounding?

I submit that such grounding can be found in the thought and work of James Madison. Not only was Madison the principal author of the First Amendment, but he also provided the clearest, most robust justification for the defense of conscience rights and religious liberty of the founding generation. But more than this, he articulated timeless principles that constitute "articles of peace" for societies around the world.[23] This achievement flowed from the way Madison drew upon theological insights about the innate human quest for transcendent meaning—the violation of which breaches fundamental rights and disturbs the social order. Remarkably, he anticipated the constitutional, historical, philosophical, and sociological grounds for religious liberty that I present in this introductory essay.

To be sure, Madison's rich corpus of work inspires contrasting interpretations, depending on the particular lens of investigation. In this volume, Muñoz focuses on the question of religious exemptions from civic duty, Tepker on the implications of equality before the law, and Green on the historical legacy of Madison's fierce opposition to religious establishments. In contrast, I zero in on his core conviction about the nature of religious obligations in a free society.

Madison's ideas flowed from a deep wellspring of religious experience and reflection in the American colonies, not just from abstract enlightenment ideas. Indeed, he drew inspiration from the heroes of conscience—Quakers, Baptists, and others—who endured persecution and developed theologies of religious liberty that would underpin his own formulations.

The most fascinating of these heroes was Roger Williams, the fiercely independent pastor and theologian of the mid-seventeenth century.[24] While initially welcomed by Puritan leaders in Massachusetts, he put himself at odds with authorities by preaching against state-enforced religion and condemning colonial charters for failing to purchase land from the Indians. Banished from Puritan Massachusetts in 1635, he went on to found Providence Plantation colony as a haven of religious liberty. While in England seeking a charter for Rhode Island, he penned his famous tract, "The Bloody Tenet of Persecution for the Cause of Religion," which was published in England in 1644.[25] In it he made the timeless argument that religious faith, to be genuine, must be free. The ground for that liberty, moreover, was "soul freedom," the doctrine that all people must have the right to follow their convictions on religious matters, because conscience itself is from God.

It is instructive to read the "Bloody Tenet of Persecution" side by side with John Locke's celebrated *A Letter Concerning Toleration*, published more than four decades later.[26] In both documents we see similar arguments about how coercion not only violates authentic Christianity—indeed, it represents a kind of heresy—but that such persecution traduces evangelization by suggesting that the good news is not compelling enough on its own. In addition, both Williams and Locke document the way persecution harms societies, unleashes convulsions, undermines economic life, and disrupts political order.

But Williams the theologian developed a far more consistent, radical, and sweeping argument for soul freedom and the rights of conscience than Locke the enlightenment philosopher. Locke would not extend toleration to Catholics because they pledge fealty to a

*Madison: theol.
heir + enlighten-
ment. pol. commit.*

foreign potentate (the Pope), or to atheists because they cannot be trusted to keep their oaths. Williams argued from entirely theological grounds that because conscience is God-given and sacred, all people—Catholics, non-believers, women, Indians, Muslims—are equally entitled, indeed called, to seek ultimate truths and to act on the transcendent obligations those truths demand. He shared with the Puritans of Massachusetts the conviction that Quakers were profoundly wrong and damned if they did not recant their heresy. But while Boston hung Quakers, Williams challenged them to theological debate.[27]

Contrary to the secularist narrative of the enlightenment triumph over fanatical religion as the foundation for religious toleration and liberal freedoms,[28] religious thinkers like Williams (and others after him) made the pivotal theological case for religious freedom. Because they spoke in the idioms of a pervasively religious culture, they paved the way for the First Amendment as surely as enlightenment skeptics and free thinkers—probably more so, as Thomas Kidd shows vividly in this volume.

Madison was as much an heir to this theological tradition as he was a child of the enlightenment. That synthesis, it seems to me, helped produce with such clarity and consistency the forceful conviction that religious liberty is foundational to the new order he helped to create. And, as I will show, it enabled him to identify and articulate a timeless principle now being validated through global events and empirical research.

Like Williams, Madison grounded religious freedom in the sacredness of conscience and the corresponding right to fulfill obligations flowing from it. Because of this conviction, Madison consistently employed the robust language of "free exercise" in defending religious liberty. Unlike Jefferson, who would only shield "religious opinions" from state regulation (as Muñoz shows), Madison's formulation suggested the right to *act* on the dictates of conscience. Unfortunately, much mischief has resulted from courts relying on Jefferson's pinched "belief–action" distinction rather than Madison's more expansive free exercise language actually contained in the First Amendment.

Remarkably, we see the clarity of this conviction from the very beginning of Madison's public career. On the eve of Independence, at the age of 25, Madison found himself embroiled in a battle to define religious liberty. The Virginia Declaration of Rights, drafted by George Mason in May of 1776, included this clause: "All men should enjoy the fullest toleration in the exercise of religion, according to the dictates of conscience." Madison was troubled by the language of "toleration," which to him suggested a fragile condescension that could be removed at will. So instead he successfully lobbied to amend the language to incorporate the "free exercise" of religion and then anchored this right in transcendent obligations. The final provision read: "That religion, or the duty which we owe to our Creator, and the manner of discharging it, can be directed only by reason and conviction, not by force or violence; and therefore all men are equally entitled to the free exercise of religion, according to the dictates of conscience."[29]

A decade later Madison would echo this sentiment in his 1785 essay, "Memorial and Remonstrance Against Religious Assessments," which serves as a kind of Ur text of American religious liberty.[30] Once again, he anchored religious liberty in the dictates of transcendent obligations: "Before any man can be considered a member of civil society, he must be considered as a subject of the Governor of the Universe." Consequently, "Religion, or the duty which we owe to our Creator . . . is precedent, both in order of time and in degree of obligation, to the claims of civil society. . . . In matters of religion," therefore, "no man's right is abridged by the institution of Civil Society."

Madison, of course, went on to introduce the Bill of Rights as amendments in the first Congress. While he failed to extend First Amendment protections to the states, he succeeded in retaining the sweeping language of "free exercise." The consistency and clarity of Madison's thought provides a key way to grasp, and apply, an essential principle of the First Amendment. Philosophically and constitutionally, religious liberty is the "first freedom" because it embodies a person's highest, especially transcendent, obligations. Indeed, the most compelling justification for religious liberty is the freedom of conscience, the freedom to fulfill obligations—especially sacred duties—which flow from an authority higher than the state. Or, as Cardinal Newman put it, "Conscience has rights because it has duties."[31] And contrary to the claim that the principle of conscience rights is inherently individualistic—that it ignores the corporate dimension of religious freedom—it extends to the freedom of the church in its institutional expression.[32]

A key measure of a free society, in sum, is the extent to which people are not forced to choose between sacred duties and citizenship privileges or obligations. This is what makes religious freedom foundational to the American constitutional order. It anchors the flowering of independent civil society, cultivates inter-religious amity, and provides a crucial limit on state power. As the Supreme Court proclaimed in its landmark 1943 case, *West Virginia v. Barnette*, there is a zone of liberty that the state cannot, and must not, violate.

To be sure, no principle can encompass every dimension of such a rich concept as religious liberty, nor does the most lucid principle release us from grappling with thorny questions and tough trade-offs. But as we will see, profound and practical constitutional implications flow from grounding of religious liberty in what I have described as this Madisonian formulation. First, it suggests that law should protect "religious freedom in full," not as a private right to worship but as the right to act on the highest obligations, the deepest human aspirations. In other words, it is a fundamental right deserving of high scrutiny and generous accommodation.

Now, the proof of a principle is its coherence and fruitfulness. The Madisonian principle I have sketched—that religious freedom is foundational, the first freedom, ontologically prior to one's obligations to the state—provides real guidance and inspiration in a host of interrelated arenas. It serves as a reliable lodestar for First Amendment constitutional law. It offers practical policy direction, as Charles Haynes shows in his account of successful efforts to craft a consensus approach on religion in the public schools. It has inspired—and continues to inspire—the popular constitutionalism of religious minorities, whose struggle to live by their transcendent lights has profoundly etched the contours of our jurisprudence. It has shaped societal norms and a culture of general religious amity—what Putnam and Campbell call "American Grace."[33] It provides genuine leverage for religious claimants with bureaucratic officials ignorant or hostile to the demands and civil benefits of religious life. It serves as a vital check on government, especially the hegemonic impulse of the modern state. Finally, it has global implications because the United States has played, and continues to play, a singular role in upholding international norms and covenants on religious rights.

POPULAR CONSTITUTIONALISM AND JURISPRUDENCE

American jurisprudence, when informed by the idea that religious liberty embodies the right to fulfill mandates of conscience, broadly accommodates religious minorities, aids in the assimilation of diverse immigrants, and checks overweening state power. On the other hand, when religious liberty is understood in limited terms as a right to religious opinions or private worship, state infringement is inevitable.

Recall the famous Flag Salute cases of the 1940s. The Supreme Court, adhering to Jefferson's belief–action distinction, originally provided no protection for Jehovah's Witness children to resist what they saw as idolatry in saluting the flag. The Court's decision in *Minersville v. Gobitis* (1940), upholding the requirement that all children do so, produced immediate harm to that religious community. Children were expelled, harassed, beaten up, or removed to expensive private schools. Witnesses refused to buckle because they fervently believed both in the obligations of their faith and in the principles of religious liberty promised in the First Amendment. Scholars at the time also saw the wider threat to religious freedom of this precedent, especially with the growing reach of the regulatory state. When the Court dramatically reversed itself three years later in *West Virginia v. Barnette* (1943), it signaled that the abridgement of conscience need not be, as William Galston put it, "unfortunate collateral damage" of law, that the state could pursue its purposes in ways that minimize the burden on religious practice. That which gives "meaning and purpose to life," as Galston concluded, must enjoy elevated status in a free society, requiring that the state justify its interference with conscience-based claims.[34]

Though questioned in certain legal and intellectual circles, this view remains a strong element of the American DNA, providing crucial levers for vulnerable religious communities, and not just through the courts. The First Amendment heritage cultivates the hope and expectation that one need not—and should not—compromise religious identity or abandon transcendent duties to participate fully in society. That promise has motivated diverse religious minorities to assert their claims in society and law.

As Rajdeep Singh and Asma Uddin demonstrate in this volume, this promise today inspires American Sikhs and Muslims to press for their rights, forges allies in that struggle, and provides real leverage in their legal and lobbying campaigns. In France, as Singh notes, the secular state insists that Sikhs violate religious duty—the wearing of the turban that signifies fidelity to God—to achieve equal rights and societal participation. But the American constitutional heritage offers the real prospect—though not without struggle—that here you can "be who you are."[35]

The story of American Sikhs especially illustrates how the struggles of religious minorities etch generous boundaries for religious free exercise and carve space for those who follow. Similarly, past efforts that curb religious freedom for one community inevitably redound to others. These are the twin lessons of the 1923 Oregon law preventing public school teachers from wearing religious garb. A legacy of the anti-Catholic campaign by the Ku Klux Klan, a bigoted law originally targeting Catholic nuns extended its tentacles over time, preventing Orthodox Jews, Muslim women who wear headscarfs, and Sikhs from teaching in Oregon public schools. Drawing upon the nation's rich heritage of conscience rights and religious liberty, Sikhs spearheaded a broad coalition of Baptists, Adventists, Catholics, Jews, Muslims, and others that overturned the law. Signifying the common ground of the campaign, a Seventh Day Adventist organization subsequently gave its annual religious freedom award to the Baptist legislator who sponsored the law sought by Sikhs.[36]

Asma Uddin, as a Muslim scholar and legal advocate, underscores how the constitutional ideal of religious liberty helps American Muslims confront discrimination and carves spaces for participation in civil society. But her account also illuminates how the generous guarantee of religious rights produces a flourishing of intellectual, artistic, and popular expressions of Islamic culture. In other words, American Muslims find they can express their Islamic faith and culture more authentically under conditions of freedom than under state-enforced, and often competing, doctrines of "proper" Islam found in many Muslim-majority societies. This would not surprise Roger Williams or James Madison.

A BRIEF HISTORY OF STRICT SCRUTINY

While popular constitutionalism draws upon the sweeping promise of religious liberty in the First Amendment, jurisprudence resides in the more arid and technical realm of legal tests and standards. But sometimes the two realms coincide.[37]

That is what occurred in the decades following the Witnesses victory in *Barnette*, as the Court developed an exacting standard by which to weigh governmental burdens on conscience rights and religious liberty. Haltingly at first, and then with greater clarity and conviction, the Court developed a relatively coherent, expansive, and popular doctrine to apply the free exercise clause. Anchoring religious liberty in the universal need—and right—to fulfill transcendent mandates, the Court employed the standard of "strict scrutiny"—the highest level of protection for fundamental rights—to weigh religious claims. Whatever one may think of the constitutional validity of such a move, it treated religious obligations with a gravity that seems consonant with the spirit of the Madisonian formulation that such obligations are ontologically prior to the claims of the state. By according such weight to religious liberty, the Court provided real leverage to religious individuals, communities, and institutions confronting the expanding regulatory reach of modern government.

The doctrine of strict scrutiny, however, never entailed the anarchy of "every conscience as a law unto itself," as critics contend. Rather, the doctrine established a test by which to adjudicate competing demands of law and religion. That test is this: when state actions impose a substantial burden on religious free exercise, the state must use "the least restrictive means of achieving a compelling governmental interest."

The Court first articulated this expansive free exercise doctrine in *Sherbert v. Verner* (1963), ruling in favor of a Seventh Day Adventist who had been fired and denied workers compensation for refusing to work on Saturday, her Sabbath. Under the compelling interest test, the government could not simply show a "plausible" or "rational" objective when its laws burdened religious liberty. The government's goal must be fundamentally important, even necessary, and in meeting that goal it must burden religious practice as little as possible.

The Court applied this standard in another landmark case, *Wisconsin v. Yoder* (1972), ruling that the Wisconsin law mandating that Amish attend school beyond the eighth grade would undermine the way of life of this religious minority. In making its decision, the Court reiterated that it will not permit encroachments on religious liberty, even by neutral laws of general applicability, unless required by compelling governmental interests "of the highest order."

Compelling state interest was the Court's free exercise standard for nearly three decades, providing grounds for litigants to gain reasonable accommodations in the application of bureaucratic mandates. Generally, the state prevailed when public health and safety were at stake. On the other hand, religious claimants often gained relief when accommodating their beliefs did not seem to contravene any compelling governmental interest, or when remedies were readily available.

The apparently settled nature of free exercise law was shattered when the Supreme Court departed from prior decisions in *Employment Division of Oregon v. Smith* (1990). The *Smith* case involved two Native Americans who sought unemployment benefits from the state of Oregon after being fired from jobs at a drug rehabilitation clinic for using peyote, a hallucinogen, as part of a traditional Indian religious ritual. The Court could have decided narrowly in favor of Oregon on the grounds that a compelling state interest required the state to uphold its criminal drug statutes.

Instead, Justice Scalia shocked legal scholars and religious leaders across the political and theological spectrum by striking at strict scrutiny itself. In his majority opinion, Scalia approvingly quoted Frankfurter's statist reasoning in *Gobitis* that conscience claims must never be allowed to trump state policy—failing to note, famously, that *Gobitis* had been overturned. Scalia feared that applying strict scrutiny to all public policy "would be courting anarchy" because many laws, in fact, "will not meet the compelling interest test." Forcing judges to weigh the importance of laws against religious beliefs, he argued, is a "luxury" we "cannot afford."

The sweeping judgment in *Smith* troubled Justice Sandra Day O'Connor, who joined in the majority decision but argued later, in her dissent in *City of Boerne v. Flores* (1997), that the ruling was "wrongly decided," and cited numerous Court interpretations of the free exercise clause that were "gravely at odds" with *Smith*. Constitutional scholars, most prominently Michael McConnell, further documented—in prodigious historical detail—the legal critique of the *Smith* decision and its profound implications for religious freedom.[38]

The ruling galvanized virtually the entire American religious landscape, in part because every faith can envision itself as a vulnerable minority in some situation. But more than this, every congregation, every religious group, every social ministry, every parochial school, every religious institution can imagine instances where the regulatory application of supposedly neutral laws would burden its freedom, conscience, and autonomy, especially if regulations were administered by officials indifferent or hostile to minority faiths or religion in general.

Scalia's attack on strict scrutiny sparked a remarkable alliance to press Congress to restore the compelling state interest test. The American Civil Liberties Union lobbied alongside the Traditional Values Coalition, the National Council of Churches with the National Association of Evangelicals, liberal Jews with fundamentalist home-schoolers, Sikhs with Southern Baptists, Mormons with tribal religionists, Muslims with Catholics—all united in their attempt to recover the guarantee of religious freedom.

The legislative result was the Religious Freedom Restoration Act (RFRA), which states that "government shall not substantially burden a person's exercise of religion even if the burden results from a rule of general applicability," unless that rule employs the "least restrictive means of furthering" a "compelling governmental interest." The law was passed almost unanimously by Congress and signed into law with much fanfare by President Clinton in 1993.

Congress acted out of its authority under Section 5 of the Constitution's Fourteenth Amendment, which gives Congress the power to "enforce" the rest of the amendment's provisions. These include the constitutional guarantee that no state may deprive any person of "life, liberty, or property without due process of law," which the Supreme Court has interpreted as "incorporating" state-level actions under the umbrella of the Constitution's religion clauses.

But just four years after the enactment of RFRA, the Supreme Court struck down its core in *Boerne v. Flores* (1997). That case involved a Catholic Church in Boerne, Texas, that outgrew its building and sought a permit to expand. The Boerne City Council, citing historic preservation, denied the application. The archbishop challenged the city government in federal court, claiming religious freedom trumped local preservation ordinances under RFRA. The Court responded by holding RFRA's application to state and local governments unconstitutional, claiming that Congress had not merely "enforced" provisions of the Fourteenth Amendment but instead had attempted to "define" what the amendment means, which the Court said was its prerogative.

In the face of broad public support for expansive guarantees of religious freedom, the Supreme Court, in effect, insisted on a more pinched interpretation. While legal scholars debated the merits of the Court's stance, this ruling sparked a number of states (including Oklahoma) to pass their own versions of RFRA, indicating the popular support for generous protections of religious liberty.

The rapid sequence from *Smith* to RFRA to *Boerne* also produced that rare phenomenon in the social world: a natural experiment. Thus, we can systematically compare what jurisprudence is like with a judicially enforced compelling interest standard (before *Smith*), without a compelling interest standard (after *Smith*, 1990–93), with it reinstated legislatively (after RFRA, 1994–97), and finally with it reinstated only in some states (after *Boerne*).

The results of the experiment are compelling, as Martin and Finke show in this volume. They first summarize early research by Finke and Wybraniec involving 1,300 free exercise cases from 1981 to 1996. Before *Smith* undercut strict scrutiny, religious litigants won favorable court decisions in 40 percent of the cases. After *Smith*, that dropped to 28 percent, but then it rebounded to more than 45 percent after RFRA was enacted legislatively.

Court cases alone, however, do not account for the profound shift in negotiating strength at the day-to-day level, where the free exercise claimant encounters a nonaccommodating bureaucrat. Under the shield of compelling interest, many disputes never reached the courts because the threat of litigation forced authorities to accommodate religious claimants. Shorn of this protection, religious claimants no longer have the leverage to shield the imperatives of their faith, or the autonomy of their institutions, from intrusive government, as we saw in the litany of examples at the beginning of this chapter.

Martin and Finke bring the empirical analysis forward by analyzing free exercise cases in state courts, to measure the impact of state level protections of religious liberty. This is vital because, in the wake of *Boerne*, half of the states have either enacted their own RFRA laws or had state Supreme Court decisions providing enhanced leverage for religious claimants seeking accommodation.[39] Martin and Finke find that standards matter. When states operate with some version of strict or high-level scrutiny, religious claimants gain relief far more often. But the authors also find that, absent a national standard, such success does not rise to the levels we saw after RFRA and before *Boerne*.

While the empirical record is clear, legal scholars continue to question the application of strict scrutiny as a proper constitutional tool, because it is often cast in legal discourse as solely a demand for "religious exemptions" from legitimate laws. We hear this view from Justice Scalia on the right to Leslie Griffin on the left,[40] and even from defenders of religious freedom, such as Philip Hamburger and Gerard Bradley.[41] Understood this way, religious freedom is vulnerable. Not only has the Supreme Court largely abandoned this test, but even some who are sympathetic to religious claims cannot find grounds for defending strict scrutiny understood this way. For example, in this volume Muñoz asserts that James Madison never intended for the first amendment to excuse a person of the obligation to follow legitimately enacted law. Even if that is the case, Madison could never have imagined the extent to which the regulatory state seeps into every nook and cranny of life, and the way law is not that which is passed by legislatures but instead flows from a host of regulatory bodies with broad delegated authority at all levels of government.

But as Cole Durham shows, religious freedom understood in Madisonian terms as the right to fulfill transcendent obligations— or, as I put it, *religious freedom in full*, not the anemic private right to worship or the truncated right under Rawls—requires that the state justify its intrusions, not the other way around.[42] In some cases this principle requires that state infringements be struck down entirely. In other cases it requires regulatory relief for religious claimants. Thus, we should dash the image of religious believers as "begging" for this exemption or that—such nettlesome people! Rather, protecting and accommodating their religious freedom should be seen as a pivotal check on the vast coercive powers of the state. This understanding of the First Amendment seems more in the spirit of Madison and Williams than the dismissal of strict scrutiny as merely a ground for granting exemptions. Moreover, those who reject the compelling interest test but believe in generous protections for religious liberty must formulate, it seems to me, a standard at least as efficacious as the one they are abandoning.[43]

THE REVENGE OF RFRA

RFRA sought to reinstate legislatively the strict scrutiny standard of adjudicating burdens on religious free exercise. At the time of its passage, most religious petitioners were seeking relief from actions of state and local agencies or schools, so the Supreme Court's ruling in *Boerne* denying RFRA's application to state and local governments was seen as a devastating blow to generous religious accommodation.

But the Supreme Court upheld RFRA's application to federal government actions. Thus, when the battle over the federal contraceptive mandate surfaced in 2012, it catapulted RFRA to the center of the legal struggle. As Robin Fretwell Wilson recounts in her chapter, the clash over the HHS regulation erupted in news, blogs, editorials, publications, proclamations, church bulletins, and letters read from the pulpits of thousands of parishes. It became the subject of congressional lobbying, litigation, presidential debates, and party platforms. That agitation propelled a national conversation about the meaning of the First Amendment, the contours of religious liberty, and the appropriate powers and limits of government.

The mandate also spawned prodigious litigation. Two years after promulgation it was challenged in some ninety-three separate lawsuits representing over three hundred institutions and individuals. Virtually all the suits invoked RFRA's compelling interest test along with the First Amendment.[44] As Wilson notes, the government had far less intrusive means of extending contraceptive coverage than mandating that religious bodies violate their conscience rights.

Initially, a number of lower courts issued injunctions against enforcement of the mandate, citing the likelihood that it would fail the test that the federal government employ the least restrictive means of achieving a compelling governmental interest. Most notably, the Tenth Circuit Court found in favor of Hobby Lobby, the Christian-owned craft chain, in its lawsuit against the government. The federal government appealed this ruling, arguing that a business is by definition a secular enterprise and thus cannot gain relief under the First Amendment or RFRA. But for the Green family, the owners of Hobby Lobby, the business has always been an integral expression of their faith. In a press statement challengiing the HHS contraceptive mandate, David Green observed that his parents were pastors, his siblings are all involved in ministry, and he sees Hobby Lobby as part of his religious vocation: "We have always operated our company in a manner consistent with Biblical principles . . . Therefore, we seek to honor him [God] in all that we do."[45]

The Court had never faced the issue of whether business owners have religious free exercise rights, so this case (and companion cases) provided an ideal opportunity to test that landmark proposition.

Ironically, when the Supreme Court ruled in favor of the Greens, on June 30, 2014, it found itself guided by the very law (RFRA), and principle (strict scrutiny), it previously spurned.[46]

Conscience protections, as Wilson notes, have a long and distinguished history, both in law and popular constitutionalism. This flows from the Madisonian logic that conscience is a demanding mentor of the highest order, and that the overweening state always presents a threat to this fundamental aspect of human dignity. As we see in the battle between the Catholic Church and other religious bodies over the HHS contraceptive mandate, the crucial concern was that the government arrogated to itself defining what motivations are sufficiently religious to earn some accommodation from the mandate. As the courts have often noted, one need not share a person's sense of sacred duty to recognize and respect it.

This idea undergirded the public campaign against the mandate. Representing the Becket Fund for Religious Liberty, Asma Uddin argued in testimony before Congress that even Jesus's ministry would not qualify as "religious" under the original HHS rule, which only accommodated religious bodies that serve their own members or those who share their beliefs. As Uddin reminded the committee, in Matthew 25 and in the parable of the Good Samaritan, Jesus teaches that we truly fulfill our obligations to God when succoring those who *are not* of our own tribe or faith.

But other traditions can be invoked as well. In the Quran, Sura 5:48 states that, had God willed, he could have created one people with one faith, but instead created many people with many faiths so that they could "vie one with another in virtue."[47] If the state supplants, undermines, or limits civil society, then believers and church institutions are not able to vie one with another in virtue, competing to see who can do the greatest works of mercy. Rather, we will increasingly see shuttered charities or secularized ones.

SAME-SEX MARRIAGE, HEIGHTENED SCRUTINY, AND RELIGIOUS LIBERTY

The concern that government will undermine religious civil society looms large in the emerging gay marriage debate. Indeed, on the heels of the revolution in attitudes and law that would redefine marriage to include same-sex unions, we have already seen the closure of religious adoption agencies, the banning of college religious clubs that adhere to traditional Christian teachings on sexuality and marriage, and fines for religious vendors of marriage services. Because marriage is deeply embedded in religion, common law, legal duties, and social benefits, its redefinition poses enormous challenges to religious conscience rights.

The issue is not, per se, the ability of gays to enter into enduring emotional unions, even to have sympathetic ministers officiate at what they define as genuine marriages. Rather, the question turns on whether there is any legitimate rationale for the state to privilege the traditional conjugal understanding of marriage. At the deepest philosophical level, therefore, the debate over same-sex marriage concerns the definition of marriage itself. Proponents of marriage as a comprehensive union of sexual complementarity argue that it is an ancient, pre-political institution rooted in the need to channel human sexuality into stable procreative unions, to the enormous benefit of children and society.[48] Under this conception, common law merely recognizes the duties and sacrifices inherent in such life-long family commitments and affords certain benefits to them. Proponents of same-sex marriage, on the other hand, argue for the imperative of equal protection of the laws for same-sex couples, and contend that no grounds exist for privileging conjugal marriage or denying full state recognition to same-sex unions. Any denial of such recognition, in this view, represents invidious discrimination.

Perceiving that public opinion and law were moving toward this new conception of marriage, The Becket Fund for Religious Liberty convened a conference exploring the implications of same-sex marriage for religious freedom and then published an edited volume presenting its findings. That volume contains contributions by four scholars who support same-sex marriage and three who do not. They agreed to suspend those policy differences and focus exclusively on what will happen to religious institutions and individuals once law recognizes same-sex unions as fully equivalent to traditional conjugal marriage. All agreed that legalizing same-sex civil marriage without providing robust religious exemptions would produce widespread conflicts to the detriment of religious dissenters.[49]

Of all the contributors, Marc Stern, then of the liberal American Jewish Congress,[50] provided the most sobering depiction of the looming collision. Though supportive of gay rights, he meticulously catalogues how law will undercut religious freedom if same-sex marriage is imposed by the courts without any provision for religious exemptions. He documents how our political system, in response to the legacy of racial oppression in American history, developed a formidable infrastructure to combat discrimination through federal and state anti-discrimination statutes, judicial rulings, and regulations on civil rights, harassment, public accommodations, commercial licenses, professional codes, government contracts, service vendors, reproductive technologies, student speech codes, and housing access. Once same-sex marriage is deemed a fundamental right, then dissenters can be subject to the full weight of this anti-discrimination infrastructure.

While Stern was not optimistic that "much can be done to ameliorate the impact on religious dissenters," he saw the best hope in legislative sensitivity to religious conscience rights. "If there is to be space for opponents of same-sex marriage, it will have to be created at the same time as same-sex marriage is recognized, and, probably, as part of a legislative package."[51]

While legislatures can carefully incorporate generous conscience protections in same-sex statutes, courts do not have the same tools in the post-Smith era. Hence, if the courts widely recognize same-sex marriage as a right rooted in fundamental equality and equal protection of the laws—the position Professor Tepker develops in this volume and the grounds upon which judges have struck down state marriage laws (including Oklahoma's)—then objections to this innovation eventually may be seen as the equivalent of racial bigotry and treated as such in law. We see intimations of this logic in Justice Anthony Kennedy's majority opinion in *United States. v. Windsor* (2013), which voided provisions of the Defense of Marriage Act denying federal benefits to same-sex couples. Despite the scholarly debate over the nature and purpose of marriage, Kennedy seems to suggest that when legislatures uphold the traditional conjugal understanding of marriage they can only be acting with malice, seeking to "disparage and injure," to "demean" and "humiliate" same-sex couples.[52]

The exquisitely difficult challenge of balancing religious liberty and marriage equality for homosexuals came out in a remarkable amicus brief filed by the American Jewish Committee (AJC) in the same-sex marriage cases (cited above) argued before the Supreme Court in the spring of 2013.[53] Featuring the legal work of Marc Stern and Douglas Laycock, both of whom participated in the Becket volume, the brief declared the AJC's support for both gay marriage equality and religious liberty. It argued that same-sex couples and religious conscience objectors "make essentially parallel claims, and both should be protected."[54]

While calling upon the Court to recognize a right to same-sex marriage, the AJC brief acknowledged the genuine threat to religious liberty if the Court strikes down laws that exclusively recognize traditional conjugal marriages. Ironically, this placed Stern in the position of making the case for the very unilateral Court action he previously showed would be least likely to provide generous conscience protections. This lent a sense of urgency to the AJC recommendation: "If this Court constitutionalizes same-sex civil marriage for the country, it must attend to the resulting issues of religious liberty."[55] In attempting to square the circle—to declare a right to same-sex marriage and protect religious conscience objections—AJC ends its brief by calling upon the Court to reconsider the rule announced in *Employment Division v. Smith*. In other words, AJC concluded that "heightened scrutiny of laws burdening the free exercise of religion would provide a means of protecting the essential interests of both same-sex couples and those with religious objections." Guided by heightened scrutiny, the Court "might conclude that there is no compelling interest in forcing religious adoption agencies to the hard choice of closing down or repeatedly violating their religious teachings on marriage."[56]

While the call for a return to heightened scrutiny of religious liberty burdens is warranted, it is not clear that a compelling interest test would be sufficient to protect religious conscience rights in the new marriage regime. If objection to same-sex marriage is deemed equivalent to the bigoted opposition to interracial marriage in the past, then the state has a compelling interest to sanction it. This is precisely why the *early* Marc Stern suggested that this issue is particularly amenable to the natural balancing instincts of legislatures.

As we see in this review of the contraceptive mandate and the legal revolution on same-sex unions, a truncated view of religious liberty in the current regulatory era will inevitably result in degraded protections for this fundamental constitutional right. Not only will this heighten societal conflict and enervate civil society at home, it will also undermine American leadership in promoting religious freedom abroad. Troubles in the cradle have global implications.

GLOBAL IMPLICATIONS

The American experiment bequeathed to the world a model of the social benefits of guaranteeing religious freedom. The United States, as Robert Putnam and David Campbell show, uniquely manages to combine strong religiosity with a high degree of inter-religious amity and tolerance. This "American grace" flows, in part, from the way the constitutional heritage gives all a stake in protecting generous contours of religious liberty.[57]

When the United States emerged as a global superpower after World War II, it also led the way in enshrining religious freedom as a universal right in international law and remains the global leader in upholding it today. In the aftermath of the Holocaust, the United States played a leading role in developing the Universal Declaration of Human Rights, through the leadership of Eleanor Roosevelt, who chaired the United Nations committee that drafted the declaration.[58] Article 18 of that foundational declaration, adopted by the United Nations in 1948, provides this ringing statement of principles:

> Everyone has the right to freedom of thought, conscience, and religion. This right includes freedom to change his religion or belief, and freedom, either alone or in community with others and in public or private, to manifest his religion or belief in teaching, practice, worship, and observance.[59]

Here we see a robust vision of religious liberty and conscience rights, embodying what I have termed *religious freedom in full*. The preface of the Declaration grounds this right in reason, conscience, and dignity—in other words, in the ontology of human experience that Madison anticipated.

The American experience and model also influenced the momentous embrace of religious freedom by the Catholic Church at the Second Vatican Council. Indeed, the celebrated American Catholic theologian, John Courtney Murray, brought insights from the American heritage in helping draft *Dignitatis Humanae* (1965), the Church's declaration on religious liberty. As Daniel Philpott and others have demonstrated, that document helped propel the global advance of freedom because it turned the Church into the principle engine of the last wave of democratization on earth.[60]

American leadership continued during the Cold War, where the denial of religious freedom was a subtext of relations between the United States and the Soviet Union. The Jackson-Vanik law of 1974 tied normalized trade relations to the freedom of Jews, and others, to emigrate from the Soviet Union. Similarly, the Helsinki Accords of 1975 tied territorial sovereignty of the Soviet Union to advancements in human rights, including religious freedom.

Most recently, Congress invoked the American tradition of religious liberty in its landmark International Religious Freedom Act (IRFA) of 1998, which makes the promotion of religious freedom a "core objective" of American foreign policy. What moved Congress to act was the striking array of religious leaders backing the initiative, leaders often at odds on other issues. In interviews I discovered that a number of these leaders forged relationships with their unlikely allies through the earlier domestic campaign to reinstate heightened legal standards for religious exercise (in the wake of the *Smith* decision) that produced the Religious Freedom Restoration Act of 1993. In other words, a coalition galvanized to strengthen *domestic* religious liberty helped fuel the *international* campaign. Though not applied vigorously by our secular State Department, IRFA's vast reporting enterprise has provided the pivotal foundation for the systematic measurement of global restrictions on religion by the Pew Research Center and the pathbreaking scholarship flowing from that enterprise.[61]

That scholarship provides empirical validation that religious freedom nourishes peaceful societies with more stable democracy, stability, inter-religious amity, women's advancement, and economic vitality.[62] If religious liberty is weakened at home, it will undermine our ability to promote such salutary "articles of peace" abroad. Indeed, prominent comparative law theorists, such as Cole Durham, increasingly critique court rulings or political decisions in the United States that depart from principles of religious liberty these advocates defend in international tribunals. Moreover, Durham's mapping of the diverse global threats to religious free exercise finds a "sweet spot" for its maximum protection in a robust policy of *accommodation*,[63] which ensures the autonomy of religious institutions and provides leverage for claimants seeking relief from policies that burden their practice. The American experience, he suggests, cultivates wide popular support for such a policy, even if trends in American law sometimes move in the opposite direction.

We live in an unprecedented time in human history, as empirical evidence and events on the ground corroborate timeless philosophical arguments about the social and political benefits of the "first freedom." Faith itself can survive discrimination or persecution; but societies suffer when expressions of conscience and faith are repressed or marginalized. Indeed, advancing religious freedom is pivotal to navigating the crucible of the twenty-first century: living with our differences in a shrinking world. Madison captured a timeless insight. We have something special here; let us preserve it for ourselves and the world.

NOTES

1. Jerry Filteau, "Catholic Charities in Boston Archdiocese to end adoption services," *Catholic News Service*, March 13, 2006, http://www.catholic-news.com/data/stories/cns/0601456.htm.
2. The Becket Fund for Religious Liberty, "Yoder v. Morristown, New York (2006–2012)," http://www.becketfund.org/yoder/ (accessed October 2, 2013).
3. The Becket Fund for Religious Liberty, "Church Wins Zoning Appeal; City Surrenders," May 3, 2012, http://www.becketfund.org/church-wins-zoning-appeal-city-surrenders/.
4. Marc Fisher, "D.C. Lets Church Tear Down Brutalist Atrocity," Raw Fisher, *The Washington Post*, May 13, 2009, http://voices.washingtonpost.com/rawfisher/2009/05/dc_lets_church_tear_down_bruta.html.
5. The Becket Fund for Religious Liberty, "Belmont Abbey College, North Carolina, (2009)," http://www.becketfund.org/bac09/ (accessed October 2, 2013).
6. Lynn Thompson, "Supreme Court Won't Take Case on 'Ave Maria' at Graduation," *The Seattle Times*, March 22, 2010; Bob Egelko, "Justices Deny Review of Graduation Music Case," *San Francisco Chronicle*, March 23, 2010.
7. Alliance Defending Freedom, "NH Court Orders Home-schooled Child into Government-Run School," August 26, 2009, http://www.adfmedia.org/news/prdetail/2950.
8. Associated Press, First Amendment Center Online staff, "Meal Prayer at Ga. Senior Center Stopped, Then Restored," May 11, 2010, http://www.firstamendmentcenter.org/news.aspx?id=22937 (accessed May 28, 2010; article no longer available at site).
9. Julia Duin, "Catholics end D.C. foster care program," *Washington Times*, February 18, 2010, http://m.washingtontimes.com/news/2010/feb/18/dc-gay-marriage-law-archdiocese-end-foster-care/?page=all.
10. Manya Brachear, "State severs foster care ties with Catholic Charities," *Chicago Tribune*, July 11, 2011, http://articles.chicagotribune.com/2011-07–

11/news/chi-state-severs-fostercare-ties-with-catholic-charities-2011 0711_1_children-with-unmarried-cohabiting-catholic-charities-civil-unions.

11. Warren Richey, "Supreme Court: Law school not obliged to recognize Christian group," *Christian Science Monitor*, June 28, 2010, http://m.csmonitor .com/USA/Justice/2010/0628/Supreme-Court-Law-school-not-obliged-to-recognize-Christian-group/(page)/1; Joshua Mercer, "Religious Liberty Increasingly Under Attack on College Campuses," *Catholic Pulse*, June 29, 2012, http: //www.catholicpulse.com/en/fortnight/cp_mercer_liberty.html; Matthew Brown, "InterVarsity Christian Fellowship gets booted off another college campus for membership policy," *Deseret News*, March 9, 2013, http://www.deseretnews. com/article/865575315/InterVarsity-Christian-Fellowship-gets-booted-off-another-college-campus-for-membership-policy.html?pg=all; Michael Paulson, "Colleges and Evangelicals Collide on Bias Policy," *The New York Times*, June 10, 2014. By the summer of 2014, Christian student groups lost recognition at San Diego State, Vanderbilt, Bowdoin, Tufts, SUNY Buffalo, Rollins, and the entire Cal State system of 23 campuses.

12. Joan Frawley Desmond, "HHS Ends Contract With Church Program for Trafficking Victims, Stressing Need for Contraception," *National Catholic Register*, October 17, 2011, http://www.ncregister.com/daily-news/hhs-ends-contract-with-church-program-for-trafficking-victims-stressing-nee/; Huma Khan, "Abortion Issue in Catholic Bishops Sex Trafficking Victim Funding," *ABC News Blogs*, December 1, 2011, 2:23 PM, http://abcnews.go.com/blogs /politics/2011/12/abortion-issue-in-catholic-bishops-sex-trafficking-victim-funding/.

13. Richard Fausset, "In Alabama, A Church Sees Its Latino Brethren Vanish," *Los Angeles Times*, December 30, 2011, http://www.latimes.com/news/nation-world/nation/la-na-alabama-church-20111230-htm1,0,2812319.htmlstory; Campbell Robertson, "Bishops Criticize Tough Alabama Immigration Law," *The New York Times*, August 13, 2011, http://www.nytimes.com/2011/08/14/ us/14immig.html?pagewanted=all&_r=1&; Debbie Elliot, "Clergy Sues to Stop Alabama's Immigration Law," *National Public Radio*, August 23, 2011, http:// www.npr.org/2011/08/23/139887408/clergy-sue-to-stop-alabamas-immigration-law.

14. Tom Hays, "NYC Churches Can Have Access to Public Schools for Religious Services, Judge Rules," *Huffington Post*, February 25, 2012, http:// www.huffingtonpost.com/2012/02/25/judge-gives-nyc-churches-_0_n_1301283.html; "Bronx Fail: 2nd Cir. Says Churches Can't Rent NYC School Facilities, But All Other Community Groups Can," Alliance Defending Freedom, June 2, 2011, http://www.adfmedia.org/News/PRDetail/4782.

15. "Islamic Center of Murfreesboro v. Rutherford County, Tennessee," The Becket Fund for Religious Liberty, http://www.becketfund.org/murfreesboro/ (accessed October 2, 2013).

16. Pew Research Religion and Public Life Project, *Rising Tide of Restrictions on Religion*, September 2013, http://www.pewforum.org/2012/09/20/rising-tide-of-restrictions-on-religion-findings/#america.

17. The Becket Fund for Religious Liberty, "HHS Mandate Information Central," plaintiffs; http://www.becketfund.org/hhsinformationcentral/ (accessed January 24, 2014). As of this date 91 suits had been filed on behalf of over 300.

18. Brian Leiter, *Why Tolerate Religion?* (Princeton, NJ: Princeton University Press, 2013).

19. John Rawls, *Political Liberalism* (New York: Columbia University Press, 1993).

20. Leslie Griffin, *Political Reason*, 22 St. John's J. Legal Comment 493 (2007); Leslie Griffin, *Fighting the New Wars of Religion: The Need for a Tolerant First Amendment*, 62 Maine L. Rev. 23 (2010); Leslie Griffin, *Good Catholics Should Be Rawlsian Liberals*, 5 Southern Cal. Interdisc. L.J. 297 (1997).

21. Leslie Griffin, *Smith and Women's Equality*, 32 Cardozo L. Rev. 1831 (2011).

22. Thomas F. Farr, *World of Faith and Freedom: Why International Religious Liberty Is Vital to American National Security* (New York: Oxford University Press, 2008).

23. Os Guinness, *The Global Public Square: Religious Freedom and the Making of a World Safe for Diversity* (Downers Grove, IL: InterVarsity Press, 2013); James Davison Hunter and Os Guinness, eds., *Articles of Faith, Articles of Peace: The Religious Liberty Clauses and the American Public Philosophy* (Washington, DC: Brookings Institute, 1990).

24. John M. Barry, *Roger Williams and the Creation of the American Soul: Church, State, and the Birth of Liberty* (New York: Penguin Group, 2012).

25. Roger Williams, "The Bloody Tenet of Persecution for Cause of Conscience," in *On Religious Liberty: Selections from the Words of Roger Williams*, ed. James Calvin Davis (Cambridge: Harvard University Press, 2008).

26. John Locke, *A Letter Concerning Toleration* (London: Hackett Publishing Company, 1689).

27. Roger Williams, *George Fox Digg'd out of His Burrowes*, in *On Religious Liberty: Selections from the Words of Roger Williams*, ed. James Calvin Davis, (Cambridge, MA: Harvard University Press, 2008).

28. This view is exemplified by the argument of Mark Lilla that liberal freedom in the modern West was fruit of the marginalization of religion. In this account, antagonism toward political theology ultimately led enlightenment actors to radically separate religion from statecraft, which forced religious people to tolerate one another and acquiesce to the modern secular state's sovereignty. See Mark Lilla, *The Stillborn God: Religion, Politics, and the Modern West* (New York: Knopf, 2007).

29. Kevin Seamus Hasson, "From Tolerance to Natural Rights: Reflections on the Battle for Disestablishment in Virginia," in *The Right to be Wrong: Ending the Culture War Over Religion in America* (San Francisco: Encounter Books: 2005).

30. James Madison, "A Memorial and Remonstrance Against Religious Assessments" (1785), http://religiousfreedom.lib.virginia.edu/sacred/madison_m&r_1785.html (accessed April 18, 2014).

31. Cardinal Newman, "Letter to the Duke of Norfolk," Section 5, Newman Reader, The National Institute for Newman Studies, http://www.newman-reader.org/works/anglicans/volume2/gladstone/section5.html.

32. Helen Alvare, Matthew Franck, and Robert George, eds., *Institutions and Conscience* (South Bend, IN: St. Augustine's Press, forthcoming).

33. Robert Putnam and David Campbell, *American Grace: How Religion Divides and Unites Us* (New York: Simon and Schuster, 2010).

34. William A. Galston, *Public Matters: Politics, Policy, and Religion in the 21st Century* (Lanham, MD: Rowman & Littlefield, 2005), chapter 9; and Galston, *The Practice of Liberal Pluralism* (New York: Cambridge University Press, 2004), chapter 4.

35. This is how Singh described the promise of the American constitutional heritage to me in an interview in 2009.

36. I was in attendance at the Seventh Day Adventist banquet presenting religious liberty awards for 2010.

37. Sarah Barringer Gordon, "The Worship of Idols: Patriotism and the End of Tim, 1935–1955," in *The Spirit of the Law* (Cambridge: Harvard University Press, 2010).

38. Michael W. McConnell, "Origins and Historical Understanding of Free Exercise of Religion," *Harvard Law Review* 103, no. 7 (May 1990): 1409–1517; Michael W. McConnell, "Free Exercise Revisionism and the Smith Decision," *University of Chicago Law Review* 57, no. 4 (Autumn 1990): 1109–53.

39. W. Cole Durham, Jr., and Robert T. Smith, "Religion and the State in the United States at the Turn of the 21st Century," in *Law and Religion in the 21st Century*, ed. Silvio Ferrari and Rinaldo Chistofori (Surry, England: Ashgate, 2010).

40. Leslie Griffin, *Smith and Women's Equality*, 32 Cardozo L. Rev. 1831 (2011).

41. Gerard V. Bradley, "Beguiled: Free Exercise Exemption and the Siren Song of Liberalism," *Hofstra Law Review* 20 (Winter 1991): 245–319; Philip Hamburger, "More is Less," *Virginia Law Review*, 90 (2004): 835–892.

42. W. Cole Durham, Jr., "Perspectives on Religious Liberty: A Comparative Framework," in *Religious Human Rights in Global Perspective: Legal Perspectives*, ed. Johan D. van der Vyver and John Witte, Jr. (The Hague, Netherlands: Martinus Nijhoff Publishers, 1996); and Durham and Smith, "Religion and the State in the United States."

43. An example of this effort is the essay by Matthew J. Frank, "Escaping the Exemptions Ghetto," *First Things* (March 2014).

44. The Becket Fund for Religious Liberty maintains an HHS Mandate Information Central that tracks the status of lawsuits against the mandate (http://www.becketfund.org/hhsinformationcentral). As of March 3, 2014, it listed 93 separate lawsuits representing over 300 religious institutions, businesses, and individuals.

45. Press statement of David Green, September 13, 2012. Becket Fund, http://www.becketfund.org/davidgreenpressstatement/.

46. *Burwell, Secretary of Health and Human Services, et al. v. Hobby Lobby Stores, Inc., et al.*, No. 13-354, decided June 30, 2014.

47. Reza Shah-Kazemi, ed., *My Mercy Encompasses All: The Koran's Teaching on Compassion, Peace & Love* (Shoemaker Hoard, 2007), 45.

48. Sherif Girgis, Ryan T. Anderson, and Robert P. George, *What is Marriage? Man and Woman: A Defense* (New York: Encounter Books, 2012).

49. Douglas Laycock, Anthony R. Picarello, Jr., and Robin Fretwell Wilson, eds., *Same-Sex Marriage and Religious Liberty* (Lanham, MD: Rowman & Littlefield, 2008).

50. Marc Stern, who is now with the American Jewish Committee, represented that institution in the amicus brief on the marriage cases.

51. Marc Stern, "Same-Sex Marriage and the Churches," in Laycock, Picarello, and Wilson, eds., *Same-Sex Marriage and Religious Liberty*, 57.

52. *United States v. Windsor*, 570 U.S. 12 (2013) (Docket No. 12–307).

53. "Amicus Curiae of the American Jewish Committee in Support of the Individual Respondents on the Merits," in the Supreme Court of the United States, October Term, 2012, *Dennis Hollingsworth et al. v. Kristin M Perry et al.*, and *United States of America v. Edith Schlain Windsor*, in her capacity as Executor of the Estate of Thea Clara Spyer, et al., Marc D. Stern, American Jewish Committee, Thomas C. Berg, M.S.L., and Douglas Laycock, Counsel of Record, University of Virginia Law School.

54. Amicus Curiae brief of the American Jewish Committee, 12.

55. Ibid., 18.

56. Ibid., 34.

56. Robert Putnam and David Campbell, *American Grace: How Religion Divides and Unites Us* (New York: Simon and Schuster, 2010).

58. Mary Ann Glendon, *A World Made New: Eleanor Roosevelt and the Universal Declaration of Human Rights* (New York: Random House, 2001).

59. United Nations, *The Universal Declaration of Human Rights*, Article 18 (1948).

60. Daniel Philpott, "The Catholic Wave," *Journal of Democracy* 15 (April 2004); Samuel Huntington, *The Third Wave: Democratization in the Late Twentieth Century* (Norman: University of Oklahoma Press, 1991).

61. "The Rising Tide of Restrictions on Religion," *The Pew Research Center's Forum on Religion and Public Life* (September 2012).

62. Brian Grim and Roger Finke, *The Price of Freedom Denied: Religious Persecution and Conflict in the Twenty-First Century* (New York: Cambridge University Press, 2011). Grim and Finke's whole book develops this argument, with Chapter 7 serving as a summary.

63. Durham, "Perspectives on Religious Liberty."

PART I

The Founding Moment and Constitutional Evolution

1   Jefferson, Madison, Henry, and the Context for Religious Liberty in Revolutionary America

Thomas S. Kidd

In the presidential election of 1800, Thomas Jefferson defeated the sitting president, John Adams, in what Jefferson styled the "Revolution of 1800." Jefferson's election was the final event of the Revolutionary era, and the first peaceful transfer of presidential power under the new Constitution. On New Year's Day, 1802, the Baptist evangelist John Leland, delighted by the election of his friend and ally to the presidency, delivered to Jefferson a prodigious gift: a 1,235-pound block of cheese. The "mammoth" cheese came from Leland's farming community of Cheshire, Massachusetts, which seems to have voted unanimously for Jefferson in the 1800 presidential election. The cheese's red crust was adorned with the motto "Rebellion to tyrants is obedience to God."

Two days later, on Sunday, January 3, Leland delivered an effusive sermon before a joint session of Congress and the president. A hostile Federalist congressman in attendance, writing in his journal, called Leland a "cheesemonger" and a "poor, ignorant, illiterate, clownish preacher." Leland spoke on the text "Behold a greater [one] than Solomon is here," with a not-too-subtle implication about his beloved president. The embarrassed Federalist congressman groaned that "such a farrago, bawled with stunning voice, horrid tone, frightful grimaces, and extravagant gestures . . . was never heard by any decent auditory before."[1]

To say that Jefferson and Leland made religious odd-fellows is an understatement. Leland had devoted his life to saving souls, and estimated at the end of his career that he had preached about eight thousand sermons. An evangelical, Leland simply confessed that "my only hope of acceptance with God is in the blood and righteousness of Jesus Christ." Although he attended church regularly as president, Jefferson did not believe that the blood of Jesus would save him, or anyone else. He always professed to be "sincerely attached" to Jesus's teachings, but Jefferson did not believe that Jesus ever claimed to be the Son of God. He similarly thought the doctrine of the Trinity was nonsense, and the "mere Abracadabra of . . . the priests of Jesus." What, then, led Leland to admire Jefferson so much that he would think to give him that big cheese?[2]

The answer to this question goes a long way toward explaining how religion helped to cement the new American nation. Although Jefferson and Leland could not have been more opposed in their personal religious views, they shared the same view of church and state. Indeed, the Baptists of New England saw Jefferson as a sort of political savior. Religious dissenters like the Baptists had long suffered persecution in Congregationalist New England, even after Patriot New Englanders fought for liberty in the Revolution. Jefferson had championed religious freedom in Virginia, where the itinerating Leland had come to know and love the future president. Jefferson the skeptical deist and Leland the fervent evangelical both believed that government should afford liberty of conscience to its citizens, and not give preference to one Christian denomination over another. These public beliefs about religion and politics made fast friends of a deist and an evangelical. To modern American eyes, this seems a most improbable alliance.

Not all conservative Christians liked Jefferson, to be sure. Many hated him because they saw him as an infidel. One called him a "howling atheist." But these critics did not represent the wave of the future. Jefferson and Leland did.

The link between Jefferson and Leland shows that in the American founding, deists and evangelicals (and a range of believers in between) united around public religious principles that keyed the success of the Revolution, and helped create America. The union of evangelicals and deists was fragile and hardly unanimous—even on religious liberty—but it proved strong enough to allow Americans to "begin the world over again," as Tom Paine put it.[3]

The public religious beliefs that helped unite Revolutionary America included the idea that all men are created equal, the importance of virtue in preserving the republic, and the role of Providence in human affairs. But this chapter focuses on the idea that lay behind Leland's cheese: religious liberty, and the disestablishment of the state churches. Across America, dissenting evangelicals led the charge against religious establishments during the Revolution, but they often gained critical assistance from liberal Christians or deists like Jefferson who shared their goals. From the Baptists of New England to the Presbyterians of South Carolina, dissenters sought to prevent state governments from giving preference to any denomination.

Everyone agreed with religious liberty in principle, but the Founders did not agree on the exact implications of religious liberty. This disagreement is perhaps best illustrated by Thomas Jefferson and James Madison's rivalry with Patrick Henry over the issue of public support for churches. Religious liberty brought together unexpected allies in the era of the founding—almost everyone supported ending persecution of religious dissenters, but people on the two poles of the American religious spectrum, evangelicals and Enlightenment rationalists (the latter including Jefferson and Madison), were more likely to support full disestablishment. More moderate, traditional Christians like Patrick Henry often advocated a continuing role for an establishment of churches.

Note that Henry had a deep background—as deep as Madison's and Jefferson's—in defending religious liberty, particularly the freedom of dissenters from persecution. In 1776, Henry played a critical role in crafting the Virginia Declaration of Rights' sixteenth article regarding religious freedom. For years, the Baptists had been petitioning the House of Burgesses for relief from the requirements of the Anglican establishment. Within days of independence, Baptists from Prince William County again petitioned the convention, arguing that since Virginia's leaders were contending for their basic liberties, they should also respect the fundamental religious rights of their fellow citizens. Disestablishing the Anglican Church would prevent internal divisions over religion in Virginia, they maintained. They insisted that they be allowed to worship God with no interference from the state, and be relieved from religious taxes that supported the Anglican Church. Henry understood that the Anglican Patriots should actively court the Baptists in order to win their support for independence. In a public letter he wrote in August 1776, Henry praised the growing interdenominational spirit in America, and declared that "the only contest among us, at this most critical and important period, is, who shall be foremost to preserve our religious and civil liberties." As Patriots, Anglicans and Baptists were "brethren who must perish or triumph together," he said.[4]

After much debate, the committee agreed to phrase the sixteenth article in these expansive terms: "That religion, or the duty which we owe to our Creator and the manner of discharging it, can be directed by reason and conviction, not by force or violence; and therefore, all men are equally entitled to the free exercise of religion, according to the dictates of conscience; and that it is the mutual duty of all to practice Christian forbearance, love, and charity towards each other." Madison also had Henry introduce an amendment to the article that seemed to imply disestablishment of the Anglican Church, in the assertion that "no man or class of men ought on account of religion to be invested with peculiar emoluments or privileges; nor subjected to any penalties or disabilities." When other delegates challenged him, however, Henry denied that this amendment was intended to end state support for the Anglican Church, although that probably was Madison's goal. Henry, unlike Madison, saw no inconsistency between state support for religion and religious freedom. In this somewhat obscure episode we see the seeds of Madison and Henry's split over religion.[5] The Declaration of Rights, in any case, had become a momentous articulation of the human rights upon which government should not intrude.

There's much to say about Henry, Jefferson, and Madison in wartime, but the war effectively put on hold Virginia's debate about religion's official role in society. After the Revolution concluded, Henry remained deeply committed to promoting public virtue in Virginia, for he and most of his revolutionary colleagues did not believe that independence would be worth anything if Virginians degenerated into immorality, selfishness, and vice. To Henry, only one public institution could adequately support virtue, and that was the church. But at the beginning of the Revolution, Virginia had stopped giving financial aid to the Anglican Church—there was little money to spare during the war—and Anglican parishes had suffered badly during the conflict. The church's financial deprivation was exacerbated by its traditional association with Britain.

At the war's end, Henry believed that the time had come to resume public funding for religion, but he knew that the state would never go back to one exclusive, established church. Instead, Henry became the champion of a so-called general assessment for religion.

Under this system, people would have to pay taxes to support a Christian church of their choosing; it could be Anglican, Presbyterian, Baptist, or whatever. (Most defenders of the assessment also agreed that tax exemptions could be given for non-Christians.) This tax would bolster not only the pastors and facilities of the churches, but their educational and social welfare functions. For Henry and the assessment's many supporters, this arrangement would honor both the public importance of religion, and the realities of Christian pluralism in the state.

Henry came out on the losing end of this issue, and Virginia decided in favor of Jefferson's Bill for Establishing Religious Freedom in 1786. Before we dismiss the value of Henry's general assessment, however, we should put his views in context, and remember that Henry was as much an activist for religious *freedom* as were Madison and Jefferson; to him, religious liberty and the question of establishment were different issues. Henry's general assessment plan was also approved by other prominent Virginia leaders such as George Washington and Richard Henry Lee. Washington expressed a common view that Christians should be made to support that which they profess to believe.[6]

Henry's general assessment plan also reveals a distinction in the Founding period between religious freedom, and separation of church and state. This distinction was important to many in the Revolutionary era, but has been blurred since the concept of separation came into modern use after World War II. Henry fully supported religious freedom, by which he meant that no one should be persecuted or disadvantaged for their religious beliefs or practices.

Separation of church and state, meaning that the government should have no connections with religion, was another matter entirely. Jefferson at times approached such a position, but even he felt comfortable permitting and even attending church services in government buildings as president, and as president he once even approved the national government assisting in the building of a church and paying the salary of a missionary among the Kaskaskia Indians. Madison developed the most far-reaching theory of separation of church and state among the Founders, but only after his retirement from politics. During those later years, Madison wrote (but did not publish) his "detached memorandum," which speculated on what real separation of church and state might require, such as the elimination of congressional or military chaplains. But the notion that government agencies could totally disengage from religion simply did not occur to most Revolutionary-era Americans, for churches were seen as the moral bulwark of the republic and a chief agency for social welfare and education.

Henry and most of his Revolutionary colleagues also would not have supported strict separation because they believed that government should promote morality. Two primary ways to do this were through punishing immorality under the law, and encouraging morality through the work of churches and schools. Modern Americans have largely ceased to see the encouragement of morality as a primary function of the state, but they have certainly not abandoned the notion that government should discourage immorality through law enforcement. Most laws, even today, are undergirded by some moral assumption or consensus. The government punishes people who kill or steal, for instance, because we think it is wrong to do those things. We are not so different from founders like Henry who saw the government as a promoter of morality, or at least a legal deterrent to immorality.

The real point of contention concerning the general assessment was whether, as a matter of conscience, people should be required by law to support a church of their choice in order to help bolster the strength of the churches and thus encourage public virtue. Jefferson and Madison cooperated with many evangelical dissenters, especially Baptists, in arguing that religion could survive, and even thrive, on a purely voluntary basis. Government support inevitably led to corruption of the church, the evangelicals believed. They did not have to think back very far—only to the early 1770s—to remember a time when Baptist preachers languished in Virginia jails for illegal preaching. That experience made the Baptists, along with Madison, who as a young man deplored the state's persecution of evangelicals, wary of official state churches.

In mid-1784, these differing visions of religious liberty clashed when the Episcopal Church boldly proposed an act of incorporation that would have given it both increased independence from state oversight and increased legal protection for church property that it held as the established church. Henry and other supporters of the church introduced the measure, but it struggled to gain support in the legislature and was postponed until the next session. The bill exacerbated the growing split between Madison and Jefferson on one side, and the ever-popular Henry on the other. Madison thought the incorporation bill was outrageous, and told Jefferson that "extraordinary as such a project was, it was preserved from a dishonorable death by the talents of Mr. Henry."[7]

Later that year, Henry and the supporters of public religion again introduced both the incorporation bill and the general assessment plan, which argued that "the general diffusion of Christian knowledge hath a natural tendency to correct the morals of men, restrain their vices, and preserve the peace of society; which cannot be effected without a competent provision for learned teachers [pastors]; and it is judged that such provision may be made by the legislature, without counteracting the liberal principle heretofore adopted and intended to be preserved by abolishing all distinctions of pre-eminence amongst the different societies or communities of Christians." Many Virginians—especially Anglicans—sent petitions to the legislature supporting the assessment. Madison spoke out against the assessment, but the tide seemed to be turning in its favor.[8]

The momentum for the assessment bill abruptly changed, however, when Henry was elected governor again on November 17, 1784. Neither the assessment nor the incorporation bill had come up for a final vote, but Henry may have thought that he could safely leave the legislature prior to their acceptance. He was wrong. Madison was quite pleased to see Henry go to the governor's mansion, and anticipated that the change of offices would prove "inauspicious to [Henry's] offspring."[9]

Although the incorporation bill passed the House, Madison managed to delay the vote on the general assessment until 1785. Then he and the bill's evangelical opponents began a public campaign against it. Madison penned the *Memorial and Remonstrance* against the assessment, and crisply stated the reasons that many Virginians, including many devout Christians, opposed the plan. Religion, he argued, "must be left to the conviction and conscience of every man; and it is the right of every man to exercise it as these may dictate. This right is in its nature an unalienable right."[10] To Madison and his Baptist allies, religious freedom required that the government give no support to any denomination. State entanglement only corrupted churches, and any action government took on behalf of a particular denomination was inherently discriminatory. Henry believed that religion's importance required its support by government;

Madison, Jefferson, and the Baptists argued that churches and individual believers (and outright skeptics, in Jefferson's case) needed to be safeguarded from government.

Ultimately, the legislature set the assessment plan aside owing to lack of popular support (the incorporation bill also foundered). Baptists across the state celebrated. As one minister put it, "This formidable imp was destroyed at the time of his formation, and never suffered to draw breath nor perform one action in this happy land of freedom." The demise of the general assessment gave Madison a new opportunity to promote the Bill for Establishing Religious Freedom. Jefferson first introduced this bill in 1779, but it lacked support until the controversy over the general assessment focused attention on Virginia's desired church–state order. In early 1786, Madison won final approval for the bill, which proclaimed that "no man shall be compelled to frequent or support any religious worship, place, or ministry whatsoever, nor shall be enforced, restrained, molested, or burdened in his body or goods, nor shall otherwise suffer, on account of his religious opinions or belief; but that all men shall be free to profess, and by argument to maintain, their opinions in matters of religion, and that the same shall in no wise diminish, enlarge, or affect their civil capacities."[11]

Henry's desire to promote religious strength through a plural establishment had generated a backlash, resulting in a remarkably modern relationship between religion and government in Virginia. The government was no longer to use tax money to help churches do their business. The Virginia model heavily influenced the First Amendment's encouragement of "free exercise of religion" and ban on a national religious establishment. As it turned out, this religious voluntarism put Christianity on a stronger basis in Virginia, and in America generally, as the era of disestablishment was followed shortly by the Second Great Awakening, the greatest period of Christian growth in American history. Evangelical churches such as the Baptists grew exponentially in the next seventy-five years prior to the Civil War.

The battle over the general assessment continued the downward spiral in Henry's relationship with Madison and Jefferson. Despite Jefferson's residence in Paris as ambassador to France, his personal animosity toward Henry grew. Jefferson's loathing for Henry had begun in 1781, when Henry had initiated an investigation into

Jefferson's behavior as governor. Jefferson had abandoned the governorship several days before the end of his term as members of the legislature fled before an invading British force led by the turncoat Benedict Arnold. When Henry proposed the investigation, the indignant Jefferson wrote that Henry had "inflicted a wound on my spirit which will only be cured by the all-healing grave." By 1784, Jefferson had come to see Henry not only as his greatest personal nemesis, but as the opponent of every worthy political goal. In his most bitter invective toward Henry, Jefferson told Madison that they needed to take their opposition to Henry to a higher authority. "What we have to do I think," Jefferson wrote, "is devoutly to pray for his death." While Jefferson probably meant this comment sarcastically, he also wrote it in one of his encrypted codes so no one else would see his morbid thoughts about Henry.[12]

Despite the failure of the general assessment, Henry remained committed as Virginia governor to the public support of religion. He responded enthusiastically to a proposal for Christianizing Native Americans presented to him by England's Selina Hastings, the Countess of Huntingdon. The countess was a key evangelical Methodist leader who corresponded with a number of American religious and political figures, including her distant relative George Washington. George and Martha Washington were so enamored with the countess that they placed an engraving of her on their bedroom wall at Mount Vernon.[13]

Sir James Jay, a prominent physician and brother of New York's John Jay, provided Governor Henry an outline of the countess's plan, including a letter from the countess to Henry. The American Revolution had opened a door for the evangelization of the Indians, she told him. Her plan sought to "introduce the benevolent religion of our blessed Redeemer among heathen and savage nations; to lead them from violence and barbarity to the duties of humanity and the arts of civil life; to provide a refuge for pious industrious people, who wish to withdraw themselves from scenes of vice and irreligion, to a country where they may spend their days in the pursuits of honest industry, and in the practice of religion and virtue." The countess wanted the legislatures of Virginia and other states with substantial frontier areas to grant lands for Christian settlers to establish new towns near the Indian tribes. There they would set up schools and churches, attracting Indians with the prospect of education and refinement. The countess would administer the licensing of Christian settlers from Europe. All she needed, she said, was for the legislatures to provide the land and tax incentives toward settlement.

Henry saw the plan as an antidote to the continuing turmoil on the frontier, which he attributed partly to Indian resistance to Christianity and what he saw as their lack of civilization. He longed to introduce more white Christian settlers who would reduce Virginia's overall dependence on slave labor. The plan would ultimately bolster public virtue, which Henry believed had woefully languished during the war. Henry advocated for the countess's plan with the state legislature, but because most of Virginia's vacant land had been deeded to Congress, he directed his appeals there, writing to Virginia's congressional delegates in 1785 and telling them that the twin goals of attracting Christian settlers and evangelizing Native Americans demanded immediate action. Similarly, Henry wrote to Joseph Martin, his prominent neighbor near Leatherwood, expressing his zeal for the plan. "She hopes to do [this] at her own expense chiefly," he said, "and to import large number of people from Great Britain and Ireland that are good whigs and strictly religious."[14]

But concerns over the settlers' political allegiances, and the means of doling out land, derailed the countess's proposal. As Richard Henry Lee told George Washington, who had also strongly recommended the plan, Congress feared that the settlers might prove to be British sympathizers, and moreover, all available land was committed for sale to pay off public debts.[15]

Henry continued to promote the plan in the Virginia legislature, but the countess's scheme was doomed, an unsuccessful instance of Henry's and Washington's continuing interest in using state power to support religion, virtue, and even missionary work. Lest we think that such ideas were peculiar to Henry and Washington, or that they faded after the adoption of the Constitution and Bill of Rights, note again that President Thomas Jefferson himself would approve federal funding for a missionary and church in Illinois. Even the great champion of total disestablishment believed that the government could employ religious workers to accomplish public goods, in this case the education and "civilization" of Native Americans. To Revolutionary-era Americans like Henry and Jefferson, that civilizing project by definition meant instructing them in Christianity.[16]

Henry's and Madison's political rivalry came to a head in 1788, when Henry became the leading Virginia Antifederalist opponent of Madison's new Constitution. As with the Bill for Establishing Religious Freedom, Henry lost the battle over the Constitution, and soon he stepped out of the political arena entirely. In retirement, Henry increasingly worried about the emerging anti-Christian implications of the French Revolution, as well as the deistic attacks on Christianity that many of the Revolution's friends championed. Increasingly serious about his own faith, Henry believed more fervently than ever that a strong republic needed robust religion to preserve it from corruption, turmoil, and violence.

Many traditional Christians in the United States had initially welcomed the French Revolution as a movement akin to their own, and one that would undermine the long-despised Catholic Church. But the French Revolution began to take an ugly anti-Christian turn in 1792, with the massacre of hundreds of priests and the conversion of some churches into Temples of Reason.

To many observers, the anti-Christianism of the French Revolution coincided with the rise of a militant new deism in America, a surge symbolized and incited by the 1794 publication of Thomas Paine's *The Age of Reason*. This pamphlet by the former hero of the American Revolution attacked traditional Christianity as a tool of political oppression. Paine's assault found an eager audience in the United States. Although it was originally published in France, where Paine had gone to support the revolution, *The Age of Reason* appeared in seventeen American editions between 1794 and 1796.[17]

The rising anti-Christian spirit of the French Revolution and the threat of deism confirmed that Henry could never align with America's pro-French Jeffersonian party. Aside from his personal history with Jefferson, and his political battles with Madison, Henry increasingly believed that he needed to defend traditional Christianity against Francophile deism. That meant keeping his distance from Jefferson's party, if not openly siding with the Federalists—but doing so would mean turning away from the Antifederalist movement he had championed less than a decade earlier. His deepening concern for Christian fidelity was reflected in a lengthy 1796 letter to his daughter Betsey:

The view which the rising greatness of our country presents to my eyes is greatly tarnished by the general prevalence of Deism which with me is but another name for vice and depravity. I am however much consoled by reflecting, that the religion of Christ has from its first appearance in the world, been attacked in vain by all the wits, philosophers, and wise ones, aided by every power of man and its triumph has been complete. What is there in the wit or wisdom of the present Deistical writers or professors that can compare them with Hume, Shaftsbury, Bolingbroke, and others? And yet these have been confuted and their fame decaying, insomuch that the puny efforts of Paine are thrown in to prop their tottering fabrick, whose foundations cannot stand the test of time.

Henry continued to believe that the success of the republic depended upon the power of virtue, which he saw as rooted in traditional religion. For Henry, the publication of Paine's *Age of Reason* was troubling because it essentially encouraged public sinfulness. Once freed from the restraints of the Bible and morality, he believed, skeptical Americans would naturally pursue selfishness and immorality. As he said in his letter to Betsey, Henry worried that he had not sufficiently identified himself as a practicing traditional Christian:

> Amongst other strange things said of me, I hear it is said by the Deists that I am one of their number, and indeed that some good people think I am no Christian. This thought gives me much more pain than the appellation of Tory, because I think religion of infinitely higher importance than politics, and I find much cause to reproach myself that I have lived so long and have given no decided and public proofs of my being a Christian. But indeed my dear child this is a character which I prize far above all this world has or can boast.[18]

Some have suggested that religion might have become more important to Henry as he grew older (at time of the publication of *The Age of Reason*, Henry was fifty-eight). Perhaps he had become more reflective about his faith, and about his country's religious commitments. But Henry also believed that with Paine's writings and Jefferson's well-known skepticism challenging the nation's spiritual foundations, Americans could no longer take their religious heritage for granted. He feared that without fidelity to long-established religious precepts, the United States would spin apart in an atheistic whirlwind, just like Revolutionary France.

Henry passed away in 1799, just before the election of his long-time nemesis Jefferson as president in 1800. The campaign of 1800 between Jefferson and John Adams tested the fragile consensus regarding the requirements for personal faith of office holders in America. In the name of religious freedom, the Constitution had banned religious tests, which left many religious Americans worried that this provision would allow skeptics and non-Christians to assume places in the national government. In the election of 1800, these fears were central to the presidential contest and to America's unfolding definition of the place of faith in its government and the lives of its leaders.[19]

Jefferson's own distinctive religious beliefs incited controversy in a way that the faith of his predecessors had not. Few Americans had raised questions about the personal beliefs of George Washington or John Adams, the first two presidents under the Constitution, even though both men were not known to profess particularly traditional Christianity. Washington commanded so much reverence, and spoke so highly of public religion, that no one would presume to criticize his personal piety or theology. He was probably a rationalist but orthodox Episcopalian, although he hardly ever spoke of his personal faith. Most Americans agreed with evangelical Baptist minister Richard Furman of Charleston, South Carolina, who extolled Washington's belief in "God's superintending providence; his special interposition in favor of the just and innocent; his attention to the prayers of his supplicating people; and the necessity of religion, for the support of morality, virtue, and the true interests of society." Without doubt, Washington believed in Providence, prayer, and public religion.

As for John Adams, while he was personally inclined toward Unitarianism (which denied the traditional Christian doctrine of the Trinity), he also affirmed the public value of religion. Adams used Christian language in official proclamations, as in a 1798 announcement of a national day of prayer and fasting, when he summoned Americans to ask God "of his infinite grace, through the Redeemer of the world, freely to remit all our offences, and to incline us, by his Holy Spirit, to that sincere repentance and reformation" which would elicit God's favor. Although some of his Republican opponents tried to accuse Adams of holding unorthodox beliefs, Adams's willingness to employ Christian rhetoric on such occasions largely shielded him from questions about his own faith.[20]

Jefferson's personal religious views became a political problem largely because of events out of his control, especially the violent anti-Christian actions of the French Revolution. Jefferson would be broadly associated with the French Revolution and its brutal assault on religion and state institutions. As Americans grew more alarmed about its implications for faith and democracy in their own country, he would be implicated by their fears.

In spite of its extraordinary assault on Christianity and tradition, most Americans responded positively to the early stages of the French Revolution, with many interpreting news of the Catholic Church's troubles through the persistent ideology of anti-Catholicism. Baptist Elias Lee of Connecticut spoke for many in America when he presented the French Revolution as the latest providential victory for liberty and republicanism: "The horn of Antichrist is broken amongst [the French], civil and religious monarchy expires, and true liberty and freedom, wafted on the wings of providence, in defiance of millions of enemies, hail a general revolution." To Christians like Lee, the revolutions in America and France possibly portended the beginning of a global campaign against civil and religious tyranny, and the imminent arrival of the millennium.[21]

Views of the French Revolution changed dramatically when the anticlericalism in France seemed to threaten traditional faith in America as well—a threat aggravated by the 1794 American publication of Paine's *The Age of Reason*. Understandably, *The Age of Reason* precipitated a heated response from Christian critics in America. The Episcopal priest Uzal Ogden of Newark, New Jersey, furiously wondered which of Paine's qualities was most conspicuous in the despicable book, "the weakness of his intellects, the depravity of his mind, or the impertinence of his conduct!" The pamphlet provoked numerous rebuttals, including a screed with the self-explanatory title *An Investigation of that False, Fabulous and Blasphemous Misrepresentation of Truth, Set Forth by Thomas Paine.*[22]

Opponents of Paine not only attacked him for his openly espoused anti-church deism, but they associated it directly with Thomas Jefferson. Jefferson indeed shared many of Paine's doubts about Christianity, although he had been reticent about expressing them. His most provocative comments on religion would come well after his tenure as president when, in personal correspondence written mostly in the 1820s, he attacked the Bible and evangelical theology in the most vicious terms, while disavowing belief in the divinity of Jesus, the miracles of the Bible, and the Trinity. But if he held those incendiary views earlier in his political career, he mostly kept them to himself.[23]

Jefferson nevertheless had a connection with Paine, an association for which his opponents reviled him. In 1791, when he was Secretary of State, he had unintentionally endorsed Paine's *The Rights of Man*, a defense of the French Revolution. Upon the book's publication, Jefferson wrote to a Philadelphia printer that he was pleased with Paine's stance against "political heresies which have sprung up among us." His remark was a not-too-subtle reference to Vice President John Adams's public criticism of the French Revolution. To his surprise, printers began using Jefferson's comment as a head note for future printings of *The Rights of Man*.[24]

Growing fears about the supposed atheism of Paine and Jefferson spilled into the American political arena in 1796, during America's first presidential election in which there were two serious candidates: Adams and Jefferson. The Framers of the Constitution had not anticipated the forming of political parties, nor did they envision public election campaigns, but George Washington's retirement unleashed unprecedented political partisanship. Neither Adams, the victor, nor Jefferson, the runner-up (and thus vice president under the Constitution's original rules), would campaign openly for the office. Others did campaign for—and against—the leading candidates, however, employing the sort of personal attacks that would fully emerge in the 1800 election. Jefferson's Federalist opponents painted him as an unbelieving friend of Paine and the French. Suspicions surfaced that Jefferson was an agent of French atheism. A writer in New York's *Minerva* newspaper asserted that "We are not Frenchmen, thank God that made us—we are not like them. And until Mr. Bache's [a Philadelphia publisher's] sale of his twenty thousand copies of the second part of Paine's *Age of Reason* shall be finished, and until the atheistical philosophy of a certain great Virginian shall become the fashion (which God of his mercy forbid) we shall never be." Federalist leaders William Smith and Oliver Wolcott blamed Jefferson's supporters for circulating *The Age of Reason*, speculating that, as president, Jefferson would invite Paine into his administration, and "this enlightened pair of philosophers would fraternize, and philosophize against the Christian religion."[25]

After 1796, during John Adams's tenure as president, the fear of French military power and atheism escalated. Adams inherited from the Washington administration an undeclared naval war with France. Once King Louis XVI was deposed and executed in 1793, the United States also reneged on debts to France, arguing that its loans were owed to the French monarchy, not the new French Republic. The French retaliated by seizing American ships in the Atlantic Ocean. Tensions between the two former allies grew worse in 1797, when American peace negotiators in Paris faced demands from French diplomats (identified by Adams as X, Y, and Z) for bribes in return for continuing the negotiations. An outraged public called for war with France. In the midst of the war fervor, the Federalist-controlled Congress passed the Alien and Sedition Acts. The Alien Act empowered Adams to take action against resident aliens in America, while the Sedition Act—an incredible assault on freedom of speech—made it a crime to publish anything of a "false, scandalous and malicious" nature against the government. A number of Jeffersonian editors and politicians were arrested under the Sedition Act.

In this tense environment, anti-Jefferson clergymen proclaimed that America was in imminent danger of a French-instigated atheistic assault. In a Fourth of July sermon in 1798, Yale College's evangelical president, Timothy Dwight, declared that the French Revolution and the expansion of infidelity represented the fulfillment of biblical prophecy, asserting that events described in the Book of Revelation, particularly the pouring out of the sixth vial of wrath described in Revelation 16, were unfolding before their eyes. He believed that the sixth vial forecast the destruction of the Roman Catholic Church, and the rise of anti-Christian philosophy in the lands where Catholicism once dominated. In this time of surging atheism abroad, Dwight argued that Americans' only hope of survival lay in maintaining traditional Christianity while avoiding alliances with the agents of godlessness. Although he did not mention Jefferson specifically, his listeners could not fail to see the implication of his words. Dalliance with the friends of France risked the imposition of atheist tyranny in America, which would, he predicted, result in "the conflagration of churches and dwellings, the total ruin of families, the butchery of great multitudes of fathers and sons, and the most deplorable dishonor of wives and daughters." The second coming of Christ was at hand. Only those who stood firm against the forces of infidelity would survive.[26] To combat these enemies, America

presumably needed a leader not only of public virtue but of orthodox personal faith.

And yet, despite all the concerns about his beliefs, Jefferson
narrowly defeated Adams in 1800. Americans drew diametrically
opposed conclusions about the religious significance of Jefferson's
election. Some Federalists saw his victory as portending apocalypse.
The *Gazette of the United States* (Philadelphia), the nation's leading
Federalist newspaper, repeatedly printed a notice in the Fall of 1800
that instructed Americans to ask themselves, "Shall I continue in
allegiance to GOD—AND A RELIGIOUS PRESIDENT; or impi-
ously declare for JEFFERSON—AND NO GOD!!!" Certain New
England Federalists reportedly hid their Bibles when they learned
that Jefferson was elected, fearing that Jefferson's minions would
come to confiscate them. Other American Christians saw Jefferson's
election in an entirely different light. The Danbury Baptist Association wrote to Jefferson in 1801 congratulating him on the election.
"We have reason to believe," the Baptists told him, "that America's
God has raised you up to fill the chair of state out of that good will
which he bears to the millions which you preside over." They prayed
that God would keep Jefferson safe and bring him "at last to his
heavenly Kingdom through Jesus Christ our glorious mediator." For
many Baptists and other Jeffersonian Republican evangelicals, Jefferson's election did not represent the triumph of infidelity—the era's
popular term for godlessness and atheism—but a great providential
victory for religious freedom.[27]

Given Jefferson's and Madison's political triumphs that often came
at Henry's expense, Patrick Henry may seem little more than a historical afterthought, especially on the issue of religious liberty. The
general assessment plan, and his support for public religion generally,
are probably among the main reasons why Patrick Henry is not better
known or understood as a Founding Father. In this debate, Henry
might indeed seem to have been on the wrong side of history, while
Jefferson and Madison's campaign for full religious freedom—sym-
bolically capped by the passage of the Bill for Establishing Religious
Freedom, and Jefferson's election as president in 1800—pioneered
the system that most Americans would come to embrace. And from
a contemporary perspective, there may seem little to recommend in
Henry's plan, as even the most conservative people of faith in America

today typically do not support the idea of tax dollars going to support churches as churches.

But Henry was probably typical of many rank-and-file Revolutionaries in his belief that religious freedom could flourish without the state totally disengaging from religion. Like George Washington and John Adams, Henry believed that religious liberty and state support for religion could go hand in hand. Indeed, neither Henry nor Jefferson believed that the state should adopt a hostile stance toward religion in public life. Although few would wish to adopt Henry's general assessment today, his notion that the state could play a role in fostering both religious freedom and religious vitality is thought-provoking. Government is probably better at discouraging immorality than promoting morality, but no republic can expect to thrive in the widespread absence of virtue. (This is a lesson that we have learned afresh with our recent financial crisis. Who could deny that a robust sense of ethical responsibility to the public good would have helped to alleviate the worst practices—junk mortgages, credit default swaps and such—behind the financial meltdown?) Religious institutions, of course, ostensibly specialize in the inculcation of virtue. Henry might suggest to us that, for the good of the republic, we might continue to seek constitutional ways to foster and protect both religious freedom and the flourishing, free exercise of faith.

NOTES

Portions of this chapter appeared earlier in my books *God of Liberty: A Religious History of the American Revolution* (Basic Books, 2010), and *Patrick Henry: First Among Patriots* (Basic Books, 2011).

1. Daniel L. Dreisbach, "Mr. Jefferson, a Mammoth Cheese, and the 'Wall of Separation Between Church and State': A Bicentennial Commemoration," *Journal of Church and State* 43 (2001): 725, 742.

2. William B. Sprague, *Annals of the American Pulpit*, vol. 6, Baptist (New York, 1969), 176; Jefferson quoted in James H. Hutson, *The Founders on Religion: A Book of Quotations* (Princeton, NJ, 2005), 123, 218.

3. Thomas Slaughter, ed., *Common Sense and Related Writings* (Boston, 2001), 113.

4. Fifth Virginia Convention, *Petition of Baptists of Prince William County*, May 19, 1776, in Robert L. Scribner, ed., *Revolutionary Virginia, the Road to Independence* (Charlottesville, VA: University of Virginia Press, 1981), 188–89;

Patrick Henry to the Ministers and Delegates of the Baptist Churches, Aug. 13, 1776, *Dunlap's Pennsylvania Packet*, Sept. 3, 1776.

5. *Virginia Declaration of Rights*, http://avalon.law.yale.edu/18th_century/virginia.asp; Edmund Randolph, *History of Virginia*, ed. Arthur H. Shaffer (Charlottesville, VA: University of Virginia Press, 1970), 254; Thomas E. Buckley, *Church and State in Revolutionary Virginia, 1776–1787* (Charlottesville, VA, 1977), 17–19.

6. Richard Henry Lee to James Madison, Nov. 26, 1784, in James Curtis Ballagh, ed., *Letters of Richard Henry Lee*, vol. 2 (New York: Macmillan, 1911), 304; George Washington to George Mason, Oct. 3, 1785, in *The Papers of George Washington Digital Edition*, ed. Theodore J. Crackel (Charlottesville: University of Virginia, 2007).

7. James Madison to Thomas Jefferson, July 3, 1784, in Gaillard Hunt, ed., *The Writings of James Madison*, vol. 2 (New York: G. P. Putnam's Sons, 1901), 59; Thomas E. Buckley, *Church and State in Revolutionary Virginia, 1776–1787* (Charlottesville, VA, 1977), 86–88.

8. *A Bill Establishing a Provision for Teachers of the Christian Religion*, in Daniel L. Dreisbach and Mark David Hall, eds., *The Sacred Rights of Conscience: Selected Readings on Religious Liberty and Church-State Relations in the American Founding* (Indianapolis, IN: Liberty Fund, 2009), 252–53.

9. James Madison to James Monroe, Nov. 27, 1784, in Hunt, ed., *Writings*, vol. 2, 94 (see n. 8).

10. James Madison, *Memorial and Remonstrance against Religious Assessments*, June 20, 1785, Document 43, in Philip B. Kurland and Ralph Lerner, *The Founders' Constitution* (Chicago: The University of Chicago Press, 1987), at http://press-pubs.uchicago.edu/founders/documents/amendI_religions43.html.

11. *Bill for Establishing Religious Freedom*, in Dreisbach and Hall, eds., *Sacred Rights of Conscience*, 250–51.

12. Thomas Jefferson to James Madison, Dec. 8, 1784, in Julian P. Boyd, ed., *The Papers of Thomas Jefferson*, vol. 7 (Princeton, NJ: Princeton University Press, 1953), 558; Kevin R. C. Gutzman, *Virginia's American Revolution: From Dominion to Republic, 1776–1840* (Lanham, MD: Lexington Books, 2007), 64.

13. Mary V. Thompson, *"In the Hands of a Good Providence": Religion in the Life of George Washington* (Charlottesville, VA, 2008), 69–71.

14. James Jay to Patrick Henry, Dec. 20, 1784; Countess of Huntingdon to Governor of Virginia, April 8, 1784; Outlines of Countess of Huntingdon's Plan, April 8, 1784, in William Wirt Henry, *Patrick Henry: Life, Correspondence, and Speeches*, vol. 3 (New York: Charles Scribner's Sons, 1891), 248–61; Patrick Henry to Virginia Delegates in Congress, Feb. 3, 1785, in Henry, *Patrick Henry*, 2:273–74; Patrick Henry to Joseph Martin, Feb. 4, 1785, Patrick Henry Papers, Library of Congress.

15. George Washington to Richard Henry Lee, Feb. 8, 1785, in Crackel, ed., *Papers of George Washington* (see n. 6); Richard Henry Lee to George

Washington, Feb. 27, 1785, in Ballagh, ed., *Letters of Richard Henry Lee*, vol. 2, 338–39 (see n. 6).

16. Edwin S. Gaustad, *Sworn on the Altar of God: A Religious Biography of Thomas Jefferson* (Grand Rapids, MI, 1995), 101.

17. Thomas Paine, *The Age of Reason* (New York: G.N. Devries, 1827), 5; Gary B. Nash, "The American Clergy and the French Revolution," *William and Mary Quarterly*, 3rd ser., 22, no. 3 (July 1965): 402.

18. Patrick Henry to Elizabeth Aylett, Aug. 20, 1796, in Henry Family Papers, Virginia Historical Society, Richmond.

19. Frank Lambert, *The Founding Fathers and the Place of Religion in America* (Princeton, NJ, 2003), 266.

20. Richard Furman, *Humble Submission to Divine Sovereignty the Duty of a Bereaved Nation* (Charleston, SC, 1800), 13; John Adams, *By the President of the United States of America, A Proclamation* (Philadelphia, 1798), broadside.

21. Elias Lee, *The Dissolution of Earthly Monarchies* (Danbury, CT, 1794), 16–17.

22. Thomas Paine, *The Age of Reason* (Boston: Thomas Hall, 1794), 4; Uzal Ogden, *Antidote to Deism* (Newark, NJ, 1795), 16; Harvey J. Kaye, *Thomas Paine and the Promise of America* (New York: Hill and Wang, 2005), 82–84; Nash, "American Clergy," 402 (see n. 17).

23. John G. West, Jr., *The Politics of Revelation and Reason: Religion and the Civic Life in the New Nation* (Lawrence, KS, 1996), 60–61.

24. Noble E. Cunningham, Jr., *In Pursuit of Reason: The Life of Thomas Jefferson* (Baton Rouge, LA, 1987), 167–68.

25. "From a Correspondent in Connecticut," *Minerva*, Sept. 3, 1796; William Smith and Oliver Wolcott, *The Pretensions of Thomas Jefferson to the Presidency Examined* (Philadelphia, 1796), 37; Robert M.S. McDonald, "Was There a Religious Revolution of 1800?" in James Horn, Jan Ellen Lewis, and Peter Onuf, eds., *The Revolution of 1800: Democracy, Race, and the New Republic* (Charlottesville, VA: University of Virginia Press, 2002), 178; Nash, "American Clergy," 409 (see n. 17).

26. Timothy Dwight, *The Duty of Americans, at the Present Crisis* (New Haven, CT, 1798), in Ellis Sandoz, ed., *Political Sermons of the American Founding Era, 1730–1805*, 2nd ed. (Indianapolis, IN, Liberty Fund, 1998), 2: 1369–71, 1386; Edward J. Larson, *A Magnificent Catastrophe: The Tumultuous Election of 1800, America's First Presidential Campaign* (New York, 2007), 167–69.

27. *Gazette of the United States*, Sept. 13, 1800; Danbury Baptist Association to Thomas Jefferson, Oct. 7, 1801, in Daniel L. Dreisbach, *Thomas Jefferson and the Wall of Separation Between Church and State* (New York, 2002), 31–32; McDonald, "Was There a Religious Revolution," 173 (see n. 25); Larson, *Magnificent Catastrophe*, 173–74 (see n. 26).

2   The Founding Fathers' Competing Visions for the Proper Separation of Church and State

Vincent Phillip Muñoz

First Amendment religion jurisprudence may have reached the height of its incomprehensibility on the last day of the Supreme Court's 2004 term. Faced with two separate cases involving Ten Commandments displays, the Court found postings of the Commandments in Kentucky courthouses unconstitutional but upheld a Ten Commandments monument on the grounds of the Texas state capitol.[1] To explain their different positions, the Court's nine justices issued ten separate opinions totalling nearly 150 pages. With one exception, every opinion included significant claims about the intentions of the Founding Fathers. Yet despite this common reliance on history, the justices invoked four different tests to determine the outcomes of the cases. Writing the majority opinion in the Kentucky case, Justice David Souter employed the "Lemon test" and claimed that the Founders' intentions dictated finding state-sponsored postings of the Ten Commandments unconstitutional. Justices Antonin Scalia and Clarence Thomas, who most thoughtfully opposed Souter, came to the opposite conclusion. They held that a proper understanding of the Founders led to a test of legal coercion, which Ten Commandments postings did not violate. For good measure, Justice Breyer, who cast the deciding vote in both cases, used a civic divisiveness test, whereas Justice O'Connor used her no-endorsement test.

One might have expected that, by now, the Founders' views would be well understood and the meaning of the Constitution's religion clauses would have been decided. The Supreme Court first turned to Thomas Jefferson to interpret the Free Exercise Clause in

1879, and since the landmark Establishment Clause case *Everson v. Board of Education* in 1947, both liberal and conservative jurists have repeatedly appealed to the Founding Fathers to guide church–state jurisprudence. The last three generations of scholarship and constitutional argument, however, have failed to reach a consensus on the historical record. If anything, the opposite has happened. Scholars and judges are more divided now than ever on how the Founders intended to protect religious liberty and what they meant by the separation of church and state.

One reason for our current confusion is that we have failed to understand that the leading Founding Fathers themselves disagreed about how best to protect religious liberty. In the rush to claim the Framers for their own side, scholars and litigators have overlooked or downplayed the fact that there is not one uniform founding position regarding the proper separation of church from state.

Our failure to account for the Founders' differences has led to two deleterious effects. First, advocates have been able to misrepresent the views of particular Founders as the "founding view" more generally. This has allowed them to draw on the authority of history without fully or adequately presenting it. Second, by assuming that there is one founding view, and that it ought to determine contemporary controversies, we have neglected to think through the Founders' arguments for ourselves. In doing so, we have failed to distinguish when their thought is profound from when it might be profoundly misguided.

Rather than deferentially appealing to our founding history, we need to learn how to critically engage it. The first step is to understand that the Founders championed different understandings of the proper separation of church and state. And there is no better place to begin than with the political thoughts of James Madison, George Washington, and Thomas Jefferson. Although they do not represent all the positions taken by members of the founding generation, these three Founders have been cited frequently by the Supreme Court. Each articulated a distinct approach to protecting the right of religious liberty.[2]

JAMES MADISON: LIBERTARIAN

No Founder has been misinterpreted and misused more than James Madison, a fact that is particularly ironic given that Madison's church–state principle is simple and straightforward. For the Establishment Clause, Madison has been cited as the constitutional foreman who built Jefferson's "wall of separation." Justice Wiley Rutledge initiated this interpretation in *Everson v. Board of Education* when he declared that Madison was "unrelentingly absolute . . . in opposing state support or aid [to religion] by taxation."[3] For most of the past two decades, Rutledge's interpretation was championed by Justice Souter, who repeatedly invoked Madison to exclude religious entities from programs financed by the government (e.g., Christian groups receiving university student activity funds) and to eliminate religion's presence in the public square (e.g., public school graduation prayers, Ten Commandments displays).[4]

For the Free Exercise Clause, Madison is said to support judicially granted exemptions from religiously burdensome laws. Michael McConnell, a former judge on the Tenth Circuit Court of Appeals and one of the nation's leading church–state scholars, has most forcefully presented this interpretation. McConnell contends that a Madisonian approach would exempt religious believers from burdensome but generally applicable laws, as long as a "compelling state interest" in the law's enforcement does not exist.[5] For example, in the peyote case *Oregon v. Smith* (1990), McConnell contends that Madison would have opposed Justice Scalia's majority opinion and, instead, would have granted members of the Native American Church an exemption from the state's drug law, allowing them to use the otherwise illegal drug in their religious ceremonies. Justice O'Connor adopted McConnell's interpretation of Madison in her 1997 opinion in *City of Boerne v. Flores*.[6]

In truth, Madison was neither a strict separationist nor pro-exemptions. Madison's principle, which he articulated in his "Memorial and Remonstrance," was that the state had an obligation to remain noncognizant of religion.[7] Just as advocates of a "color blind" constitution believe that the law should not take race into account, Madison said the state could neither legitimately privilege nor punish individuals or groups on account of their religious professions and actions (or the lack thereof).

Madison thought a "religion blind" constitution followed from a proper understanding of social compact theory and the place of the right to religious liberty within it. His emphasis on individual rights, however, was not opposed to religious duties. In fact, Madison's church–state philosophy begins by recognizing human obligations to the divine. "It is the duty of every man to render to the Creator such homage and such only as he believes to be acceptable to him," Madison declares. This duty, he continues, "is precedent, both in order of time and in degree of obligation, to the claims of Civil Society." Because men have a duty to the Creator to worship according to conviction and conscience, Madison says that they have an inalienable natural right to do so. The state, accordingly, cannot legitimately take cognizance of religion.[8]

This understanding of religious freedom led Madison to oppose religious tests for political office and the abridgement of civil rights on account of religion.[9] It also led him to remonstrate against special taxes to fund religious ministers and to declare his opposition to taxpayer-funded legislative and military chaplains.[10] Madison opposed legislation that imposed special disabilities or extended particular benefits on account of religion.

Madison's resistance to taxpayer funding of religious ministers has been cited by separationists like Justice Souter to indicate that Madison opposed all government aid to religion. But what Madison actually opposed was the singling out of religious groups and individuals for special privileges. His principle of noncognizance requires that religious citizens be treated no better than nonreligious citizens, but it also means that they be treated no worse: no special privileges for religion and no particular penalties.

For this reason, a Madisonian approach would forbid special exemptions for religious citizens from generally applicable laws. To grant exemptions on account of religion requires that the state take cognizance of religion. A better approach from a Madisonian point of view would be to use nonreligious criteria for exemption eligibility. Property tax exemptions for nonprofit organizations, for example, would allow religious and nonreligious groups to receive the same benefit on equal terms. It would also avoid state officials' need to determine what groups are (and are not) authentically religious.

As noted, Madison derived noncognizance from his understanding of man's religious duties and his corresponding natural rights, but he also thought it was politically prudent. The early history of Christianity, Madison said, demonstrated that it, at least, did not need the support of government to flourish. In 1823, more than three decades after the adoption of the First Amendment, Madison claimed: "We are teaching the world a great truth that Governments do better without kings and nobles than with them. The merit will be doubled by the other lesson: that Religion flourishes in greater purity without, than with the aid of government."[11]

In contemporary political terms, Madison was a libertarian in church–state matters. He thought that religion did not need state support. If anything, he believed government aid tended to corrupt religion by making it dependent on and beholden to state authorities. These practical observations were supported by his natural rights political philosophy. For Madison, theory and practice agreed that that the state should remain noncognizant of religion.

GEORGE WASHINGTON: CONSERVATIVE

When one examines George Washington's politics regarding religion, one cannot help but be struck by how different they were from Madison's. While Madison attempted to make government noncognizant of religion, Washington consistently sought to use governmental authority to encourage religion and to foster the religious character of the American people. Washington, for example, initially was not opposed to Patrick Henry's general assessment bill, the proposed tax to fund religious clergymen in Virginia that sparked Madison to write the "Memorial and Remonstrance." Writing to George Mason, a leading assessment foe, Washington explained,

> Altho [sic], no man's sentiments are more opposed to *any kind* of restraint upon religious principles than mine are; yet I must confess, that I am not amongst the number of those who are so much alarmed at the thoughts of making people pay towards the support of that which they profess, if of the denominations of Christians; or declare themselves Jews, Mahomitans or otherwise, and thereby obtain proper relief.[12]

Washington's strong endorsement of military chaplains reflects a second difference from Madison. Madison thought taxpayer-funded chaplains violated constitutional principles. Such a thought probably never crossed Washington's mind. As commander-in-chief of the Continental Army, Washington sought not only to procure chaplains for his soldiers but also to ensure that the Continental Congress offered a salary generous enough to attract "men of abilities."[13] Chaplains, he believed, helped to improve discipline, raise morale, check vice, and fortify courage and bravery, as well as to secure respectful obedience and subordination to those in command.

As president, Washington inaugurated the tradition of declaring special days of prayer and thanksgiving, which brings forth another sharp divergence from Madison. Madison followed the first president's example, but after he left the presidency Madison wrote that official religious proclamations violated the spirit of the Constitution.[14] Washington took no such view. His first proclamation began by recognizing "the duty of all nations to acknowledge the providence of Almighty God, to obey His will, to be grateful for His benefits, and humbly to implore His protection and favor."[15]

Washington's official religious presidential proclamations not only reflect his understanding of the nation's duties, they also display his deliberate intention to sanctify solemn public statements and occasions. All of Washington's most important public addresses include religious language. A significant portion of his First Inaugural Address, to take just one notable example, is a prayer.[16]

The use of taxes to support religion, the appointment of military chaplains, the propriety of issuing religious presidential proclamations, and the deliberate inclusion of sacred language in public ceremonies reflect the distance between Washington and Madison on the proper disposition of government toward religion. Washington did not think that state actors must or should be noncognizant of religion. He agreed that religious worship was a natural right and that the purpose of government was to secure the rights of man, but he did not translate those general principles into Madison's specific limitations on the powers of government. Whereas Madison's libertarianism aimed to privatize religion, Washington sought to adorn the public square with vestments of sacred obligation and religiously inspired moral character.

It should not be surprising, then, that Washington's most definitive statement on church and state pertains not to the limits of state power but rather to the propriety of governmental support of religion. In his Farewell Address, Washington declared:

> Of all the dispositions and habits which lead to political prosperity, Religion and morality are indispensable supports. In vain would that man claim the tribute of Patriotism, who should labor to subvert these great pillars of human happiness, these firmest props of the duties of Man and citizens. The mere Politician,

equally with the pious man ought to respect and to cherish them. A volume could not trace all their connections with private and public felicity.

Religion and morality are indispensable because, Washington explains a few lines later, "'Tis substantially true, that virtue or morality is a necessary spring of popular government." Virtue and morality are needed for public felicity, because without them, Washington asks, "where is the security for property, for reputation, for life, if the sense of religious obligation desert the oaths, which are the instruments of investigation in Courts of Justice?"[17]

Washington venerated virtue and morality because they prompt citizens to act in a decent, truthful, and law-abiding manner. Virtuous citizens govern themselves and they respect the rights of others, thereby reducing the need for security through the coercive force of law. Virtue and morality are indispensable because they make limited government possible.

And religion, Washington thought, was indispensable for cultivation of virtue and morality:

> And let us with caution indulge the supposition, that morality can be maintained without religion. Whatever may be conceded to the influence of refined education on minds of peculiar structure, reason and experience both forbid us to expect that National morality can prevail in exclusion of religious principle.[18]

Washington concedes that a few may be good on account of their "refined education," but he suggests that most men require religion to fortify their character. Washington therefore endorsed the use of religion to nurture patriotic and moral citizens, something that Madison thought was unnecessary and illegitimate. From Washington's perspective, Madison's position ignored the reality that republican government needs religion. To separate religious morality from state support would imprudently destabilize the foundation of the moral character upon which republican government is built.

For Washington, the right of religious liberty meant only that individuals should not be coerced to practice a religion to which they did not subscribe. As he declared in one of his letters to the Quakers, individuals "remain responsible only to their Maker for the Religion, or modes of faith, which they may prefer or profess."[19]

Government endorsement of religion, and even the funding of it, especially if it was directed to the taxpayer's own religion, did not violate Washington's understanding of the right to religious freedom.

Washington's embrace of positive state action does not mean he approved of sectarianism. In his public speeches and writings, he deliberately avoided specifically Christian language, even though most Americans at the time were Christian. His First Inaugural Address includes fervent supplications to "that Almighty Being who rules over the universe," homage to "the Great Author of every public and private good," and humble supplications to "the benign Parent of the human race." Washington sought to teach the young country that the American system of government, as he wrote to the Hebrew Congregation at Newport, "gives to bigotry no sanction, to persecution no assistance." When he called on Congress to pass legislation authorizing military chaplains, he wanted chaplains of every denomination so that each soldier could attend his own religious services. If military commanders expected church attendance, soldiers should be provided clergymen of their own denominations. When President Washington addressed the American people using religious language, he spoke in a tongue that all Americans could appreciate and understand.

If we were to translate Washington's politics into a legal doctrine, it would be similar to those who suggest a "secular purpose" rule for Establishment Clause jurisprudence. A Washingtonian approach would allow government to support (or hinder) religion as long as the state possesses a legitimate secular reason for its actions. Washington probably would have disliked the term "secular purpose," as the term itself can seem unnecessarily hostile toward religion; instead he might have favored "civic policy" or "the civic good"—government may support (or hinder) religion insofar as it does so in a manner that supports a legitimate civic good.

Washington would have fervently disagreed with today's strict separationists, who claim that government may not favor religion over irreligion. He also would have disagreed, though less emphatically, with nonpreferentialists, who claim government may support religion if it supports all religions equally. Washington's position is a bit more discriminating. Government should support religion because religion supports republican government. By implication, a Washingtonian approach would allow government not to support those religions that maintain principles hostile toward republicanism or advocate behavior contrary to good citizenship. That said, Washington also believed that when the state endorsed religion, it ought to be as ecumenical as possible.

On the question of exemptions from burdensome laws, Washington clearly would have favored legislative and executive accommodations of religion. As a military commander, he treated Quaker pacifists with the utmost care and respect. Yet in all his dealings with the Quakers, Washington never suggested that they had a natural or constitutional right to be exempt from legitimate, generally applicable laws. If anything, he suggested the opposite. In his aforementioned 1789 letter to the Quakers, Washington declared that "while men perform their social duties faithfully, they do all that society or the state can with propriety demand or expect." In the letter's next paragraph, he chided the Quakers for failing to share with others the burden of common defense.[20] When the state remained within its legitimate sphere, Washington suggested that it should, if possible, accommodate the demands of religious conscience, but that it did not have an obligation to do so.

Washington's prudential conservatism aimed to create a cooperative relationship between religion and government while keeping distinct the different ends of church and state. Insofar as religion could help nourish the moral citizenship that made limited democratic government possible, he believed the state could and should endorse religion. At the same time, Washington always maintained that individuals possessed a natural right to practice their religion according to the convictions of conscience and that, within its own exclusive sphere, religion ought to remain free of government interference.

THOMAS JEFFERSON: PROGRESSIVE

If Washington was on the right in matters of religious liberty, Thomas Jefferson was on the progressive left. Placing Jefferson on the church–state political spectrum is difficult, however, because he is a bundle of contradictions. As in other areas in his life, so too with religious freedom: Jefferson said one thing but did something else.

What Jefferson publicly declared is encapsulated in his statute for religious freedom, the Virginia bill that was adopted by his home state in 1786.[21] In it, Jefferson recognizes five overlapping rights: (1) that no individual shall be compelled to frequent or (2) support any religious worship, place, or ministry; (3) that individuals shall not suffer or be punished by the state on account of religious opinions or beliefs; (4) that individuals shall remain free to profess and by argument maintain their opinions in matters of religion; and (5) that an individual's civil capacities shall not be diminished, enlarged, or affected by his religious opinions. While not the same as Madisonian noncognizance, protection of these rights would lead to the same results in many cases.

The complication with Jefferson is that the political actions he undertook to separate church and state were inconsistent with the rights he articulated. To take just one example, Jefferson repeatedly attempted to deprive clergymen of the right to hold public office, which contradicts the spirit, if not the letter, of the rule that an individual's civil capacities not be diminished on account of religious profession. Jefferson first designed to limit clergymen's civil rights in his 1783 draft constitution for Virginia.[22] When the proposal crossed Madison's desk, Madison said that it "violate[d] a fundamental principle of liberty by punishing a religious profession with the privation of a civil right."[23] Jefferson, however, was undeterred. Two years later in a private letter, he said the exclusion was needed because if clergymen were eligible to sit in the legislature, they would probably form its majority. That outcome had to be prevented, Jefferson continued, because the *esprit de corps* animating the clergy "has been severely felt by mankind, and has filled the history of ten or twelve centuries with too many atrocities not to merit a proscription from meddling with government."[24]

Jefferson failed to write his exclusion into the Virginia state constitution, but his efforts to restrict clergymen's civil rights and reduce their societal influence would resurface. In an 1817 bill establishing elementary education in the state, Jefferson sought a legal prohibition against clergymen serving on the board of visitors.[25] He did not want the clergy directing or influencing Virginia's public schools. "History," Jefferson had written in 1813, ". . . furnishes no example of a priest-ridden people maintaining a free civil government."[26]

The legal exclusion of clergymen from political office was just one aspect of Jefferson's larger church–state reformation project. He also sought the transformation of Americans' religious opinions through public education. Jefferson insisted that young schoolchildren not read the Bible in Virginia's public schools. Young minds, he said, "are not sufficiently mature for religious inquiries." He recommended instead that children be taught morality with "the most useful facts from Grecian, Roman, European and American history."[27] Jefferson wanted Scripture banned from the curriculum so children's minds and imaginations would be kept free of miraculous truths and revealed dogmas, superstitions that he believed would inhibit the critical analysis of religion that he wanted more advanced students to undertake.

When planning his beloved University of Virginia, Jefferson designed the curriculum to minimize clerical influence. Instead of a professor of divinity, which was standard at the time, Jefferson proposed a professor of ethics.[28] This would allow the university to teach morality without sectarianism and without hiring a member of the clergy. When Jefferson made his first round of faculty appointments, he caused a public stir by selecting a number of professors known for their heterodox religious opinions. Evangelical Christians' distrust of Jefferson ran so deep that Joseph Cabell, Jefferson's legislative ally in establishing the university, warned his friend that the clergy suspected "that the Socinians [Unitarians] are to be installed at the University for the purpose of overthrowing the prevailing religious opinions of the country."[29]

Jefferson was particularly keen to subjugate clerical influence in education because he thought that it stood as a barrier to progress in human thinking. He embraced the basic Enlightenment critique of religion and religious authority: that church authorities invented theological doctrines to disarm human reason and then used those dogmas and the power of the state to suppress the ideas and individuals that might threaten clerical power and influence. If men were freed from the artificial constraints that the clergy had imposed, Jefferson believed they would be guided by science and reason alone. He was a true progressive insofar as he believed that to secure progress, one only had to remove the "monkish ignorance" that arrested its development.

Jefferson's trust in the natural progress of reason is what led him, at the end of his life, repeatedly to predict that most Americans would become Unitarians. In 1822, he wrote, "I rejoice that in this blessed country of free inquiry and belief, which has surrendered it's [sic] creed and conscience to neither kings nor priests, the genuine doctrine of only one God is reviving, and I trust that there is not a young man now living in the US. who will not die a Unitarian."[30] Later that same year, he claimed "that the present generation will see Unitarianism become the general religion of the United states [*sic*]."[31] Unitarianism, for Jefferson, represented the rejection of what he called the "hocus-pocus phantasm" of the Trinity and the episco-pal structures of authority necessary to perpetuate it. His predic-tion of a general acceptance of Unitarianism signalled his faith in the triumphs of reason over dogma and equality over hierarchy.

When the Supreme Court constructed Jefferson's "wall of sepa-ration" out of the First Amendment's text[32]—and then used that metaphor to remove prayer and Bible reading from the public schools,[33] eliminate religious symbols from the public square,[34] and prohibit religious organizations from receiving public funds—it resumed the liberal project that Jefferson himself began (and expected to be completed within a generation or two of his death). Like the modern Court, Jefferson did not aim to be neutral toward religion. He intended his "wall" to restrict clerical authority, thereby diminishing the influence of irrational dogmas and institutions in American society. He sought to create a system of public education that would foster rationalism in religion and politics. Although Jeffer-son articulated natural rights principles in his famous Virginia Statute, his approach to religious liberty is better characterized as a politics that seeks, like modern liberalism itself, to aid the natural march of progress by transforming and overcoming traditional religion, thereby emancipating individuals to develop their minds and spirits accord-ing to the dictates of reason alone.

THE FOUNDERS' DISAGREEMENT AND FIRST AMENDMENT JURISPRUDENCE

Whatever the merits of history-based jurisprudence, the leading Founders' disagreement means that no single church–state position can claim the exclusive authority of America's founding history, and that no one Founder's position can be assumed to reflect the original meanings of the religion clauses. We should view jurisprudential appeals to any one Founder with a large dose of circumspection, especially if that appeal claims to represent "the views of the Founders." It is easy to pick and choose from the leading Founders to support different church–state jurisprudential results. Want to keep Bible reading out of public schools? Refer to Jefferson. Need a quotation to support religion in the public square? Washington's Farewell

Address works perfectly. Too often a single quotation or an example from one Founder is used to imply that the entire founding generation stood for a particular understanding of religious liberty.

The quintessential example of Founder abuse is *Everson v. Board of Education*, the 1947 Establishment Clause case. In *Everson*, Justice Hugo Black asserted, without *any* compelling evidence, that the framers of the Constitution intended the First Amendment to achieve the same purpose as Jefferson's Virginia Statute for Religious Freedom.[35] Then, in a second bald assertion, he distilled the meaning of Jefferson's principle from his 1802 "wall of separation" letter to the Danbury Baptist Association.[36] Justice Black's selective history has been the cornerstone of the separationist jurisprudence that has guided much of the past sixty-plus years of Establishment Clause litigation. *Everson* remains a standing precedent to this day.

In a fundamental way, Justice Black got Jefferson right, but his claim that Jefferson's position represented the true meaning of the Establishment Clause was pure fiction. Jefferson had nothing to do with the actual drafting of the First Amendment. His closest ally on church–state matters, James Madison, sharply criticized a central tenet of his approach. Few members of the founding generation shared his anticlericalism. To use Jefferson's "wall of separation" metaphor for the Establishment Clause was to rewrite the First Amendment, not to interpret it.

Justice Black's use of Jefferson is not atypical of how the Founders are employed in church–state jurisprudence. A few fragments from the founding era replace actual historical investigation and sustained constitutional reasoning. After long deliberation, one might find Jefferson's approach to religious liberty to be wise, prudent, and consistent with the Constitution's text and underlying purposes. But to show that it is any of these things requires a serious effort to present convincing reasons and arguments, not careless sloganeering. Throwing down a few Jefferson quotations as judicial trump cards simply does not suffice.

Because they disagreed, the leading Founders advanced arguments to defend their positions, and they made those arguments using philosophical reasoning and political considerations that can be as applicable today as they were over two hundred years ago. Understanding those arguments and considerations can help us think through the proper relationship between church and state for our times. The best type of originalism would take the Founders' competing positions seriously, evaluate their strengths and weaknesses, and integrate their most persuasive arguments with the Constitution's text and underlying principles. This approach to jurisprudence would be more honest insofar as judges would not cloak their substantive positions within an appeal to history. It would also be more true to the spirit of the Founders themselves, who sought to draft a constitution worthy of our sustained reflection and deliberate choice.

NOTES

This chapter is adapted from Vincent Phillip Muñoz, *God and the Founders: Madison, Washington, and Jefferson* (New York: Cambridge University Press, 2009).

1. *McCreary County v. American Civil Liberties Union*, 545 U.S. 844 (2005); *Van Orden v. Perry*, 545 U.S. 677 (2005).

2. For views of other members of the founding generation, see Daniel Dreisbach, Mark David Hall, and Jeffry H. Morrison, eds., *The Forgotten Founders on Religion and Public Life* (Notre Dame, IN: University of Notre Dame Press, 2009).

3. *Everson v. Board of Education*, 330 U.S. 1, 40 (1947). Jefferson's metaphor of a "wall of separation" was used by Justice Black in his majority opinion in *Everson*. Black also cited Madison (at 12) to support his interpretation.

4. See Justice Souter's opinions in *Rosenberger v. University of Virginia* (1995), *Lee v. Weisman* (1992), and *McCreary County v. American Civil Liberties Union* (2005).

5. Michael W. McConnell, "The Origins and Historical Understanding of Free Exercise of Religion," *Harvard Law Review* 103 (1990): 1453, 1462–63.

6. *City of Boerne v. Flores*, 521 U.S. 507, 549 (1997).

7. The text of Madison's "Memorial and Remonstrance" can be found in Vincent Phillip Muñoz, *God and the Founders: Madison, Washington, and Jefferson* (New York: Cambridge University Press, 2009), 223–28.

8. "Memorial and Remonstrance," Article 1. For an elaboration of this interpretation, see *God and the Founders*, chapter 1.

9. James Madison, *The Writings of James Madison*, vol. 5, ed. Gaillard Hunt (New York: G. P. Putnam's Sons, 1900–1910), 288.

10. Elizabeth Fleet, "Madison's 'Detached Memoranda,'" *William and Mary Quarterly*, 3rd ser., 3 (1946): 560.

11. James Madison to Edward Livingston, July 10, 1822, in *Writings of James Madison*, vol. 9, 102–103. See also Madison's Letter to Edward Everett, March 19, 1823, in *Writings of James Madison*, vol. 9, 127.

12. Washington's emphasis. George Washington to George Mason, October 3, 1785, in *The Writings of George Washington*, vol. 28, ed. John C.

Fitzpatrick (Washington, DC: U.S. Government Printing Office, 1938), 285. Washington wrote to Mason on account of Mason's sending to Washington a copy of a memorial and remonstrance against Henry's bill. It is fair to assume that Mason sent Washington Madison's "Memorial and Remonstrance," although it is unclear from Washington's letter, which refers only to "a memorial and remonstrance." Madison published his "Memorial and Remonstrance" anonymously, and several other petitions against the bill were also circulating at that time.

13. George Washington to the President of Congress, December 31, 1775, *Writings of George Washington*, vol. 4, 197–98, requesting an increase in the salary of military chaplains to $33 a month. On July 29, 1775, the Continental Congress, in its first official act regarding army chaplains, passed a resolution providing for a salary of $20 a month, the same as captains. For a discussion of Washington's military requests and orders pertaining to religion, see Paul F. Boller, *George Washington & Religion* (Dallas: Southern Methodist University Press, 1963), 49–60.

14. Fleet, "Madison's 'Detached Memoranda,'" 558–62.

15. George Washington, "Proclamation. A National Thanksgiving," October 3, 1787, in James D. Richardson, *A Compilation of the Messages and Papers of the Presidents: 1789–1897*, vol. 1 (Washington, D.C.: U.S. Government Printing Office, 1896), 64.

16. George Washington, "First Inaugural Address," April 30, 1789, *Papers of George Washington*, vol. 2, Presidential Series, ed. Dorothy Twohig (Charlottesville, VA: University Press of Virginia, 1987–), 174.

17. Farewell Address, September 19, 1796, *Writings of Washington*, vol. 35, 229. Washington's Farewell Address was not a speech but a long letter addressed "To the PEOPLE of the United States," first published in *American Daily Advisor*, Philadelphia's largest newspaper, on September 19, 1796. For a discussion of the drafting and publication of the Farewell Address, see Matthew Spalding and Patrick J. Garrity, *A Sacred Union of Citizens: George Washington's Farewell Address and the American Character*, Introduction by Daniel J. Boorstin (Lanham, MD: Rowman & Littlefield Publishers, Inc., 1996), 45–61.

18. Farewell Address, September 19, 1796, *Writings of Washington*, vol. 35, 229.

19. George Washington to the Society of Quakers, October 1789, *Papers of George Washington*, vol. 4, Presidential Series, ed. Dorothy Twohig (Charlottesville, VA: University Press of Virginia, 1987–), 266.

20. Ibid.

21. The text of Jefferson's Virginia Statute for Religious Freedom can be found in Muñoz, *God and the Founders*, 231–34.

22. *The Papers of Thomas Jefferson*, vol. 6, ed. Julian P. Boyd (Princeton, NJ: Princeton University Press, 1953), 297. Jefferson published his draft constitution as an appendix to *Notes on the State of Virginia*.

23. Madison, *Writings of James Madison*, vol. 5, 288.

24. Letter to Chastellux, September 2, 1785, in *Papers of Thomas Jefferson*, vol. 8, 470.

25. "An Act for Establishing Elementary Schools," 1817, in *The Writings of Thomas Jefferson*, vol. 9, ed. H. A. Washington (Washington, DC: Taylor & Maury, 1854), 490.

26. Letter to Alexander von Humboldt, December 6, 1813, in *Thomas Jefferson: Writings*, ed. Merrill D. Peterson (New York: The Library of America, 1984), 1311.

27. *Notes on the State of Virginia*, Query XIV, in *The Portable Thomas Jefferson*, ed. and Introduction by Merrill D. Peterson (New York: Penguin, 1975), 197.

28. *Jefferson: Writings*, 462–64.

29. Cabell to Jefferson, August 5, 1821, in John G. West, *The Politics of Reason and Revelation*, 63 n.265.

30. Jefferson's emphasis. Thomas Jefferson to Benjamin Waterhouse, June 26, 1822, in *Jefferson's Extracts from the Gospels*, ed. Dickenson W. Adams (Princeton, NJ: Princeton University Press, 1983), 405–406.

31. Letter to James Smith, December 8, 1822, in *Jefferson's Extracts from the Gospels*, 409.

32. *Everson v. Board of Education*, 330 U.S. 1 (1947).

33. *Engel v. Vitale*, 370 U.S. 421 (1962); *Abington School District v. Schempp*, 374 U.S. 203 (1963).

34. See, for example, *County of Allegheny v. American Civil Liberties Union*, 492 U.S. 573 (1989).

35. *Everson v. Board of Education*, 330 U.S. 1, 13 (1947). For an account of Justice Black's methods and motivations regarding his *Everson* opinion, see Donald L. Drakeman, *Church, State, and Original Intent* (New York: Cambridge University Press, 2010), chap. 3.

36. *Everson v. Board of Education*, 330 U.S. 1,16 (1947). For a more recent interpretation of Jefferson's wall, see Daniel L. Dreisbach, *Thomas Jefferson and the Wall of Separation Between Church and State* (New York: New York University Press, 2003).

3 The First School Prayer Debate and Its Impact on Modern Church–State Doctrine

Steven K. Green

Few constitutional issues have been as contentious as those concerning prayer and Bible reading in the public schools and the public funding of religious schools. In the 1940s, the U.S. Supreme Court asserted authority over these issues for the first time (via the incorporation of the Bill of Rights through the Due Process Clause of the Fourteenth Amendment) and proceeded to announce one controversial ruling after another. In 1947, a slim Court majority upheld the constitutionality of minor forms of public financial assistance for children attending parochial schools, yet suggested that more significant aid would violate notions of church–state separation. The following year the Court struck down a program of religious instruction in the public schools, declaring that "a state cannot consistently with the First [Amendment] utilize its public school system to aid any or all religious faiths or sects in the dissemination of their doctrines."[1] Few holdings were as contentious, however, as the 1962 and 1963 decisions banning ceremonial prayer and Bible reading in the public schools. There, the Court struck down the widespread practice of daily religious exercises, eliciting an outcry from many who insisted that the justices had "thrown the Bible out of the schools" and, in the process, had disregarded the nation's religious heritage. Evangelist Billy Graham charged the decision was but "another step toward the secularism of the United States," and lamented: "God pity our country when we can no longer appeal to God for help." Political leaders also criticized the holding, with North Carolina senator Sam Ervin, a self-described constitutional expert (who would later gain fame during the Watergate hearings), insisting that "the Supreme Court has made God unconstitutional." Few people defended the decisions, at least publicly.[2]

The public scrutiny given the Court's prayer and Bible reading holdings was an episode previously unmatched in American constitutional history. Only the desegregation holding in *Brown v. Board of Education* (1954) received the same level of media attention and engendered a public debate about the meaning of a constitutional principle. *Christianity Today* reported that, during the pendency of the prayer cases, the Supreme Court received as many as fifty letters a day in favor of prayer and Bible reading, and Congress twice held public hearings on the issue. Responding to the outcry, members of Congress introduced a proposed constitutional amendment to prohibit schools and other government institutions from prohibiting public prayers or Bible readings. When Congress held hearings on the proposed amendment in 1964, more than one hundred people testified, with the overwhelming majority favoring the amendment. Overall, the Bible reading controversy "attracted the widest attention and the largest following," asserted one religious magazine, and for many people it represented "America's greatest battle." But more was at stake than mere Bible reading; as one religious leader remarked, the controversy raised the "greater question" of "whether the United States will continue to give honor and respect to God in national life."[3]

The constitutional controversy was not resolved until Congress narrowly voted down the proposed school prayer amendment in November 1971. Even though the high court would go on to reaffirm the substance of the 1963 decisions in later rulings, the issue of religious expression in our nation's schools has remained a contentious issue and, for many people, has never been resolved. To this day, legal conflicts arise over issues such as student-led prayer at school events, the on-campus distribution of religious materials, and the teaching of evolution, to name a few. The legal touchstone for all of these controversies remains the 1962 and 1963 prayer and Bible reading cases.[4]

As the above quotations demonstrate, the "school prayer" controversy is part of a larger debate over the public role of religion in America. While the specific conflicts can be highly significant for the teachers, students, and parents involved, they are merely manifestations of a greater religious–ideological divide that has gripped the United States for much of its history. This debate asks several crucial questions: What were the sources of republican principles upon which the nation was founded, and did religion serve as a significant influence on the founding? What assumptions did the Founders make about the role of religious expression and moral virtue in the new nation, and to what extent can a nation exist independent of a religious foundation? To what extent (if any) should a democratic government acknowledge the religious traditions and facilitate the religious faith of its people, and how would such state action avoid devolving into the sectarian preferences and strife that has plagued so many nations?

Fueling this ideological debate and the specific church–state controversies are historical claims and assumptions. Although those claims vary, two are most common: that the Founders intended to create a secular republic with a regime of separation of church and state; and that the Founders were chiefly concerned about abolishing coercive religious establishments and sect preferences but still envisioned America as a Christian nation, one where the government would support and reinforce religious values and traditions. Promoters of the secularist position point to the actions and writings of leading Founders such as Thomas Jefferson and James Madison, whose ideas were embraced by the modern Supreme Court between the 1940s and 1990s.[5] In contrast, proponents of the religionist position claim that a consensus existed in America over the role of religion in public education and in public life from the founding period through the mid-twentieth century. They claim that when the Supreme Court finally entered the legal fray in the late-1940s, it embraced an inaccurate model of church–state relations, one that was promoted by an intellectual elite suspicious of religion and its value to democratic society. Specifically for the issue of prayer and Bible reading, religionist proponents claimed that those practices were relatively common throughout the nation's history, and uncontroversial until the Court declared them outcasts. As a result, religionists assert that the high court should renounce its more separationist holdings and affirm a tradition of religious accommodation.[6]

Because proponents of this latter position are contesting the dominant narrative adopted by the Supreme Court and endorsed by the majority of scholars, they have been most active in reexamining the nation's history. This revisionist project questions the influence of those actors of the dominant narrative—Jefferson and Madison—and argues that they were more atypical than typical of contemporary attitudes during the founding period. Conservative scholars, such as Daniel Dreisbach and Mark David Hall, have sought to rehabilitate the religious bona fides of the Founders, including rational theists like Jefferson and Benjamin Franklin, as part of an alternative narrative in which the Founders envisioned an active role for religion in public affairs. Adopting a different track, Columbia University Professor Philip Hamburger published an influential work in 2002, *Separation of Church and State*, where he maintained that church–state separation was not only an alien idea for most members of the founding generation, but that it represents an illiberal concept, one that arose chiefly during the nineteenth century to maintain a Protestant hold on the culture by suppressing Catholics and their institutions. These critiques reinforce a larger movement within academia that challenges the secularization thesis that dominated most of the twentieth century. This post-secularization critique, represented in the works of James Davison Hunter, among others, maintains that the culture has never been secularized, such that the nation is not represented by the image portrayed in the holdings by the modern Supreme Court.[7]

Both the secularist and religionist accounts of our history are correct, but only halfway. Most accounts of church–state relations in America have focused on the founding period—with background about colonial practices—and then they jump forward in time to analyze the modern Court's church–state cases. This approach is due in part to our national obsession with the founding period, to uncovering the "original intent" or "original meaning" behind the founding documents and then allowing those interpretations to control or direct our understanding of constitutional principles. Yet this approach is triply flawed. First, it overstates the importance of a brief fifteen year period in our history, as if long-developing notions of democracy, freedom, equality, and civic virtue reached their apex between 1775 and 1790 and then ceased developing. It ignores the long evolution of ideas and the myriad, incremental experiences that shaped eighteenth century republican theory.[8] Second, it suggests a past that was *unified* and *positive*—that we can capture those "agreed-upon historical truths" if only they can be identified (and that these "truths" should be accepted uncritically). Finally, an originalist perspective is untrue to the Founders themselves, who saw history and the political theories they were espousing as an evolving process, not as something static or completed. Many in the founding generation believed that the nation had yet to achieve the ultimate state of religious freedom. As one example, in 1790 the Pennsylvania legislature revised its revolutionary constitution of 1776, strengthening its no-establishment clause while removing many religious disqualifications for public office-holding. Reflecting on the changes, Noah Webster predicted that the revisions were merely "a prelude to wiser measures; people are just awakening from delusion. The time will come (and may the say be near!) when all test laws, oaths of allegiance, abjuration, and partial exclusions from civil offices will be proscribed from this land of freedom."[9]

Agitation for expanding religious freedoms continued after the ratification of the First Amendment, with people contesting the "mild and equitable" establishments in New England and the common use of religion as a disqualifier of civic participation that existed in the new states. As late as 1822, James Madison bemoaned that there "remain[ed] in others a strong bias towards the old error . . . some sort of alliance or coalition between government and religion." Thus some forty years after the adoption of the First Amendment, Madison still believed that pressure for a union of church and state was a "danger [that] cannot be too carefully guarded against." Webster and Madison were correct, as many old errors persisted into the nineteenth century. The subsequent history of the United States has been one of a gradual expansion of religious freedom and diversity.[10]

In addition to amplifying the significance of the founding period—and seeing the values it pronounced as being relatively static—both secularists and religionists have generally given short shrift to the events of the nineteenth century (Professor Hamburger excepted), portraying it as a period when the majority of Americans shared a limited concept of church–state separation, one that promoted a Victorian attitude about religious morality in public life. Under the separationist narrative, the Protestant Empire of the nineteenth century, in which prayer and Bible reading prevailed in public schools and an evangelical ethos dominated the culture, is depicted as a period of regression from the founding principles, with the original separationist values being rediscovered by the scribes of the modern Supreme Court. In contrast, religionists claim the religiosity of the nineteenth century is pervasive evidence of the true founding settlement on church–state matters, one that the modern Supreme Court ignored or renounced. While both groups are correct in identifying a prominent public role of religion during the nineteenth century, they are wrong in assuming that attitudes toward church–state matters during that period were either uniform or static. In actuality, the nineteenth century was a highly dynamic period in American religious history, with various actors contesting not only the dominant Protestant narrative but advancing contrasting visions of church–state relations. The events of the century facilitated an evolution in ideas about church and state that bridged the gap between the founding and modern era and laid the basis for the Court's more separationist decisions.[11]

The nineteenth century is thus key to our understandings of church–state relations. I argue that there were various phases of disestablishment in American history. The first took place during the founding period and was one of political disestablishment (others have called it institutional disestablishment). During this time, 1775–1800, the formal ties between religion and government were severed and religious institutions were privatized. In addition, political disestablishment grounded the country's political values chiefly on secular, rational principles. This was a highly significant event in governance and human rights, when the nation and majority of states rejected the centuries-old assumptions and arrangements concerning the relationship between the sacred and profane spheres. Adherence to religious belief became a private matter, and religious toleration— with an eye toward religious equality—became the accepted norm. Still, this first disestablishment was in many ways modest, with states retaining religious-based laws and policies, such as maintaining religious qualifications for public office holding and oath taking, and enforcing Sunday laws on religious grounds. Many people understood this formal disestablishment as having little effect on the role of religion in the broader culture. At this point, disestablishment was chiefly political, not cultural.[12]

A second disestablishment occurred during the nineteenth century, one that was neither as dramatic nor as obvious as the first. In many ways, however, its impact on American law and society was as significant as the earlier political disestablishment. This second phase involved a legal and institutional disestablishment, a gradual process of secularizing the law and the institutions of state and local governments. Leading the way was a secularizing movement in the law, one facilitated by a desire for the law to respond to changing commercial and demographic pressures. In the drive to make the law more professional and responsive to a developing economy, lawyers and judges began to divorce the law from its moral and religious trappings. Contract law stopped caring about which party was at fault in a breach, now focusing on what was the agreed-upon price for a default. To not fulfill a contract or some other financial obligation stopped being seen a moral failing and became merely a business matter. Probate law abandoned its prohibition against honoring "irreligious" bequests deemed inconsistent with Christian principles. Blasphemy prosecutions, still common during the first third of the century, died off because of a growing discomfort over the law punishing expressions of religious heterodoxy. No longer would the law protect the dominant majority's religious sensibilities in the absence of a true public disturbance (i.e., disorderly conduct), now measured objectively. And over time, prosecutions for "profaning the Sabbath" decreased, and the religious justifications for Sunday laws shifted to health and safety rationales. This impulse helped secularize not only the substance and institution of the law, but also changed the way in which people envisioned its role in reinforcing religious norms. Whereas at the beginning of the nineteenth century judges commonly referred to Christianity as "forming part of the common law," by century's end that phrase and concept had fallen into disfavor. While remnants of morality remained in a handful of legal fields, such as criminal and domestic law, well into the twentieth century, overall the law became unconcerned with moral questions. The law, as an institution, became amoral.[13]

While this development in the law took place chiefly in mill-run areas of the law—contract, probate, nuisance—judges and litigants grasped the constitutional significance of these changes. Legal efficiency and predictability were often the driving forces for judges abandoning religious justifications, yet the constitutional implications were never far below the surface. Judges and lawyers appreciated that notions of church–state separation and religious equality were evolving, and many saw the changes as a positive and progressive event. In prohibiting lawyers from inquiring into a witness's religious beliefs as a way to discredit his testimony, the Kentucky Court of Appeals opined in 1882 that the purpose of its new rule "was to make the divorce between church and state irrevocable." Similarly, in disclaiming any authority to settle a property dispute between two factions of a church by examining church doctrine, the Vermont Supreme Court in 1846 declared that "Civil courts in this country have no ecclesiastical jurisdiction. . . . This doctrine inevitably results from that total separation between church and state . . . which is essential to the full enjoyment of the guaranteed rights of American citizenship." And in rejecting a religious rationale for enforcing a Sunday law, the Ohio Supreme Court in 1853 asserted Sunday was merely a civil day of rest from labor. "We have no union of church and state," the court opined, "nor has our government ever been vested with authority to enforce any religious observance, simply because it is religious." Increasingly, parties recognized that the secularizing thrust in the law had constitutional implications as well.[14]

The chief cultural institution to undergo a gradual secularization was the nation's public schools, and the religious transformation in public education helped to accelerate the second disestablishment more than any other factor. This episode requires some background.

Following the American Revolution, public education in America was practically nonexistent. Quasi-public schools—meaning schools open to most children—operated in some New England towns, but they generally were not free, charging tuition to parents. Most other education was private in nature, through tutors or in academies, and limited to children of the wealthy and propertied classes. In a few eastern cities, churches and religious groups operated "charity schools" for poor and destitute children, but those opportunities were limited and generally not available to the larger number of children of farming and working-class families. Regardless of its availability, the content of education was chiefly religious (excluding the elite academies), dependent on children reading religious texts and reciting catechisms.[15]

In the decades following the American Revolution, political and civic leaders began to advocate for a system of schools accountable to the public which would be free and open to children from all economic and social classes. Reformers, such as Benjamin Rush and Noah Webster, believed that a *common* education was necessary to transmit civic values for self-governance and to make children industrious. Early on, a handful of states established modest "school funds" in their treasuries to encourage towns to organize common schools. Also during the early nineteenth century, "free school societies" emerged in cities to provide a common education for poor and working-class children, many belonging to a growing immigrant class. To make these schools attractive and accessible to all children, education reformers quickly settled on the concept of a "nonsectarian curriculum," one that emphasized reading, writing and arithmetic over the more doctrinal curriculum taught in the denominational schools. Still, all education reformers believed that a common education must include instruction in religious and moral values. At this point, no one could conceive that moral education could be divorced from religion, and moral education was indispensable for instilling those necessary elements of civic virtue and industry in the future generation. Thus, one of the "primary objects" of non-sectarian education, wrote one advocate, was "to inculcate the sublime truths of religion and morality contained in the Holy Scriptures . . . without observing the particular forms of any religious society."[16]

Despite its name, and overall goal of avoiding doctrinal differences, early nonsectarian education was highly religious, representing a form of watered-down Protestantism that merely discarded the doctrines that divided Protestant denominations—predestination, for example. Notions of human sinfulness and salvation were appropriate areas of instruction since they were commonly shared Protestant doctrines. These topics were taught through Bible readings, catechisms, and worship activities, and pan-Protestant themes infused reading and history texts; "a sense of God permeate[d] all books as surely as a sense of nationalism," writes Ruth Miller Elson. In the early decades of the century before the rise in Catholic or Jewish immigration, few people objected to the religious content of non-sectarian education.[17]

This model was not static, however. The nineteenth century in America was a dynamic period in so many ways, the most important aspects here being religious and demographic. Whereas most church-going Americans in 1800 affiliated with long-established denominations—Congregationalist, Presbyterian, Episcopal—the religious complexion by 1850 was considerably more diverse. Not only were Baptists and Methodists now dominant, they faced competition from a variety of heterodox faiths: Shakers, Adventists, Mormons, Transcendentalists, Freethinkers, and Catholics. The idea that a consensus existed over commonly shared religious values—particularly those to be taught in public schools—was becoming illusive. In addition, the ethnic composition of America was changing, chiefly due to immigration. The nation's complexion was shifting from being a people of British stock to including a larger percentage of Irish, Germans, Jews and Latinos, all of whom not only spoke different languages and practiced different religions, but also held different cultural attitudes from the dominant Anglo-American Protestant class. These forces, not to mention evolving economic and geographic factors, all challenged the emergent public school system and the assumptions upon which a nonsectarian curriculum relied.

In response to these forces, nonsectarianism went through three phases during the nineteenth century. The first phase, just described, continued in many locations through the 1840s (longer in communities that were religiously homogeneous). In such instances, the curriculum reflected and reinforced distinctly Protestant values, commonly of an evangelical variety. Once again, this version was "nonsectarian" only in the sense that the curriculum avoided matters that divided Protestant denominations. In addition, many schools engaged in religious instruction for the distinct purpose of instilling religious fealty among the children. A second phase of nonsectarianism slowly emerged during the 1830s and 1840s, led by reformers such as Horace Mann, Secretary of the Massachusetts Board of Education. As part of his efforts to standardize and professionalize public education in Massachusetts, Mann campaigned against the instruction in common Protestant doctrines and the role of schools in instilling religious fealty. Instead, Mann urged schools to practice unmediated Bible reading which, he believed, would inspire children to be virtuous and religious on their own. "The diversity of religious doctrines, prevalent in our community, would render it difficult to inculcate any religious truths," Mann wrote. Still, Mann believed that schools should retain the Bible as a sourcebook for teaching those "fundamental principles of Christianity," which he believed to be universal. A system of nonsectarian education

> earnestly inculcates all Christian morals; it founds its morals on the basis of religion; it welcomes the religion of the Bible; and, in receiving the Bible, it allows it to do what it is allowed to do in no other system—*to speak for itself.* But here it stops, not because it claims to have compassed all truth, but because it disclaims to act as an umpire between hostile religious opinions.[18]

Exposing children to religion remained the goal, but only to those universal values of God's love and goodness.

Mann's modifications initially drew objections from all sides. Orthodox Protestants thought the changes discarded essential religious doctrines that could and should be taught in public schools. A growing number of Catholics, Jews, and freethinkers also objected that Mann's "universal" Christianity was based on Protestant assumptions about the perspicuity of scripture and was essentially Protestant in character. One evangelical critic charged that Mann's nonsectarianism was a "grand instrument in the hands of freethinkers, atheists, and infidels," while a Catholic bishop called them "*sectarian* free-schools" because of their Protestant assumptions. Depending on one's perspective, Mann's nonsectarianism was either too religious or not religious enough.[19]

The nation's expanding religious pluralism was on Mann's side, however. Over time, Protestants slowly acceded to the new form of nonsectarianism. For moderates and liberals, it respected rights of religious conscience, while for evangelicals, half a loaf was better than no loaf. But nothing unified Protestant support behind Mann's system more than the growing Catholic opposition to public education and its Protestant complexion. Importantly for all Protestants, Mann's system preserved a minimal Protestant character of education—and most crucial, the King James Bible—while it counteracted Catholic objections to its remaining religious content, or so Protestants and educator hoped. Protestants could never fully comprehend that Catholics objected to a more-secular-oriented educational system as much as they opposed a overtly Protestant one.[20]

The institutionalization of nonsectarianism in public education, and its growing acceptance among Protestants, was a leading factor in the decision by the Catholic Church to establish a system of parochial schooling in mid-century. Initially, in the early years, many Catholic had leaders supported the common free schools and recommended attendance by Catholic children. This was due in part to the fluidity of early public schooling, where the lines between public and private operation were not always clear, and the religious complexion of schools frequently reflected the local religious flavor. But also, Catholic officials initially had few objections to the use of religion in public education. The Philadelphia *Catholic Herald* in 1834 affirmed that "religion must be the foundation and the topstone of education," and recommended that "the Bible should be studied more diligently than any other volume, and . . . the spirit of religion should pervade even the common school."[21] As one historian has noted, "[p]rior to 1840, there was no strong Catholic protest against the Common School Movement. On the contrary, many Catholic leaders were at first sympathetic to the movement and indeed participants in it."[22]

That amicable situation deteriorated with the influx of Catholic immigrants into the United States after the 1830s. Protestant leaders and nativists began to raise alarms that a foreign "Romanism" posed a threat to republican government and, in turn, to public education. This concern caused many Protestants to resist any further reduction in the Protestant character of common education, which they considered to represent the bulwark of American values. At this same time, Catholic leaders began to raise objections to having Catholic children exposed to the Protestant-oriented exercises. Bishops also increasingly objected to the use of popular textbooks that portrayed Catholicism in a negative light, as well as to the evangelizing efforts of groups such as the American Bible Society and the American Home Mission Society. These textbooks, promoted by the societies, praised the virtues of Protestant culture while they disparaged Catholic culture and faith: Protestantism was identified with progress, republicanism, and individual conscience, whereas Catholicism was commonly associated with superstition, despotism, and mindless obedience to authority. As the Catholic Bishops charged in an 1840 pastoral letter, they could "scarcely point out a book in general use in the ordinary schools . . . wherein covert and insidious efforts are not made to misrepresent our principles, to distort our tenets, to vilify our practices and to bring contempt upon our Church and its members." After years of urging Catholic parents to send their children to Catholic schools, in 1852 the bishops called for "the establishment and support of Catholic schools," admonishing parents to "make every sacrifice which may be necessary for this object."[23]

Even before the impasse, some Catholic leaders, led by New York Bishop John Hughes, had begun to agitate for a share of the public school funds for Catholic schools. These efforts also unified the various Protestant factions and secularists, who argued that Catholic funding threatened the financial stability of public education (and to their favored position) while it violated church–state separation. For public school supporters, nonsectarianism provided a ready defense to Catholic requests for a share of the school funds for their emerging parochial schools: public funds should pay only for universal *nonsectarian* education rather than for private *sectarian* schooling. Catholics continued their efforts to obtain a share of the school funds throughout the remainder of the century. However, they were met with massive resistance by Protestants and secularists who agreed on two essential points: their support for public education and their mutual distrust of Catholic schooling. These two interrelated controversies—Bible reading and religious school funding—embroiled the nation throughout the pre– and post–Civil War years, and the issue became so prominent that it acquired its own short-hand name: "the School Question."[24]

The Civil War temporarily diverted attention away from the School Question. But the controversy did not go away, and Catholic immigration only increased during the war years. Following the war, ongoing Catholic complaints about religious exercises led several urban school districts to disband unmediated prayer and Bible reading. In the most famous incident, the Cincinnati Board of Education banned Bible reading in its schools in 1869. Bible supporters quickly challenged the action and succeeded in having the practices temporarily restored by a three-judge trial court, but only over the stinging dissent of Judge Alphonzo Taft, father of the future president and chief justice. Judge Taft insisted that the no-preference clause of the state constitution prohibited the Protestant-oriented religious exercises. To hold that Protestants "are entitled to any control in the schools . . . or that they are entitled to have their mode of worship and their Bible used in the common schools . . . is to hold to the union of Church and State, however we may repudiate and reproach the name," Taft wrote. The state constitution afforded "absolute equality before the law, of all religious opinions and sects," he asserted. "No sect can, because it includes a majority of a community or a majority of the citizens of the State, claim any preference whatever." Taft's opinion was a bellwether, though it built on understandings of church–state separation that had been developing over the years. On appeal, the Ohio Supreme Court agreed with Taft, reinstating the school board's ban on Bible reading. Speaking for a unanimous court, Justice John Welch wrote that the national and state constitutions had "at last solved the terrible enigma of 'church and state'" that had plagued other nations.

Disestablishment meant more than simply forbidding government tax support of religion or prohibiting religious preferences. It meant that religious matters were "not within the purview of human government," Welch declared. Religious instruction in the schools was "eminently one of those interests, lying outside the true and legitimate province of government." Significantly, Welch rejected arguments that nonsectarian instruction was exempt from the above interpretation because it affirmed "universal" religious principles. Even if the state supported only a general Christianity through its policies, it would still be "a first step in the direction of an 'establishment of religion'; and I should add, that the first step in that direction is a fatal step, because it logically involves the last step."[25]

The Ohio Supreme Court decision, coming some ninety years before those of the U.S. Supreme Court, was pathbreaking in that it rejected popular assumptions about the duty of government to promote a system of morals derived from religion. Even though the decision was initially an outlier, it was instrumental in shaping public attitudes about church–state relations. An emerging chorus of educators, secularists, and liberal Protestant leaders began to call for an education system that was not just nonsectarian but secular. Compulsory Bible reading in the schools was "not in accordance with American doctrine of the liberty of conscience" and should be abolished, wrote the nation's best-known preacher, Henry Ward Beecher. "It is too late to adopt the church–state doctrine."[26]

Although a handful of school districts followed Ohio's lead in abolishing Bible reading, a greater number chose to water down the religious content of the exercises even more, hoping to appease Catholics, Jews, and secularists. These actions effectively turned the Bible reading into rote exercises done now for the purpose of instilling moral character, not religious devotion. This trend ushered in the third phase of nonsectarianism, of using the Bible for reputedly nonreligious goals. Some schools used the Bible as a textbook for teaching reading, history, or literature. This compromise satisfied few people. Critics charged the "literary, historical, and moral truths of the Bible cannot be truly taught without involving the teaching of its religious truths," while others simply condemned the entire enterprise. As stated by University of Chicago theologian Shailer Mathews, to teach the Bible "merely as a piece of literature . . . is worse than not teaching it at all."[27] Even Catholics, who otherwise objected to the King James Bible, found the trend emblematic of the moral decline of American education. Writing in 1881, Rochester Catholic Bishop Benjamin McQuaid quipped that New York had made "great progress in eliminating every semblance of religious instruction in its common schools." Where the Bible was read at all, he noted, it was done "in a very perfunctory way."[28]

Religious exercises did not die out in the nineteenth century; on the contrary, rote, unmediated, and sometimes even devotional prayer and Bible reading remained common practices among the nation's public schools, particularly in rural areas or places with greater religious homogeneity. But as a result of the Ohio decision and a handful of subsequent state court decisions striking prayer and Bible reading on church–state grounds, there was no longer a presumption that such practices were constitutional. As the Wisconsin Supreme Court opined in 1890, it "could not doubt that the use of the Bible as a *textbook* has the tendency to inculcate sectarian ideas and is sectarian instruction." In its holding, the Wisconsin court expressly rejected arguments that the practices were justified on grounds they instilled moral character or simply recognized the nation's religious heritage. Bible reading was inherently religious, regardless of its purported justifications, the court declared; as a result, it was "eminently one of those interests, lying outside the true and legitimate province of government." In reporting on the Wisconsin ruling, the *New York Times* opined that it represented the inevitable direction for public education, particularly if "the common school system [wishes to] maintain . . . its integrity."[29]

The number of late nineteenth and early twentieth century cases outlawing religious exercises in public schools was never large, but they, in conjunction with actions by urban school boards deemphasizing or eliminating religious exercises, created the perception that schools were becoming secularized. A national survey conducted by the Woman's Christian Temperance Union in 1887 confirmed the perception, noting that the Bible was not being read in schools in 175 counties out of 254 reporting. Where religious exercises persisted, stated the WCTU report, the Bible frequently was "not so generally read as formally." A series of late-century reports by the U.S. Commissioner of Education documented this phenomenon, noting that not only was religious instruction in decline, but so too was the use of the Bible as a textbook for teaching morals or literature. Even the amount of time schools devoted to character and moral instruction had declined considerably. In his 1895 government report, Commissioner William T. Harris concluded that

[outside] New England there is no considerable area where [the Bible's] use can be said to be uniform. This condition has come about as much by indifference as by opposition. . . . There has been a change in public sentiment gradually growing toward complete secularization of the Government and its institutions.

. . . Secularization of the schools is accepted or urged by many devout people who deem that safer than to trust others with the interpretation of the laws of conscience.[30]

Summarizing the secularizing trend of the previous century, a 1912 Columbia Teachers College study stated that "over the century there has been a gradual but widespread elimination of religious and church influences from public education." In every state, the study continued, "religious instruction was either entirely eliminated or else reduced to the barest and most formal elements." The study attributed this transformation to two factors. The first was a "conviction that a republic can securely rest only on an educated citizenship." The second was "a sacred regard by the state for the religious opinion of the individual citizen."[31]

This secularizing trend, or the perception that one existed, produced a backlash in the early 1900s. Coinciding with the rise of Protestant fundamentalism, legislatures in sixteen states, chiefly in the South and Midwest, enacted laws requiring or authorizing non-sectarian Bible reading in the schools. But the legislative reaction to secularization was not able to halt the overall trend, which was spurred on by a new group of education reformers led by John Dewey who advocated for an increasingly pragmatic, and secular, system of public education. By the time the U.S. Supreme Court ruled on school prayer and Bible reading in 1962–63, less than forty percent of the nation's public schools conducted any form of religious exercises, a fact ignored by critics of the Court's decisions.[32]

Critics of the Court's school prayer decisions also ignored, or were unaware of, the nineteenth century transition away from public school religious instruction, a trend that helped institute another level of disestablishment in America. (This was despite a reference to the 1873 Ohio Supreme Court ruling in the Court's 1963 decision.) Because this historical transformation conflicted with the popular narrative about the nation's religious heritage, the Court was accused of making new law rather than seen as building on an existing body of jurisprudence. Seen in their historical context, the modern Court's prayer and Bible reading decisions were actually cautious; they merely affirmed a trend rather than breaking new ground. This distinguishes the prayer and Bible-reading decisions from the Court's approach in *Brown v. Board of Education*, which dramatically reversed a system of racial segregation.[33]

The nineteenth-century transition in the School Question thus brought about a fuller conception of disestablishment in America. It demonstrated that legal understandings of religious freedom have not been static. At the same time, that transition was not without its faults. The School Question unfortunately became embroiled in nativist reactions to Catholic immigration, which at times overshadowed the important constitutional issues at stake. But that past should not obscure the sincere efforts of others to make the public schools truly accessible to children of all religious faiths by limiting and then eliminating religious exercises. The School Question controversy was thus a crucial element in our nation's second disestablishment. As important, it helped lay the foundation for modern Supreme Court jurisprudence and the cultural disestablishment of the second half of the twentieth century. That became the nation's third disestablishment.[34]

NOTES

1. McCollum v. Board of Education, 333 U.S. 203, 211 (1948).

2. Engel v. Vitale, 370 U.S. 421 (1962); Abington School District v. Schempp, 374 U.S. 203, 312–13 (1963); "Tempest Over School Prayer Ban," *Christianity Today*, July 20, 1962, 46; "Repercussions of Supreme Court Prayer Ruling" (ibid., August 3, 1962, 25); *New York Herald Tribune*, July 5, 1962, 18; William E. Boles and Edward N. Beiser, "Prayer and Politics: The Impact of Engel and Schempp on the Political Process," *Journal of Public Law* (1964): 475–503; Bruce Dierenfield, *The Battle Over School Prayer* (Lawrence, KS: University of Kansas Press, 2007).

3. Statement of Carl T. McIntire, Hearings on School Prayers before the Committee on the Judiciary, House of Representatives, 88th Cong., 2d Sess. (1964), 1299; *Christian Crusade* (May 1964), 24; Steven K. Green, "Evangelicals and the Becker Amendment," *Journal of Church and State* 33 (Summer 1991): 555–64.

4. Santa Fe Independent School District v. Doe, 530 U.S. 290 (2000); Lee v. Weisman, 505 U.S. 577 (1992); Edwards v. Aguillard, 482 U.S. 578 (1987); Wallace v. Jaffree, 472 U.S. 38 (1985).

5. Leonard W. Levy, *The Establishment Clause* (New York: Macmillan, 1986); Isaac Kramnick and R. Laurence Moore, *The Godless Constitution: The Case against Religious Correctness* (New York: W.W. Norton, 1996).

6. James M. O'Neill, *Religion and Education under the Constitution* (New York: Harper, 1949); Chester James Antieau, Arthur T. Downey, and Edward C. Roberts, *Freedom from Federal Establishment: Formation and Early History of*

the First Amendment Religion Clauses (Milwaukee, WI: Bruce, 1964); Robert L. Cord, *Separation of Church and State: Historical Fact and Current Fiction* (Grand Rapids, MI: Baker Book House, 1982); Gerard V. Bradley, *Church–State Relationships in America* (Westport, CT: Greenwood Press, 1987).

7. Daniel L. Dreisbach, *Thomas Jefferson and the Wall of Separation between Church and State* (New York: New York University Press, 2002); Daniel L. Dreisbach, Mark D. Hall, and Jeffry H. Morrison, eds., *The Forgotten Founders on Religion and Public Life* (Notre Dame, IN: University of Notre Dame Press, 2009); Philip Hamburger, *Separation of Church and State* (Cambridge, MA: Harvard University Press, 2002); James Davison Hunter, *To Change the World: The Irony, the Tragedy, and the Possibility of Christianity in the Late Modern World* (New York: Oxford University Press, 2010).

8. See generally, Gordon S. Wood, *The Creation of the American Republic, 1776–1787* (New York: Norton, 1969); Bernard Bailyn, *The Ideological Origins of the American Revolution* (Cambridge, MA: Harvard University Press, 1967).

9. Noah Webster, "On Test Laws, Oaths of Allegiance and Abjuration, and Partial Exclusions from Office" (March 1787), in *The Founders' Constitution*, vol. 4, ed., Philip B. Kurland and Ralph Lerner (Chicago: University of Chicago Press, 1987), 636.

10. Madison to Edward Livingston, July 10, 1822, in *James Madison on Religious Liberty*, ed., Robert S. Alley (Buffalo: Prometheus Books, 1985), 82–83; Steven K. Green, "A 'Spacious Conception': Separationism as an Idea," *Oregon Law Review* 85 (2006): 443–80; David Sehat, *The Myth of American Religious Freedom* (New York: Oxford University Press, 2011).

11. See Steven K. Green, *The Second Disestablishment: Church and State in the Nineteenth Century* (New York: Oxford University Press, 2010).

12. Ibid., 160–203; Mark Douglas McGarvie, *One Nation Under Law* (DeKalb, IL: Northern Illinois University Press, 2004), 13, 47–66.

13. Green, *The Second Disestablishment*, 205–47 (see n. 11).

14. Ibid.; Bush v. Commonwealth, 80 Ky. 244, 24 (1882); Smith v. Nelson, 18 Vt. 511 (1846); Bloom v. Richards, 2 Ohio St., 387, 404 (1852).

15. Carl Kaestle, *Pillars of the Republic: Common Schools and American Society* (New York: Hill and Wang, 1983), 13–29; David Nasaw, *Schooled to Order: A Social History of Public Schooling in the United States* (New York: Oxford University Press, 1979), 30, 34; Noah Feldman, "Non-Sectarianism Reconsidered," *Journal of Law & Politics* 18 (2002): 65–117.

16. William Oland Bourne, *History of the Public School Society of the City of New York* (New York: William Wood, 1870), 6–7, 636–46.

17. Kaestle, *Pillars of the Republic*, passim; Ruth Miller Elson, *Guardians of Tradition: American Schoolbooks of the Nineteenth Century* (Lincoln: University of Nebraska Press, 1964), 41.

18. Horace Mann, *The Common School Journal* 1 (November 1838): 14; Horace Mann, *Twelfth Annual Report of the Board of Education, Covering the Year 1848* (Boston: Dutton & Wentworth, 1849), 116–17.

19. Ellwood P. Cubberley, ed., *Readings in Public Education in the United States* (Boston: Houghton Mifflin, 1934), 202–12; Fredrick Packard to Horace Mann, Sept. 11, 1838, reprinted in "Appendix A," in Raymond B. Culver, *Horace Mann and Religion in the Massachusetts Public Schools* (New Haven: Yale University Press, 1929), 270, 281.

20. Steven K. Green, *The Bible, the School, and the Constitution: The Clash that Shaped Modern Church–State Doctrine* (New York: Oxford University Press, 2012), 30–91.

21. *Catholic Herald*, January 30, 1834, reprinted in Vincent P. Lannie and Bernard C. Diethorn, "For the Honor and Glory of God: The Philadelphia Bible Riots of 1840," *History of Education Quarterly* 8 (Sept. 1968): 48.

22. Lloyd P. Jorgenson, *The State and the Non-Public School* (Columbia: University of Missouri Press, 1987), 73.

23. Elson, *Guardians of Tradition*, 47–53 (see n. 17); "The Pastoral Letter of 1840," in Peter Guilday, ed., *The National Pastorals of the American Hierarchy (1792–1919)* (Washington: National Catholic Welfare League, 1923), 124–25, 134; "The Pastoral Letter of 1852" (ibid., 191).

24. Vincent P. Lannie, *Public Money and Parochial Education: Bishop Hughes, Governor Seward, and the New York School Controversy* (Cleveland, The Press of Case Western Reserve University, 1968); Green, *The Bible, the School, and the Constitution*, 45–91 (see n. 20).

25. Robert G. McCloskey, ed., *The Bible in the Public Schools: Arguments in the Case of John D. Minor, et al. versus The Board of Education of the City of Cincinnati, et al.* (Cincinnati: Robert Clarke, 1870; New York: De Capo Press, 1964), 414–16; Board of Education v. Minor, 23 Ohio St. 211, 250–54 (1873).

26. Board of Education v. Minor, 23 Ohio St. 211 (1873); Green, *The Bible, the School, and the Constitution*, 93–135 (see n. 20).

27. "The Bible and the Common Schools," *The Biblical World* 20 (October 1902): 243–47; "The Use of the Bible in Public Schools: A Symposium," *The Biblical World* 27 (January 1906): 48–62.

28. Benjamin J. McQuaid, "Religion in Schools," *North American Review* 132 (April 1881): 332–44; Green, *The Bible, the School, and the Constitution*, 117–18, 236 (see n. 20).

29. State ex rel. Weiss v. District Board of School Dist. No. 8, 44 N.W. 967, 973 (Wis. 1890); "The Bible in Schools," *New York Times*, March 20, 1890, 4.

30. "Respecting Establishments of Religion and Free Public Schools," in *In Defense of the Public Schools* (Philadelphia: Aldine Press, 1888), 95; William T. Harris, *Report of the Commissioner of Education for the Year 1894–1895*, vol. 2

(Washington, DC: Government Printing Office, 1896), 1656; R. Laurence Moore, "Bible Reading and Nonsectarian Schooling: The Failure of Religious Instruction in Nineteenth-Century Public Education," *Journal of American History* 86 (March 2000): 1585–86.

31. Samuel Windsor Brown, *The Secularization of American Education* (New York: Teachers College, Columbia University, 1912), 1–4.

32. Richard B. Dierenfield, *Religion in American Public Schools* (Washington, DC: Public Affairs Press, 1962), 39–61.

33. Abington School District, 374 U.S. at 214–15.

34. Ray Allen Billington, *The Protestant Crusade, 1800–1860, A Study of the Origins of American Nativism* (New York: Macmillan, 1938); Green, *The Bible, the School, and the Constitution,* 71–91 (see n. 20).

PART II

Societal Implications of Constitutional Principles

4 Defining and Redefining Religious Freedom

A Quantitative Assessment of Free Exercise Cases in the U.S. State Courts, 1981–2011

Robert R. Martin and Roger Finke

American history is steeped in struggles over how and where to draw the boundaries of religious freedom. Despite the First Amendment's guarantee that Congress shall make no law prohibiting the free exercise of religion, conflicts between the interests of government and the exigencies of religious worship and expression are seemingly inevitable. In both past and present, these conflicts have proved critical to our understanding of how free exercise rights are to be defined, for, like other constitutional liberties, the terms and limits of free exercise rights have been clarified only through the labors of those who put them to the test.

In every historical era, it is often the efforts of religious outsiders, whose practices run up against the commands of secular law, that have refined our understanding of what constitutes protected religious exercise. Catholics, Jews, and a host of Protestant sects were among the first to gauge the scope of religious rights; indeed, the earliest recorded state court decision on the subject involved the rights of Catholic clergy in the early years of the nineteenth century.[1] Newer faiths reinvigorated the process during the late nineteenth and early twentieth centuries. In contesting federal polygamy law in 1878, the Church of Jesus Christ of Latter-day Saints presented the Supreme Court with its first chance to test the scope of free exercise rights.[2] For their part, the Jehovah's Witnesses were involved in twenty-three Supreme Court rulings on free exercise rights from 1938 to 1946 alone, prompting Supreme Court justice Harlan Fiske Stone to note that "Jehovah Witnesses ought to have an endowment in view of the aid which they give in solving the legal problems of civil liberties."[3]

By the latter decades of the twentieth century, a standard for defining the boundaries of religious freedom had taken shape. Relying on the strict scrutiny standard of judicial review, or what is commonly known as the compelling interest test, courts balanced the gravity of the government's interest in applying laws burdening religious exercise against the severity of those burdens.[4] Then, in 1990, in its ruling in *Employment Division, Department of Human Resources of Oregon v. Smith*,[5] the Court did away with this balancing standard under most circumstances, holding that religious exemptions to laws were not to be granted so long as these laws were facially neutral and generally applicable. Subsequent decades have deepened the struggle over the legitimacy of religious exemptions in American law, pitting those who wish to uphold the *Employment Division v. Smith* precedent against those seeking to return to the earlier balancing standard. This struggle has resulted in lengthy discussions and bold predictions about the consequences of the alternative free exercise standards, yet systematic assessments of these consequences have been lacking.

This chapter offers a quantitative assessment of court decisions resolving disputes over the free exercise of religion from 1981 to 2011. Relying on content analysis of thousands of court opinions from two major data collections, this assessment reviews the standards used in these decisions, the consequences of relying on different standards for the outcomes of these decisions, and how trends in outcomes and use of these standards have varied over time. Before we begin this assessment, however, we offer two overviews that situate the current debates within a broader historical context. The first is a brief overview of the historical origins and consequences of religious freedoms in America. This historical account reviews the consequences of the dramatic shift in religious freedoms that accompanied independence. The second is a more extended overview of the major court cases that laid the foundation for the current legal and legislative debates over religious freedoms. From *Reynolds* to *Smith* and beyond, we present a review of the milestone Supreme Court decisions and their aftermath. After laying this groundwork, which is necessary in order to understand the current debates, we turn to our analysis of court decisions to assess the standards used and the decisions received in religious free exercise cases. We find

that fluctuating judicial and legislative standards for religious freedoms have immediate and powerful effects on the standards employed
in subsequent cases as well as on the outcome of the cases themselves, especially in cases involving minority religions.

THE NEW RELIGIOUS ECONOMY

When investigating government involvement in religion around the
globe, Jonathan Fox observed that the relationship between religion
and state in America is characterized by a greater degree of separation than in any of the other 174 nations he studied.[6] Fox argued
that, owing to the lack of government subsidies to religious groups
and the absence of formal, targeted restrictions on worship, the United
States government plays less of a role in the religious sphere than
does the government of any other country. But what are the origins
of this dramatic degree of separation, and what are its consequences?

Contrary to some nostalgic notions, this strict separation of church
and state and the strong assurances of religious freedoms were made
possible through an unlikely alliance of rationalists such as Thomas
Jefferson and evangelical sects such as the Baptists.[7] Both sides of
this tenuous alliance bemoaned the paradigm of state establishment
of churches in pre- and post-Revolutionary America, but while
rationalists sought to free the state from religious controls and
concerns, evangelical leaders wished to free the religious sphere
from state influence. From these divergent yet complementary
motives emerged the religious guarantees of the First Amendment,
protecting the free exercise of religion from state interference on
the one hand, and preventing establishment of a religion supported
by the federal government on the other. While established churches
continued to operate in several states, they faded with time and
gave way to a religious landscape where all faiths were free to operate
but could not rely on government entities for support.

The results of this experiment in religious freedom would rapidly
become clear. When European scholars and church leaders visited
nineteenth century America, they marveled at the consequences of
the new religious freedoms they observed. Referring to this as a new
religious economy and a "voluntary principle," they were quick to
comment on how this principle resulted in more religious groups and
more religious activity. When Reverend Andrew Reed was sent to

assess the church of America in 1834, he wrote to the Congrega-
tional Union of England and Wales that "[c]hurches have been revived
where they languished, and they have been created in abundance
where they did not exist."[8] Perhaps the most celebrated European
visitor of the early nineteenth century, Alexis de Tocqueville made
similar observations. He commented that upon his arrival in the
United States, "It was the religious atmosphere which first struck
me." When he asked others to explain this atmosphere, he reported
that "they all attributed the peaceful influence exercised by religion
over their country principally to the separation of Church and state."[9]

In similar fashion, two of the earliest surveys of American religion attributed the high level of religious activity and the growing
number of sects in the United States to this voluntary principle. Initially written for European audiences, *America* by Philip Schaff[10]
and *Religion in America* by Robert Baird[11] both concluded that the
"facts" seemed obvious: religious freedoms increased the involvement
of the people and stimulated evangelical activity. Schaff and Baird
were keenly aware of the charges coming out of Europe against the
new voluntary principle, and Schaff acknowledged that the "shady
side" of the new sect system "changes the peaceful kingdom of God
into a battle-field, where brother fights against brother."[12] Yet both
writers were clear that the new freedoms were a powerful force in
shaping the religious history of America.

Although the establishment of religious freedoms in the new
nation often falls in the shadows of the Great Awakenings, a few
historians have highlighted the consequences of these freedoms.
Indeed, the prominent historian Sidney Mead wrote that the religious freedoms ushered in by the Revolutionary Era provided the
"hinge upon which the history of Christianity of America really
turns."[13] So were Mead, Schaff, Baird, and the European visitors correct? Did these new religious freedoms reshape the religious landscape?

Historical data suggests that these freedoms exerted a powerful
effect on the vitality of American churches. As shown in Figure 4.1,
rates of religious affiliation doubled in the roughly 75 years between
independence and 1850. Less than a fifth of the American population belonged to a church in 1776, a time when state-established
churches were the dominant form of religious organization. Three-
quarters of a century later, nearly a third of Americans belonged to
a church, and adherence rates generally remained on an upward tra-
jectory through the twentieth century.

Figure 4.1. Rates of church adherence, 1776–2000, United States.

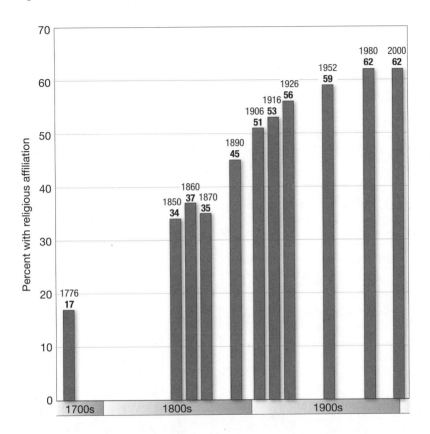

Source: Roger Finke and Rodney Stark, *The Churching of America: Winners and Losers in Our Religious Economy,* 2nd ed. (New Brunswick, N.J.: Rutgers University Press, 2005), 23.

Equally noteworthy is that this dramatic growth was not uniform across religions and denominations. Figure 4.2 illustrates how many of the dominant faiths during the period of state-established religion lost considerable ground to more energetic upstart faiths by the mid-nineteenth century. Episcopalians and Congregationalists, both beneficiaries of official recognition and establishment in the colonial era, were hit especially hard; their overall share of religious adherents in the country decreased dramatically by 1850. Free to profess and spread their faiths without state encumbrance, upstart

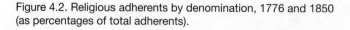

Figure 4.2. Religious adherents by denomination, 1776 and 1850 (as percentages of total adherents).

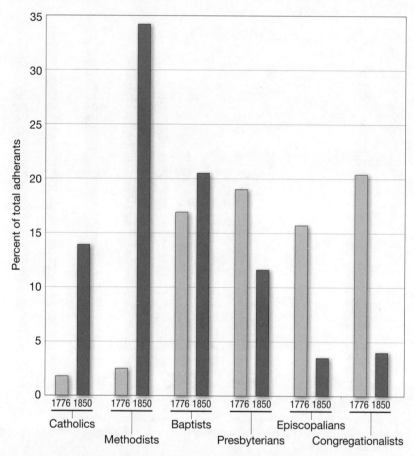

Source: Roger Finke and Rodney Stark, *The Churching of America: Winners and Losers in Our Religious Economy,* 2nd ed. (New Brunswick, N.J.: Rutgers University Press, 2005), 56.

groups more than made up for the decline of the old establishment churches, as Baptists, Catholics, and especially Methodists saw major surges in membership during this period.

While the last hundred years have not witnessed shifts in religious freedom as dramatic as the sudden surges experienced by the new nation, the twentieth century witnessed a series of landmark judicial and legislative actions that redefined the scope of free exercise rights in meaningful ways. In the section that follows, we present a historical primer detailing how the legal opportunity structure for those alleging violations of their free exercise rights has developed, paying particular attention to Supreme Court decisions and legislative actions that have had far-reaching effects on how the boundaries of free exercise rights are defined.

FREE EXERCISE AND THE COURTS

Every year, great numbers of people and organizations invoke the free exercise guarantees of the First Amendment and comparable provisions in state constitutions as a means of resolving conflicts between their legal and religious obligations. The standards used to adjudicate these conflicts vary by place, time, and the subject matter of the dispute, and are characterized by a remarkable amount of heterogeneity. Below we review a few of the most influential court decisions and legislative responses that set the terms of the present-day skirmishes over religious freedoms.

Early Free Exercise Jurisprudence: 1878–1963

Despite the ratification of the Bill of Rights at the end of the eighteenth century, it was not until 1878 that the first case addressing the scope of the First Amendment's Free Exercise Clause was heard by the Supreme Court. That case, *Reynolds v. United States*,[14] established the precedent that while government cannot regulate religious belief, it may choose to restrict religious behavior when pursuing vital interests. The *Reynolds* case hinged on whether or not a Mormon who had two wives could be punished for violating anti-polygamy laws, even though he cited the taking of multiple wives as a matter of religious obligation. The Court held that the polygamy laws were valid as a means of upholding a moral and democratic society, and that under the Free Exercise Clause, Mormons had to comply with these laws.[15]

Yet the precedent established in *Reynolds* was not to become the guiding standard for evaluating free exercise claims through most of the twentieth century. The government's license to limit free exercise was narrowed considerably in 1940 when the Court held in *Cantwell v. Connecticut*[16] that religious practices could only be restricted by government if they constituted a "clear and present danger" to the public order.[17] Restrictions on religious practice were now only permissible if they could be justified as necessary to protect the safety of the public at large. In the absence of a specific threat to the public, religious behavior could not be limited.

The Rise of the Compelling Interest Test: 1963–1990

In 1963, the Supreme Court established a new standard for settling claims, one that was dominant in free exercise jurisprudence for the next few decades. In *Sherbert v. Verner*,[18] the Court heard the case of a Seventh-day Adventist who lost her job because she refused to work on Saturdays, when members of that faith keep the Sabbath. After being unable to find another job that would accommodate her religious obligation, she applied for unemployment compensation in South Carolina and was denied on the grounds that she could find employment if only she would work on Saturdays. In the face of this denial, she sued the state on the grounds that her rights to the free exercise of religion were being violated. The Court found in favor of the Seventh-day Adventist, and in doing so developed the compelling interest test for ruling on free exercise cases. Under this test, a claimant must establish that a government authority, through law or action, has imposed a substantial burden on their sincerely held religious beliefs. If this condition is met, the claimant is granted relief unless the government authority can justify the imposition of this burden in the name of a compelling government interest, an interest of paramount importance. Furthermore, even if it can meet this threshold, the government authority must demonstrate that the method used to further its compelling interest imposes the lowest feasible level of restriction on the claimant's religious practice; in other words, it must show that it is pursuing the least restrictive means of furthering its compelling interest. This judicial standard still permits restrictions on religious behavior, but it does so in a way that places a high value on religious exercise and mandates that these rights not be limited unless it is absolutely necessary to do so.[19]

The *Sherbert* test was used once more by the Court in the 1972 *Wisconsin v. Yoder* case,[20] in which a number of Amish asked for permission to withdraw their children from the public schools after eighth grade, an impermissible request under the state of Wisconsin's compulsory education laws. Applying the legal standard established in *Sherbert*, the Burger Court held that the state did not have a compelling interest in forcing the children to attend public schools beyond the eighth grade, and decided in favor of the free exercise claimants.[21] This standard remained in effect until 1990, when the Supreme Court issued a striking decision that appeared to reverse its jurisprudence from the previous half-century.

A Conflict in Interpretation: 1990–1997

In 1990, the Supreme Court surprised observers[22] by dramatically narrowing the applicability of the compelling interest test described in the *Sherbert* opinion for making judgments in most free exercise cases. In *Employment Division of Oregon v. Smith*,[23] two substance abuse rehabilitation counselors were fired for taking part in a peyote ritual, a component of the Native American Church's worship services. Because peyote use was banned in Oregon, their subsequent unemployment compensation claims were rejected; this led the counselors to sue the state on free exercise grounds.[24] Their claim ultimately reached the Supreme Court, where the Court's majority opinion rejected the counselors' free exercise claim without making any attempt to balance the counselors' free exercise rights against the interests of the state. The majority's decision relied instead on the principle that the ban on peyote was a law that was neutral regarding religion (i.e., that it was not designed to discriminate) and that was generally applicable to all; according to the majority, religious exemptions to such laws are not permitted under the Constitution.[25]

Writing for the majority, Justice Scalia attempted to square this new standard with the Court's rulings on earlier free exercise cases by arguing that those cases had been exceptions to the standard the Court had laid out a century earlier in *Reynolds v. United States*. According to Scalia, these cases had involved either hybrid combinations of free exercise claims and claims based on other rights (e.g., the rights of parents to be responsible for their children's education in the *Yoder* case) or individualized assessments made by the government (e.g., whether to grant unemployment benefits, as in the *Sherbert* case). These types of cases were to remain subject to the compelling interest test.[26] But as legal scholar Michael W. McConnell observed, the decision had the effect of replacing the general standard for adjudicating free exercise claims with "a bare requirement of formal neutrality. Religious exercise is no longer to be treated as a preferred freedom; so long as it is treated no worse than commercial or other secular activity, religion can ask no more."[27]

The decision provoked a hostile reaction from a diverse and unlikely coalition of actors. A petition in opposition to the decision was signed by a kaleidoscopic array of religious bodies (from the Unitarian Universalist Association to the Baptist Joint Committee on Public Affairs), constitutional scholars, and think-tanks, and was delivered to the Court.[28] In a stinging rebuke of the *Smith* decision, both houses of Congress passed the Religious Freedom Restoration Act (RFRA) in 1993 by nearly unanimous margins, mandating that the *Sherbert* test be used by courts to adjudicate free exercise cases.[29] The Court answered in 1997 with its decision in *City of Boerne v. Flores*,[30] holding that RFRA as it applied to the state courts was unconstitutional, and that Congress had overstepped its bounds in instructing state courts on how to interpret the Constitution.[31]

Present-Day Patchwork: 1997 to 2012

The *Boerne* decision reaffirmed at the state level the rational basis legal standard articulated in *Smith*, although it offered little guidance on how federal free exercise cases should be resolved. Nearly a decade would pass before the Supreme Court declared in its 2006 *Gonzales v. O Centro Espirita Beneficente Uniao do Vegetal* decision[32] that RFRA was constitutional as it applied to cases in federal courts. Since 1997, several steps have been taken to restore the compelling interest test articulated in *Sherbert*. First, in reaction to the decision that RFRA could not be applied in state jurisdictions, some states have enacted legislation or constitutional amendments enshrining the principles of the original RFRA in state law.[33] In general, these so-called mini-RFRAs codify the compelling interest test in law by stating that the free exercise of religion in a given state may not be substantially burdened by facially neutral and generally applicable laws, unless it is done so in the name of a *compelling government interest* that is pursued using the *least restrictive possible means*.[34] Second, Congress passed the Religious Land Use and Institutionalized Persons Act (or RLUIPA) in 2000, a measure requiring states to use the compelling interest test articulated in *Sherbert* in free exercise cases that involve prisoners' rights and land use restrictions on religious organizations; RLUIPA requires this at both the state and federal levels.[35] Prior to RLUIPA, prisoners' free exercise claims were subject to a rational basis standard; prison officials only needed to demonstrate that their restrictions on inmates' religious liberties were reasonably related to a legitimate penological interest.[36] The bricolage response to the *Boerne* decision at the federal level was largely a result of resistance from civil rights groups to the possibility of Congress passing the original RFRA again in a way that might be more likely to pass constitutional muster. Pushback was especially strong from groups that were concerned about the potential impact the law might have on gays and lesbians who could conceivably find themselves the victims of discrimination justified in the name of religious belief.[37]

As a result, religious freedom claims made in the federal courts are subject to the compelling interest test articulated in the *Sherbert* opinion (and later codified in RFRA), and the courts at the state level are generally subject to the rational basis test articulated in the *Smith* opinion. However, there are several exceptions in which the compelling interest test can be applied at the state level:

- The case involves a land use or zoning claim, or it involves the rights of prisoners or others housed in a government-run institution.
- The claim is made in a state that has enacted mini-RFRA legislation.
- The claim is based on a "hybrid" combination of free exercise rights and other types of rights, or the claim involves the government making individualized assessments on matters implicating the free exercise of religion. This exception was included in the text of the *Smith* opinion, and has been interpreted by some jurists as legitimate grounds for using the compelling interest test.[38]

Finally, there is one additional condition under which a test that balances religious burdens and government interests may be used. Each of the fifty states has its own constitution, and each state's constitution contains a provision guaranteeing the free exercise of religion. The state courts are free to interpret their own constitutions as they see fit, and some state supreme courts have held that, when claimants invoke the protections of their state free exercise clauses, courts should use some form of balancing test to evaluate their claims, be it the compelling interest test or another standard that requires religious burdens and government interests to be balanced against one another.[39] This panoply of judicial exceptions and patchwork of legislation actions has led Durham and Smith to argue that "a significant additional measure of free exercise protection has been re-established."[40]

Thus, present-day free exercise cases are typically subject to one of two classes of legal standards. Under one class—as articulated in the *Smith* opinion—no accommodations can be made on free exercise grounds if facially neutral, generally applicable laws burden religious exercise. Under the other—as articulated in the *Sherbert* opinion as well as in an array of state court precedents—accommodations may be made on free exercise grounds if burdens on religious exercise outweigh the value of a government interest that leads to those burdens.

Using our extensive coding of court cases, we review in the following section the implementation of these standards on religious freedom and the consequences they have for the outcome of the court cases. Did the *Smith* decision limit favorable rulings on religious freedoms as charged? If so, did RFRA and the state mini-RFRAs serve to restore a balance of rulings that is more favorable to free exercise claimants?

FREE EXERCISE GUARANTEES: EVIDENCE FROM QUANTITATIVE DATA

Our quantitative findings are based on two major data collections on religious freedom court cases. Both collections code information on the groups involved, the standard used for deciding the case, and the outcome of the case. Together these collections span thirty years and account for over two thousand cases, allowing us to offer a review of the standards used in a wide range of cases and the outcomes that resulted. This analysis permits us to assess the effects of the shifting boundaries of religious freedom. We explore how free exercise guarantees affect both larger faiths and those on the outside of the mainstream, how judicial and legislative actions influenced subsequent decisions in free exercise cases, and whether the standard of review alters the likelihood that a free exercise claimant will receive a favorable decision.

Smith and RFRA, 1981–1997

Taken together, the *Employment Division v. Smith* case of 1990 and the 1993 passage of RFRA present an ideal opportunity to explore how judicial and legislative actions can alter the protections provided by legal guarantees of religious freedom. The chain of events surrounding the decision and the subsequent legislative action allows for the comparison of judicial decisions in free exercise cases during three distinct time periods: (1) the period prior to the *Smith* ruling (before April 1990), when the compelling interest test remained in effect; (2) the period in the aftermath of the *Smith* ruling, when the compelling interest test was deemed inapplicable to most cases (April 1990 through March 1993); and finally, (3) the period after the passage of RFRA, when the compelling interest test was restored at all levels (March 1993 through June 1997).[41] The three time periods offer a natural quasi-experimental design for testing the consequences of judicial and legislative actions on the protection of religious freedoms. Taking advantage of this research opportunity, John Wybraniec systematically coded over two thousand court cases involving First Amendment religious freedom claims from 1981 to 1997 at all levels of the judiciary.[42] The opinions that Wybraniec coded were derived from thorough analysis of the *Religious Freedom Reporter*, a journal published from 1981 to 2002 that compiled court opinions from both professional legal databases and reports from outside contributors.[43]

The results of this extensive coding effort confirmed a common expectation: religious outsiders are disproportionately likely to turn to the courts for protection. Observers have long noted the presence of minority religions in Supreme Court cases. From the Mormons in *Reynolds* to the Seventh-day Adventists in *Sherbert* to the members of the syncretistic Brazilian faith involved in *Uniao do Vegetal*, religious minorities have been at the forefront of clarifying the scope of religious rights for more than a century.[44] Their involvement in these cases often stems from the outlawing of these groups' religiously inspired behavior, from the use of sacramental narcotics to polygamy.

Results gleaned from Wybraniec's coding indicate moreover that while religious minorities are far more likely to turn to the courts for protection, they are far less likely to receive a favorable ruling in so doing. Whereas 21 percent of all U.S. church members were in mainline Protestant denominations during this period, those in the mainline denominations were involved in only 4 percent of the religion cases. In sharp contrast, minority religious groups make up only about 18 percent of the church membership in the United States, but they account for nearly 62 percent of the free exercise cases coming to the courts, and nearly one-half of all court cases on religion—yet they receive less favorable rulings. From 1981 to 1997 they received favorable rulings in 37 percent of their cases, compared with 70 percent for mainline Protestants. Thus, as expected, religious minorities more frequently turn to the courts for protection, despite receiving a lower rate of favorable rulings.[45]

But what was the impact of *Smith* and RFRA? It appears that the consequences of the *Smith* decision were swift and immediate.[46] Limiting our attention to the 1,171 cases specifically concerned with free exercise issues, Figure 4.3 reveals that the percentage of favorable decisions declined from 40 percent prior to *Smith* to 28 percent following *Smith*, and rebounded to over 45 percent after RFRA was passed. Were these changes related to the courts' use of the compelling interest test? Figure 4.4 shows that the courts' use of the compelling interest test follows a nearly identical pattern. Some 24 percent of free exercise cases at all levels used this test prior to the *Smith* decision, but this number fell to 12 percent following *Smith*. With the passage of RFRA, however, the use of the compelling interest returned to its approximate pre-*Smith* level at 25 percent. Thus, the consequences of the *Smith* decision resulted in an immediate reduction in the use of the compelling interest test and a far lower rate of favorable free exercise decisions.

But even this drop in favorable rulings underestimates the impact of *Smith*. Religious groups were less likely to initiate free exercise claims in the period following *Smith* but prior to RFRA, dropping from 7.1 free exercise cases initiated per month prior to *Smith* (from 1981 to 1990) to only 3.2 cases in the post-*Smith*, pre-RFRA period. Without access to free exercise exemptions in the law, religious groups quickly curtailed their attempts to seek redress. This finding is consistent with concerns raised by colonial Baptists during the late seventeenth and earlier eighteenth centuries. Historians tell us that Baptists chose not to appeal their cases to the courts because they had no representation "on the bench, none at the bar, and seldom any on the juries."[47] The religious minorities of the late 1900s had far greater protections than the colonial Baptists, but the principle

Figure 4.3. Percentage of favorable decisions by legal period (*N* = 1,171).

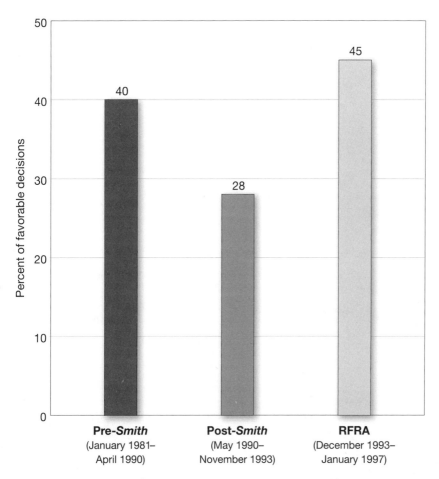

Source: Amy Adamczyk, John Wybraniec, and Roger Finke, "Religious Regulation and the Courts: Documenting the Effects of Smith and RFRA," *Journal of Church and State* 46 (2004): 250.

remains the same: when religious minorities receive fewer favorable rulings and appear to receive less protection from the courts, they initiate fewer court actions. This, in turn, may influence courts' perceptions of the scope of religious practice—that is, with religious groups turning less often to the courts requesting exemptions, the courts may be less aware of how laws of general applicability may burden religious exercise.[48]

Figure 4.4. Percentage of decisions citing compelling interest (*N* = 1,171).

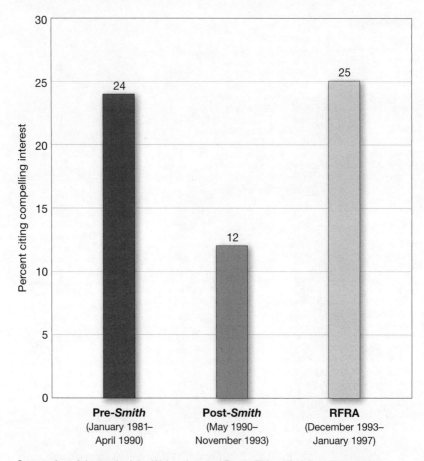

Source: Amy Adamczyk, John Wybraniec, and Roger Finke, "Religious Regulation and the Courts: Documenting the Effects of Smith and RFRA," *Journal of Church and State* 46 (2004): 250.

Following the *Smith* decision, the reduction in free exercise claims, the increase in unfavorable rulings, and the reduced use of the compelling interest test all weighed most heavily on religious minorities relying on the courts for protection. Justice O'Connor explains: " . . . [T]he First Amendment was enacted precisely to protect the rights of those whose religious practices are not shared by the majority and may be viewed with hostility. The history of our free exercise doctrine amply demonstrates the harsh impact majoritarian rule has had on unpopular or emerging religious groups such as the Jehovah's Witnesses and the Amish."[49]

Using multivariate models with this same data, Wybraniec and Finke found that Justice O'Connor is right: minority religions are especially burdened by receiving reduced access to redress in free exercise cases.[50] When controlling for region, level of court, legal period, citation of the compelling interest test, and whether an individual or group brought the case forward, they found that minority religious groups were significantly less likely than mainline Protestant churches to receive favorable decisions. With the exception of Native American religions, the odds that sects, cults, and Muslims will receive a favorable ruling are about one-third of the odds for mainline Protestants. Christians with unidentified affiliations, members of the Jewish faith, and Catholics were also less likely to receive a favorable decision when compared to mainline Protestant groups.[51]

Smith, RLUIPA, and state mini-RFRAs, 1997–2011

Wybraniec and Finke's analysis ends in 1997, just as the Supreme Court ruled in *City of Boerne v. Flores* that the rational basis test outlined in *Smith* is applicable to state courts. This analysis also falls before RLUIPA and the many mini-RFRAs passed by states. Each of these events raises new questions about the standards now used at the level of the state courts and the consequences of these standards. As reviewed earlier, the *Smith* test is largely in effect when state courts rule on free exercise cases, although several exceptions were noted: (1) if the case's subject matter allows it to be heard under the RLUIPA; (2) if a state has passed a mini-RFRA; (3) if the claim falls under the hybrid rights exception that some have found in Justice Scalia's opinion in *Smith*; or (4) if a state court interprets its own state's constitution to mandate use of a test balancing government interests against burdens on religion.

To assess how often state courts use a balancing test and the consequences of using this standard, the first author used the LoislawConnect research database to locate all published religious free exercise cases that were handed down at the state level between June 1997 (when the Court issued its decision in *City of Boerne* invalidating RFRA at the state level) and the end of 2011.[52] Because legislative attempts to shift the boundaries of free exercise rights over the last few decades have focused primarily on supplanting rational basis tests with balancing tests in such cases, we focus exclusively on cases decided using one of these types of standards. This focus limits our consideration to 225 cases from nearly every state in the country. Each case was then coded for the final outcome of the case and the legal standard used in making the decision, as well as for the specific legal precedent or piece of legislation articulating the legal standard.

In the final sample, 44 percent of the cases were ruled upon using the rational basis standard (most often the *Smith* precedent) and the remaining 56 percent of cases were decided using some kind of balancing standard (often the compelling interest test articulated in the *Sherbert* decision). The high proportion of total cases using this type of standard suggests that in the wake of RFRA's invalidation at the state level, legislative efforts and state-level precedents have made a significant impact on restoring pre-*Smith* balancing standards.

As Figure 4.5 indicates, however, the rate of favorable rulings in state courts was low between 1997 and 2011. Only 24 of the 225 free exercise cases in the higher state-level courts that were resolved using a rational basis or balancing test, or about 1 in 9, resulted in favorable decisions for the party making the free exercise claim. Free exercise claimants lose their cases about 88 percent of the time, even after all the legislation passed at the state and federal levels aimed at restoring religious freedoms. It makes little difference whether the case is heard at the appellate or state supreme court, as roughly equal proportions of the favorable decisions were handed down at each of these levels.

The odds of winning such a case are long, but does the legal standard that claimants face make a difference in the outcome? The data suggest that it does. As shown in Figure 4.6, nearly one in six, or about 17 percent, of all the cases settled using a balancing test resulted in favorable decisions for the claimants. By contrast, only one in twenty, or 5 percent, of all the cases decided using the rational basis test were decided favorably for free exercise claimants. Given the small number of total wins for free exercise claimants, this means that only five cases in the state appellate and supreme courts that were decided using the *Smith* test or some analogue between mid-1997 and 2011 yielded favorable rulings for the claimants. The low success rate in cases decided using a rational basis test should not

Figure 4.5. Success of free exercise claims in the state courts, 1997–2011.

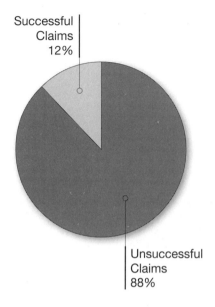

Source: Opinions from state appellate courts, June 25, 1997, through December 31, 2011. Accessed through LoislawConnect. *N* = 225.

be surprising: to prevail under the *Smith* test, claimants essentially must argue that the law in question discriminates on the basis of religion. Success under these circumstances is rare, but it does occur, as in the Supreme Court's decision in *Church of the Lukumi Babalu Aye v. City of Hialeah*.[53] In this decision, the Court held that a Hialeah, Florida, city ordinance prohibiting ritual animal sacrifice had the effect of forbidding a proposed Santeria church from operating within city limits; the ordinance unconstitutionally prohibited the church members' religious exercise and ran afoul of the Free Exercise Clause.

Finally, even though claimants were more than three times as likely to win if their cases were decided using a balancing test, the 17 percent success rate on balancing-test cases is still quite low. Even though RLUIPA and the mini-RFRAs were enacted in hopes of, to appropriate RFRA's title, "restoring religious freedom," free exercise claimants must overcome many pitfalls to receive a favorable decision. The compelling interest test, for instance, involves the use of

Figure 4.6. Comparing outcomes of free exercise cases by test used, 1997–2011.

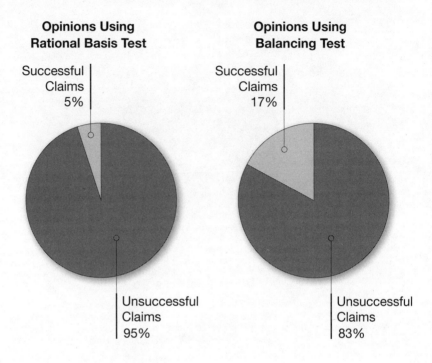

**Opinions Using
Rational Basis Test**

Successful
Claims
5%

Unsuccessful
Claims
95%

**Opinions Using
Balancing Test**

Successful
Claims
17%

Unsuccessful
Claims
83%

Source: Opinions from state appellate courts, June 25, 1997, through
December 31, 2011. Accessed through LoislawConnect. *N* = 225.

strict scrutiny, which is in theory the most rigorous legal standard
available for preserving First Amendment rights. It requires that
the state cite a compelling interest as justification for limiting a
party's free exercise. The recent data collection efforts indicate a
tremendous amount of variation in what state courts determine to
be compelling interests. State interests that courts found to be compelling include, as we might expect, the protection of children from
abuse, saving lives, and ensuring public safety. However, they also
include such specific interests as completing a trial without a three-
day delay in deliberations,[54] maintaining a zoning district as a single-
family residential zone,[55] reducing the likelihood of smoke-related
litigation in a prison,[56] and, in a case regarding a billboard in Kentucky, public safety and "aesthetics."[57]

Furthermore, many of these cases did not require the state to justify its actions owing to a compelling interest, because courts often found that claimants failed to prove that their free exercise rights were burdened *substantially*. The threshold for determining whether a burden on religious exercise rises to a "substantial" level is variable. In the absence of specific precedents informing the substantive basis for a case, the substantiality threshold is relatively arbitrary, and judges appear to use considerable discretion in determining whether this threshold is met. In short, legislative efforts to raise the legal bar for the state in justifying limitations of people's free exercise rights have made a real impact on the outcomes of such decisions, but the relatively low success rate of cases where courts balance religious rights against government demands indicates that free exercise claimants remain at a stark disadvantage in the face of generally applicable, religiously neutral laws.

CONCLUSION

Relative to the rest of the world, the United States remains a stronghold of religious liberty, yet as the findings we describe here show, not all religious groups have equal success at earning redress when they feel their liberties have been violated. While differences in how religious minorities' court cases are resolved are hardly analogous to bans on religious worship and practice in other countries, even slight limitations on religious practice have important consequences.

Indeed, Laycock has argued that had certain cases in the American court systems been resolved differently, the outcomes of those cases may have led the religious groups involved to change their practices or else be outlawed.[58] Had the state of Oregon not passed an exemption for the religious use of peyote in the wake of the *Smith* case, the sacramental use of the substance by Native American faiths would have been banned, depriving adherents of one of the core components of their worship. More dramatically, the International Society for Krishna Consciousness (ISKCON)—also known as the Hare Krishnas—were sued in 1977 by a devotee and her mother on multiple charges, including emotional distress, false imprisonment, and wrongful death (*George v. International Society for Krishna Consciousness*), and would have had to sell all of their temples and monasteries to pay the amount dictated by the jury.[59] Appeals of the decision reduced the amount ISKCON was responsible for, but had the case been resolved differently, ISKCON in its present form would have ceased to function in the United States. Given that these examples involve minority religions, the denial of their free-doms might not seem far-reaching or significant for most. Yet a growing body of research is finding that the consequences of denying religious freedom ripple far beyond religious minorities. From the early American example previously offered to many global events, the consequences of religious freedom are many.

Taking an international view, Fox and Tabory found that higher levels of government restriction on religion in countries across the globe are associated with lower levels of service attendance.[60] Gill's 1998 study of countries in Latin America, meanwhile, revealed that levels of pluralism and Protestant sect growth were greater where levels of government regulation of religion were lower.[61] But the consequences go far beyond religious practice. The denial of reli-gious freedoms holds a strong relationship with religious persecution, social violence, and the denial of other civil liberties.[62] These findings suggest that governmental limitations on religious practice have profound effects on countries' religious sectors and the larger civic order. Whether looking at America or across the globe, religious free-doms are remarkably fragile and vulnerable, yet the consequences of the freedoms are powerful and far-reaching. The boundaries of free exercise in America continue to be tested, contracted, and expanded, but our findings demonstrate that even subtle shifts can have dramatic consequences.

NOTES

1. Michael W. McConnell, "The Origins and Historical Understanding of Free Exercise of Religion," *Harvard Law Review* 103, no. 7 (1990): 1504. According to McConnell, the earliest state court decision involved the 1813 subpoena of a Catholic priest in New York to testify in the matter of a man who confessed a theft to the priest. Saying at trial that he would rather die than disclose the subject of a sacramental confession, the priest refused to testify, and the court supported his refusal.

2. *Reynolds v. United States*, 98 U.S. 145 (1878).

3. Shawn F. Peters, *Judging Jehovah's Witnesses: Religious Persecution and the Dawn of the Rights Revolution* (Lawrence, KS: University of Kansas Press, 2000), v.

4. *Sherbert v. Verner*, 374 U.S. 398 (1963).

5. *Employment Division, Department of Human Resources of Oregon v. Smith*, 494 U.S. 872 (1990).

6. Jonathan Fox, *A World Survey of Religion and the State* (New York: Cambridge University Press, 2008).

7. Sidney Mead, *The Lively Experiment: The Shaping of Christianity in America* (1963; repr., New York: Harper & Row, 1976); Roger Finke, "Religious Deregulation: Origins and Consequences," *Journal of Church and State* 32 (1990): 609–26.

8. Andrew Reed and James Matheson, *A Narrative of the Visit to the American Churches*, vol. 2 (London: Jackson and Walford, 1835), 137, 141.

9. Alexis de Tocqueville, *Democracy in America and Two Essays on America*, trans. Gerald Bevan (London: Penguin Books, 2003), 345.

10. Philip Schaff, *America: A Sketch of Its Political, Social, and Religious Character* (Cambridge, MA: The Belknap Press, 1855).

11. Robert Baird, *Religion in America; or, An Account of the Origin, Progress, Relation to the State, and Present Condition of the Evangelical Churches in the United States. With Notices of the Unevangelical Denominations* (Glasgow: Blackie and Co., 1844).

12. Schaff, *America,* 99, 102.

13. Mead, *The Lively Experiment*, 52.

14. *Reynolds*, 98 U.S. 145.

15. Ronald B. Flowers, *That Godless Court? Supreme Court Decisions on Church-State Relationships*, 2nd ed. (Louisville, KY: Westminster John Knox Press, 2005).

16. *Cantwell v. Connecticut*, 310 U.S. 296 (1940).

17. Flowers, *That Godless Court?*, 25.

18. *Sherbert*, 374 U.S. 398.

19. Flowers, *That Godless Court?*, 31–33.

20. *Wisconsin v. Yoder*, 406 U.S. 205 (1972).

21. Flowers, *That Godless Court?*, 34.

22. Michael W. McConnell, "Free Exercise Revisionism and the *Smith* Decision," *The University of Chicago Law Review* 57, no. 4 (1990), 1109–53; Jesse H. Choper, "Separation of Church and State: 'New' Directions by the 'New' Supreme Court," *Journal of Church and State* 34, no. 2 (1992), 363–75.

23. *Employment Division of Oregon*, 494 U.S. 872.

24. Kenneth Marin, "*Employment Division v. Smith:* The Supreme Court Alters the State of Free Exercise Doctrine," *American University Law Review* 40 (1990–91), 1431–76.

25. Douglas Laycock, "Free Exercise and the Religious Freedom Restoration Act," *Fordham Law Review* 62, no. 4 (1994), 883–904.

26. John P. Forren, "Revisiting Four Popular Myths About The Peyote Case," *Journal of Constitutional Law* 8, no. 2 (2006), 209–53.

27. McConnell, "Free Exercise Revisionism and the *Smith* Decision," 1153.

28. James E. Wood, Jr., "Abridging the Free Exercise Clause," *Journal of Church and State* 32 (1990), 749–50.

29. Laycock, "Free Exercise and the Religious Freedom Restoration Act," 883–904.

30. *City of Boerne v. Flores*, 521 U.S. 507 (1997).

31. Jerold L. Waltman, *Religious Free Exercise and Contemporary American Politics: The Saga of the Religious Land Use and Institutionalized Persons Act of 2000* (New York: Continuum, 2011).

32. *Gonzales v. O Centro Espirita Beneficente Uniao do Vegetal*, 546 U.S. 418 (2006).

33. Nicholas Nugent, "Toward a RFRA That Works," *Vanderbilt Law Review* 61 (2008), 1052.

34. As of 2010, fifteen states have enacted mini-RFRAs. These are Arizona, Connecticut, Florida, Idaho, Illinois, Louisiana, Missouri, New Mexico, Oklahoma, Pennsylvania, Rhode Island, South Carolina, Tennessee, Texas, and Virginia. In addition, Alabama has incorporated the language of RFRA into its state constitution via amendment. Eugene Volokh, "Religious Exemption Law Map of the United States," July 9, 2010, *The Volokh Conspiracy* (2010), accessed March 5, 2014, http://www.volokh.com/2010/07/09/religious-exemption -law-map-of-the-united-states/.

35. Ted G. Jelen, *To Serve God and Mammon: Church-State Relations in American Politics*, 2nd ed. (Washington, DC: Georgetown University Press, 2010), 84–85.

36. *Turner v. Safley*, 482 U.S. 78 (1987); *O'Lone v. Estate of Shabazz*, 482 U.S. 342 (1987).

37. Waltman, *Religious Free Exercise and Contemporary American Politics.*

38. See *Scott v. State*, 80 S.W.3d 184 (Texas 2002); *Triplett v. Livingston County Board of Educ.*, 967 S.W.2d 25 (Ky.App.1997).

39. When reading state-level free exercise cases, the first author has come across a multitude of cases wherein claimants invoked the protections of both the state and federal free exercise clauses; in many of these cases, claimants' First Amendment claims were subjected to the *Smith* test and their state constitutional claims were subject to a balancing test.

40. W. Cole Durham, Jr., and Robert T. Smith, "Religion and State in the United States at the Turn of the Twenty-first Century," in *Law and Religion in the 21st Century: Relations Between States and Religious Communities*, ed. Silvio Ferrari and Rinaldi Cristofori (Burlington, VT: Ashgate, 2010), 94.

41. Note that this last period is prior to the Court's clarification in *City of Boerne v. Flores* in June 1997, when the status of the compelling interest test was further muddied.

42. John Wybraniec, "The Battle Over Religious Freedom: Court Decisions and the Religious Economy in the United States" (Ph.D. diss., Purdue University, 1998). See also John Wybraniec and Roger Finke, "Religious Regulation and

the Courts: The Judiciary's Changing Role in Protecting Minority Religions from Majoritarian Rule," *Journal for the Scientific Study of Religion* 40 (2001), 427–44; Amy Adamczyk, John Wybraniec, and Roger Finke, "Religious Regulation and the Courts: Documenting the Effects of *Smith* and RFRA," *Journal of Church and State* 46 (2004), 237–62.

43. Wybraniec, "The Battle Over Religious Freedom," 68.

44. Donald Black, *The Behavior of Law* (New York: Academic Press, 1976), 114. Insights from the sociology of law suggest that this should be expected. As Black has observed, those who are considered outsiders in a given society are less likely to enjoy the full benefits of law than those who enjoy greater respectability. Those with less societal influence have less of an ability to normalize their behaviors in law, and are more apt to encounter incidents when their preferred practices fall outside of the law.

45. Wybraniec and Finke, "Religious Regulation and the Courts," 434–35.

46. However, while writing for the majority in *City of Boerne v. Flores* (521 U.S. 507, 1997), Justice Kennedy asserted that laws of general applicability very rarely burden the free exercise of religion in America. See Ira C. Lupu, "The Failure of RFRA," *University of Arkansas at Little Rock Law Journal* 20 (1997–98), 589; and James E. Ryan, "*Smith* and the Religious Freedom Restoration Act: An Iconoclastic Assessment," *Virginia Law Review* 78, no. 6 (1992), 1417.

47. See William G. McLoughlin, *New England Dissent 1603–1833* (Cambridge, MA: Harvard University Press, 1971).

48. Professor Drinan makes the similar point that we will not know what happens to religious individuals and persons if RFRA is not reinstated in some form. As he explains, "[a]t the local level, zoning commissions will quietly deny access to Jewish temples, controversial denominations, or Catholic schools. Appeals will not be taken nor will there be any public outcry. The number of individuals who will seek to vindicate their rights under the *Smith* decision will be small." Robert F. Drinan, "Reflections on the Demise of the Religious Freedom Restoration Act," *Georgetown Law Journal* 86 (1997–98), 115–16.

49. *Employment Division*, 494 U.S. at 902.

50. Wybraniec and Finke, "Religious Regulation and the Courts," 437.

51. Ibid. Aside from religious affiliation, legal period, and citing of the compelling interest test, the only other significant predictor was level of court.

52. Legal databases such as LoislawConnect publish only those state decisions handed down by appellate courts and courts of last resort, such as state supreme courts. As a result, free exercise cases heard in state trial courts were not captured by this coding effort. In all, 456 state-level free exercise cases were coded, of which 225 were identified as being resolved using one of the two legal standards identified above. LoislawConnect, accessed August 7, 2013, http://www.loislaw.com/pns/index.htp.

53. *Church of the Lukumi Babalu Aye v. City of Hialeah*, 508 U.S. 520 (1993).

54. *People v. Hall*, 2 A.D.3d 227 (1st Dept [New York], 2003).

55. *Libolt v. Town of Irondequoit Zoning Bd.*, 66 A.D.3d 1393 (4th Dept [New York], 2009).

56. *Roles v. Townsend*, 64 P.3d 338 (Idaho 2003).

57. *Harston v. Commonwealth*, 2010-CA-000615-MR (Ky.App. 3-4-2011).

58. Laycock, "Free Exercise," 883–904.

59. *George v. International Society for Krishna Consciousness*, 213 Cal. App. 3d 729 (1989).

60. Jonathan Fox and Ephraim Tabory, "Contemporary Evidence Regarding the Impact of State Regulation of Religion on Religious Participation and Belief," *Sociology of Religion* 69 (2008), 245–71.

61. Anthony J. Gill, *Rendering Unto Caesar: The Catholic Church and the State in Latin America* (Chicago: University of Chicago Press, 1998).

62. Brian Grim and Roger Finke, *The Price of Freedom Denied: Religious Persecution and Violence* (Cambridge, UK: Cambridge University Press, 2011); Roger Finke and Jaime Harris, "Wars and Rumors of Wars: Explaining Religiously Motivated Violence," in *Religion, Politics, Society and the State*, ed. Jonathan Fox (Boulder, CO: Paradigm Publishers, 2012).

5 Religious Liberty in the Public Schools

Toward a Common Vision for the Common Good

Charles C. Haynes

> Congress shall make no law respecting an establishment of religion, or prohibiting the free exercise thereof.
>
> *Religion clauses of the First Amendment*
> *to the U.S. Constitution*

More than two hundred years after the ratification of the First Amendment to the U.S. Constitution, America's need to articulate a shared understanding of the role of religion in public life has never been more urgent—or more challenging.

The United States is today the most religiously diverse society in the world and, among developed nations, one of the most religious. Moreover, culture wars involving deep religious convictions make our increasingly crowded public square an often angry place where citizens shout past one another across seemingly unbridgeable distances.

If we hope to sustain and strengthen America as one nation of many faiths and beliefs in the twenty-first century, we must renew our commitment to the guiding principles of the religious liberty clauses of the First Amendment. The rights and responsibilities that flow from the First Amendment provide the civic framework that enables Americans to debate differences, to understand one another, and to forge public policies that serve the common good.

Nowhere is it more important to reinvigorate a shared understanding of religious liberty than in public schools, the principal institutions charged with preparing young people for citizenship in a pluralistic democracy. By teaching and modeling First Amendment rights and responsibilities, schools become laboratories for democratic freedom, places where people of all faiths and none learn to treat one another with fairness and respect.

Getting religion and religious liberty right in public schools is critical to the future of the American experiment in democratic freedom. That's why I have spent much of the past two decades working with educational, religious, and civil liberties groups to find common ground on the role of religion in public education.

Our success in reaching agreement on many contentious issues has been in no small measure due to the vision of the First Amendment articulated in the Williamsburg Charter, a restatement of religious liberty principles drafted by representatives of America's leading faiths and signed by some two hundred leaders from every sector of American life in 1988.

As Os Guinness, principal drafter of the Charter, reminds us, a religious consensus in America is neither possible nor desirable, but agreement on constitutional principles is not only possible but urgently needed, especially in the public school arena. A principled compact that spells out the rights and responsibilities required by our commitment to religious liberty provides a civic unity that serves the interest of America's diversity.[1]

In this chapter, I first describe the consensus reached in recent years about the constitutional role of religion in public schools, and then indicate where work still needs to be done to address remaining differences.

RESTORERS VS. REMOVERS

The failure to live up to the promise of religious liberty for much of American history has created widespread confusion and controversy about the constitutional role of religion in public schools. As a result, extreme voices from both ends of the ideological and religious spectrum often shape how schools address (or fail to address) religion and religious liberty.

On one end of the ideological spectrum are "restorers," those who seek to a return to an era when one religion was widely preferred in school policies and practices. For much of the nineteenth century—and well into the twentieth century—public schools could fairly be described as semi-established Protestant schools.

Despite the U.S. Supreme Court rulings of the 1960s ending state-sponsored religious practices, some public school officials continue to cling to vestiges of that bygone era by promoting the dominant religion in the community. Rather than accept the Court's decisions and focus on constitutional ways in which religion may be expressed in public schools—particularly by students—restorers continue to push for school endorsement of (their) religion by doing such things as posting the Ten Commandments in school hallways or offering prayers over the intercom.

On the other end of the spectrum are "removers," those who appear determined to turn public schools into religion-free zones in the name of church–state separation. After the Supreme Court struck down state-sponsored prayer and devotional Bible reading, many public school officials became removers, less out of hostility toward religion than fear of controversy. They have often misapplied the Court's decisions by excluding appropriate study about religions and censoring student religious expression protected by the First Amendment.

In some school districts today, removers continue to resist including more study about religions in the curriculum, arguing that public school teachers cannot be trusted to be fair and objective when discussing religion. In addition, they often oppose policies designed to protect students' religious expression, fearing that students and local churches will use these polices as a vehicle for evangelization in public schools.

Both "restorers" and "removers"—whose approaches to religion in public education have shaped much of our history—are acting in ways that are unjust and, in many instances, unconstitutional.

THE NEW CONSENSUS

Despite our difficult history of getting religious liberty wrong, many public schools today are working hard to get religious liberty right. In fact, I would argue that there is more study of religions and more student religious expression in public schools today than at any time in the last 100 years. Religion is coming into public schools—but mostly through the First Amendment door.

Many factors have contributed to this change over the past two decades, including court decisions, litigation, and the work of advocacy groups on all sides. But two developments may be highlighted for having played an especially critical role in reshaping the role of religion in public education:

First, passage of the Equal Access Act in 1984—and the subsequent U.S. Supreme Court decision upholding the constitutionality of the Act (*Board of Education v. Mergens*, 1990)—has led to the formation of hundreds, if not thousands, of student-initiated and student-led religious clubs in secondary public schools throughout the country. Although implementation of the Equal Access Act has not been without controversy, even most early critics now agree that it has generally worked to give students appropriate opportunities to express their faith in schools while simultaneously ensuring that public school officials remain neutral toward religion.

Second, over the past two decades, broad coalitions of religious, civil liberties, and educational organizations have issued a series of common ground statements on the constitutional and educational place of religion in public schools. This new consensus first emerged in the late 1980s when I joined with Oliver Thomas, then of the Baptist Joint Committee, to convene religious liberty advocates and education leaders in an effort to find common ground.

The first agreements on "religion in the curriculum" and "religious holidays" in the late 1980s were followed by a series of additional common ground documents, including "A Joint Statement of Current Law" in 1995 (coordinated by lead drafter Marc Stern, then of the American Jewish Congress, and endorsed by 35 religious and civil liberties groups), "Public Schools and Religious Communities" in 1998, and "The Bible and Public Schools" in 2000.[2]

The new consensus gave impetus to an effort by the Clinton administration to break new ground by drafting and disseminating legal guidance on the constitutional role of religion in public education. Drawing on the broadly supported Joint Statement, the U.S. Department of Education (DOE), headed by Secretary Richard Riley, issued "Religious Expression in Public Schools: A Statement of Principles" in 1995. The guidance outlines the ways in which students may express their faith during the school day, including expressing their religious views in class discussion, sharing their faith with classmates, and reading their scriptures during their free time. At the same time, the guidelines remind school officials that students do not have the right to have a captive audience listen or to compel other students to participate in their prayers or religious discussions.

It is worth recalling that the 1995 U.S. DOE guidelines were crafted during a period of debate in Congress over a "prayer amendment" to the Constitution proposed by Rep. Ernest Istook (R-OK) that critics believed would return schools to the days of teacher-led prayer. To counter arguments for such an amendment, the Clinton administration sought to educate the public about the many ways in which student religious expression, including prayer, was sufficiently protected under current law.

When the DOE guidance was updated in 1998, the White House took the opportunity to add new documents on religion in schools that would address a broader audience and have greater impact. At the request of Secretary Riley, I coordinated the writing of two additional consensus statements with broad support from religious, education, and civil liberties groups: "A Teacher's Guide to Religion in Public Schools" and "A Parent's Guide to Religion in the Public Schools." In addition, a DOE publication entitled "How Faith Communities Support Children's Learning in Public Schools" was drafted to provide examples of successful collaborations between public schools and religious communities in mentoring programs, after-school activities, and other initiatives. In January 2000, President Clinton directed the DOE to send a packet with all of these agreements to every public school principal in the United States.

The DOE guidelines were updated and revised once again in 2003 to comply with a provision of the No Child Left Behind Act of 2001 directing the DOE to issue new guidance concerning student prayer in public schools.

GETTING RELIGION RIGHT

As a result of the new consensus articulated in the common ground documents and the DOE guidance, educators need no longer choose between imposing religion in public schools and banishing it altogether. The First Amendment answer shaped by the common ground statements of the past two decades is to find the proper role for religion in public education by fully and fairly applying religious liberty principles in every school.

What schools look like when they get religion right under the First Amendment is most clearly summarized in *Religious Liberty,*

Public Education, and the Future of American Democracy, a vision statement released in 1995 that was endorsed by 24 major organizations and widely disseminated throughout the country. Drafted in 1994 when Ron Brandt of the Association for Supervision and Curriculum Development and I convened religious, civil liberties, and educational leaders, the statement articulates civic ground rules for resolving differences over religion in public schools. The key provision of the resulting agreement is found in principle four:

> Public schools may not inculcate nor inhibit religion. They must be places where religion and religious conviction are treated with fairness and respect. Public schools uphold the First Amendment when they protect the religious liberty rights of students of all faiths or none. Schools demonstrate fairness when they ensure that the curriculum includes study about religion, where appropriate, as an important part of a complete education.[3]

Across our differences, we agreed that there is a role for religion in public schools that upholds both the "no establishment" and "free exercise" provisions of the First Amendment. The Constitution does not bar religion from schools, but rather opens the door to appropriate student religious expression and to academic study of religion while simultaneously keeping school officials from taking sides in religion.

The 1995 vision statement enjoys broad support across the religious and ideological spectrum. Both the Christian Coalition and People for the American Way are on the list of endorsers. The Christian Educators Association International is listed, but so is the National Education Association. The National Association of Evangelicals, the Catholic League for Religious and Civil Rights, and the Anti-Defamation League join with the American Association of School Administrators, the National Parent Teacher Association (National PTA), and the National School Boards Association to endorse these guiding principles.

Fortunately for the vitality of public education, it is still possible for Americans to articulate a common vision for the common good across differences that are often deep and abiding. After a long history of fighting over the role of religion in public schools, we now have broad consensus that under current law students have the right to

- pray in public schools, alone or in groups, as long as the activity does not disrupt the school or infringe on the rights of others;
- share their faith with others and to read their scriptures;
- express personal religious views in class or as part of a written assignment or activity. when it's relevant to the discussion and meets the academic requirements;
- distribute religious literature in school, subject to reasonable time, place and manner restrictions; and
- form student-led religious clubs in secondary schools if the school allows other extracurricular clubs.[4]

We also have reached broad agreement that study *about* religions is not only constitutional, it is an essential part of a good education. Of course, this means that public schools must teach about religion objectively or neutrally; their purpose must be to educate students about a variety of religious traditions, not to indoctrinate them for or against any religion.

TAKING RELIGION SERIOUSLY IN THE CURRICULUM

Study about religion in public schools has come a long way since the first consensus statement in 1989. State social studies standards, for example, are now fairly generous to religion, in stark contrast to the virtual silence about religion in state curriculum frameworks of the 1980s. As a result, many history textbooks have expanded treatment of religions beyond the bare mention of religion typical of earlier editions.[5]

Despite these improvements, much of the public school curriculum—beyond modest inclusion in history and literature—continues to neglect study of religion. As Warren Nord and I have argued elsewhere, public education's failure to take religion seriously in the curriculum is neither neutral nor fair under the First Amendment. Genuine neutrality under the Establishment clause would require exposing students to religious as well as secular ways of understanding the world. A curriculum that largely ignores religious worldviews sends a message to students that religion is irrelevant in the search for truth.[6]

Moreover, religious convictions—for better and for worse—play a central role in shaping events and public policies at home and abroad. If we have learned nothing else in the past decade, we now know that religion *matters* in the twenty-first century. Unfortunately, most students in America's schools have few meaningful opportunities to engage issues that address the role of religion and belief in society. In many classrooms and much of the curriculum, religious diversity is the ignored diversity.

Failure to take religion seriously could have profound consequences for our society. As we have seen since the horrific events of September 11, 2001, ignorance is a root cause of intolerance, contributing to religious prejudice and discrimination. Study about religions in schools, therefore, is vitally important for creating respect and understanding among students of all faiths and beliefs.

Serious treatment of religion will necessitate significant reforms in education to ensure that each teacher has sound academic resources for teaching about religion and receives adequate preparation in the study of religion as it relates to the subject they teach. Every social studies teacher, for example, should be required to take at least one course in religious studies. Age-appropriate textbooks and supplementary materials that reflect the best scholarship in the field will need to be developed.

As an illustration of what can be done, I will highlight one promising new program called *Face to Faith*, which has great potential to deepen the conversation about religions and religious freedom in public school classrooms.

Sponsored by the Tony Blair Faith Foundation, *Face to Faith* dares to go where few have gone before by giving students across the world meaningful opportunities to learn from one another about their religions and cultures. Through videoconferencing and online community, students connect directly with their peers to discuss how various religions address global issues—and to share their own faiths and beliefs through open, respectful dialogue. Launched in 2009, *Face to Faith* is already in more than 1,200 schools in 29 countries, including more than 200 public and private schools in the United States.[7]

This innovative use of technology in the classroom does more than increase religious and cultural literacy; it changes hearts and minds. "*Face to Faith* has opened my eyes to the fact that although we come from different places and cultures, we are all more alike than different," reports a student at Brighton High School in Canyons School District, Utah. "The opportunity to participate in this program has blown all the misconceptions that I held out of the water and caused me to try harder to understand people from all places and circumstances."

Face to Faith puts a human face to faith by giving American students direct access to young people of many faiths, beliefs, and cultures in other parts of the world. High school students in Tacoma, Washington, for example, recently engaged students in the Palestinian Territories in a lively exchange about their differences and similarities.

"The dialogue that surfaced regarding misunderstandings about people of the Muslim faith," reports the school's principal, "broke down misperceptions. That's at the heart of what this learning experience is all about."

As important as it is to increase religious literacy, a larger aim of *Face to Faith* is to remove barriers that prevent young people from negotiating differences—especially differences in faith and belief—with civility and respect. By focusing on dialogical skills and cooperative learning, *Face to Faith* builds civic character by preparing students to speak sensitively, listen carefully, and use rights-respecting language.

American schools are implementing *Face to Faith* in a variety of ways. In some schools, social studies teachers integrate the program in their history, global studies, or civics classes. In others, *Face to Faith* is part of an elective course in World Religions or is available as an extracurricular club.

The early success of *Face to Faith* in schools across the country is a positive sign that growing numbers of public schools are ready to take religion seriously. I am optimistic that this project and similar initiatives will be adopted in the coming decade by many more American schools, advancing First Amendment principles by encouraging student voice, promoting religious freedom, and educating for understanding among students of different faiths, beliefs, cultures, and nationalities.

THE CHALLENGES AHEAD

Although the common ground achieved over the past two decades has made a significant difference in how public education addresses religion, much work remains to be done. Far too many school districts continue to muddle along with outdated policies—or no policies at all—that leave them vulnerable to conflicts and litigation. Some school officials are afraid to fully implement the new consensus, even when pushed to do so by the U.S. Department of Education. And many teachers remain unprepared or unwilling to tackle teaching about religions, whatever the standards or textbooks require.

Moreover, pockets of resistance to common ground solutions from both restorers and removers continue to trigger fights and lawsuits.

In 2011, for example, the third Tennessee school district in as many years settled with the American Civil Liberties Union by finally promising to do what national agreements and U.S. Department of Education guidelines have called on public schools to do for years. Among other violations, Sumner County school officials had distributed Bibles in elementary schools, endorsed religion in the presence of students, and organized prayers over the loudspeaker. Under the settlement, the district agreed that school personnel would no longer promote religion, but students would be able to express their religious views in ways that are constitutionally protected— exactly the common ground solution already in place in many parts of the country.[8]

On the other end of the spectrum, some school districts still mistakenly treat student religious expression as government speech, apparently because they are afraid of letting any religious expression through the schoolhouse door. From the Pennsylvania school district that would not allow a child to dress as Jesus for the Halloween parade, to the New Jersey school that barred a student from singing "Awesome God" in the talent show, most of these fights are absurd and unnecessary—not to mention expensive. Here again, if these districts had in place policies and practices consistent with the First Amendment and current law, they would not only avoid lawsuits, they would rebuild trust and support in their communities where it has been lost.

School districts that are successfully negotiating religious conflicts have strong policies that address a broad range of issues involving religion in schools. Such policies say "yes" to a role for religion, even as they say "no" to school-sponsored religious practices. Sound First Amendment policies support teaching about religions in ways that are academically and constitutionally sound, and offer clear guidance on how current law addresses student religious expression, distribution of religious literature, and student religious clubs.[9]

WHERE WE STILL DISAGREE

Common ground on some issues, of course, does not necessarily guarantee common ground on all issues. Culture-war differences still spark fights and lawsuits in many communities. Let me briefly describe three of the most contentious areas of disagreement that we are still working to resolve: conflicts over issues involving sexual orientation; controversies surrounding some Bible electives; and debates over where to draw the line on student religious expression at school-sponsored events.

In many parts of the country, few debates are more divisive than arguments over how schools should handle issues concerning sexual orientation, including student religious views on homosexuality. In 2012, for example, a gay high school student in Ohio won a court settlement allowing him to wear his "Jesus is not a homophobe" T-shirt. Meanwhile, in other communities, Christian students have battled for the right to proclaim their own views about homosexuality. In 2008, two of these students won a court decision lifting their school's ban on wearing "be happy, not gay" T-shirts at a Chicago high school.

In some public schools a "Day of Silence" to encourage support for gay, lesbian, bisexual, and transgender students is countered by a "Day of Dialogue" (formerly "Day of Truth") to encourage conservative religious students to speak out for their religious convictions. The first is sponsored by the Gay, Lesbian & Straight Education Network (GLSEN) and the second by the conservative Focus on the Family.

Beyond T-shirt wars and dueling days, conflicts over lesbian, gay, bisexual, and transgender (LGBT) issues involve the curriculum, recognition of student clubs, and other aspects of school life. In 2006, the First Amendment Center released a consensus guide recommending a process for addressing these questions in local school districts. "Public Schools and Sexual Orientation: A First Amendment Framework for Finding Common Ground" was drafted by Wayne Jacobsen, an evangelical leader in California, and me, with the help of GLSEN and the Christian Educators Association International—two organizations with widely divergent views on homosexuality, but with a shared commitment to civil dialogue.[10] To date, however, only a small number of districts have followed the advice in these guidelines and proactively worked for common ground on this issue.

In an effort to provide an additional tool for resolving conflicts over student speech on all sides of this and other controversial issues, the First Amendment Center joined with the American Jewish Congress and fifteen other religious and education groups in 2012 to release "Harassment, Bullying and Free Expression: A Guide to Safe and Free Public Schools."[11] This publication is designed to help school officials implement effective anti-bullying policies while simultaneously upholding free speech and free exercise of religion.

Over the past decade, conflicts have also broken out in school districts across the country, particularly in rural areas, over proposals for elective Bible courses. This is not surprising, given our long history of fighting over the role of the Bible in public schools, from the "Bible wars" of the nineteenth century to the lawsuits of the twenty-first. If the issue was only Bible literacy, then finding agreement on the importance of learning about the Bible might be easy. After all, how can students understand much of what they see in museums, read in literature, or encounter in history and current events if they are biblically illiterate?

Unfortunately, however, much of the recent pressure for Bible courses comes from the National Council on Bible Curriculum in Public Schools, a Christian conservative organization that appears to have a religious agenda. According to studies conducted by Mark Chancey, professor of religious studies at Southern Methodist University, the National Council's curriculum materials unconstitutionally promote one religious view of the Bible. School districts adopting this curriculum risk winding up in court.[12]

An alternative approach emerged in 2005 when the Bible Literacy Project released a new textbook, *The Bible and Its Influence*, in an effort to provide an academically sound presentation of the themes, narratives, and characters of the Hebrew Scriptures and New Testament. Although not without its own critics, the Bible Literacy Project textbook is supported by a broad range of scholars and religious liberty experts, and is now being used by many school districts without controversy.

Although public schools in most states can offer Bible electives now if they so choose, some legislators want to encourage more Bible courses by providing state support and incentives. A number of states, including Georgia, Texas, Tennessee, South Carolina, Arizona, and South Dakota, have enacted "Bible bills"—and other states are likely to follow suit.

Of course, Bible literature and history can (and should) be part of the public school curriculum—but only if the material is taught objectively using scholarly materials. Most of the state Bible bills, however, give little or no guidance on what constitutional and educational safeguards schools should put in place to ensure that Bible courses are academic, not devotional. And little provision is made to prepare teachers or to provide scholarly resources for teaching about the Bible.

Here again, the First Amendment Center has published consensus guidelines on how to address the Bible in public schools. Released in 2000, "The Bible and Public Schools: A First Amendment Guide" is endorsed by a broad range of national groups, from the Christian Legal Society to People for the American Way.[13] The Society of Biblical Literature has also weighed in on this issue, publishing "Teaching the Bible," a resource for public school teachers engaged in teaching about the Bible (http://www.sbl-site.org/educational/teachingbible.aspx).

A third cluster of conflicts in many public schools involves student religious expression before captive audiences at school-sponsored events. In recent years, differences over if and when to draw the line on student religious expression at school-sponsored events have sparked fights and lawsuits. Beyond mentioning their religious beliefs or affiliations (which most legal experts agree is permissible under current law), do students have the right to speak extensively about their faith or offer a prayer at school events, or does such speech put the school in the position of unconstitutionally endorsing religion?

According to the 2003 U.S. Department of Education guidelines on "constitutionally protected prayer," student speakers chosen on the basis of neutral criteria who retain "primary control" over their speeches may not be restricted because of the religious or anti-religious content of what they say. Although some lower court decisions support this approach, some civil liberties groups argue that current law does not fully support this application of the First Amendment.[14]

In recent years, some state legislatures—frustrated by the reluctance of many school officials to provide a forum for student religious speech, including prayers—have enacted legislation encouraging school policies that reflect the 2003 DOE guidelines and allow more student religious expression at school-sponsored events. For example,

Texas enacted the Religious Viewpoints Antidiscrimination Act in 2006, and Florida Governor Rick Scott signed a similar bill in 2012.

Not surprisingly, many school administrators and school boards are reluctant to adopt policies urged by DOE guidance and various state laws that would create a "free speech" forum at graduations and assemblies. Turning over the microphone to student speakers can be a risky business for school officials, especially when religion is involved.

CONCLUSION

Despite these remaining areas of disagreement, new consensus on many, if not most, religion in schools issues that have long divided Americans creates an historic opportunity to get religion right—or close to right—in public education. After more than 150 years of shouting past one another about the place of religion in public schools, we finally have a model for finding considerable common ground.

The single most important step any school district can take is to proactively develop sound policies and practices (with the full participation of parents and all members of the school community) that reflect the constitutional safe harbor provided by national agreements on religious freedom in schools.

After more than 20 years of mediating these issues in local communities around the country, I can say with confidence that school districts with sound First Amendment policies and practices are much less likely to experience conflicts and lawsuits over issues related to religion in schools.

If American schools and communities seize the opportunity provided by the new consensus, a common vision for the common good may yet be realized in public education—and in our nation— as we confront the difficult task of continuing to forge one nation out of many peoples and faiths in the twenty-first century.

NOTES

1. For a full discussion of the meaning and significance of the Williamsburg Charter, see Os Guinness, *The Case for Civility: And Why Our Future Depends On It* (New York: Harper One, 2008).

2. For the text of the consensus guidelines and the list of endorsers, see Charles C. Haynes and Oliver Thomas, *Finding Common Ground: A First Amendment Guide to Religion and Public Schools* (Nashville, TN: First Amendment Center, 2011), http://www.firstamendmentcenter.org/madison/wp-content/uploads/2011/03/FCGcomplete.pdf.

3. Haynes and Thomas, *Finding Common Ground*, 12.

4. The U.S. Department of Education guidelines on student religious expression in public schools are reprinted in Haynes and Thomas, *Finding Common Ground*, 59–76.

5. Susan L. Douglass, *Teaching about Religion in National and State Social Studies Standards* (Nashville, TN: Council on Islamic Education and First Amendment Center, 2000).

6. Warren A. Nord and Charles C. Haynes, *Taking Religion Seriously across the Curriculum* (Alexandria, VA: Association for Supervision and Curriculum Development, 1998). See also Warren A. Nord, *Does God Make a Difference? Taking Religion Seriously in Our Schools and Universities* (New York: Oxford University Press, 2010).

7. For more information about *Face to Faith* and the Tony Blair Faith Foundation, see www.tonyblairfaithfoundation.org.

8. *American Civil Liberties Union v. Sumner County Board of Education* was settled on May 2, 2011.

9. For examples of good policies on religion in public schools, see Haynes and Thomas, *Finding Common Ground*, chap. 15.

10. *Public Schools and Sexual Orientation: A First Amendment Framework for Finding Common Ground*, http://www.firstamendmentcenter.org/madison/wp-content/uploads/2011/03/sexual.orientation.guidelines.pdf.

11. American Jewish Committee and Religious Freedom Education Project/First Amendment Center, *Harassment, Bullying and Free Expression: A Guide to Safe and Free Public Schools*, http://religiousfreedomeducation.org/rfep/wp-content /uploads/2012/05/FAC-Harassment-Free-Expression-BROCHURE.pdf.

12. For a discussion of the controversy over Bible electives, see Mark A. Chancey, "A Textbook Example of the Christian Right: The National Council on Bible Curriculum in Public Schools," *Journal of the American Academy of Religion* 75, no. 3 (September 2007): 554–81.

13. The Bible Literacy Project, Inc., and First Amendment Center, *The Bible and Public Schools: A First Amendment Guide* (Nashville, TN: First Amendment Center, 1999), http://www.firstamendmentcenter.org/madison/wp-content/uploads/2011/03/bible_guide_graphics.pdf.

14. For the full text of the U.S. Department of Education guidance issued in 2003, see Haynes and Thomas, *Finding Common Ground*, 59–66.

PART III

Exploring Contemporary Challenges

6   The Erupting Clash between Religion and the State over Contraception, Sterilization and Abortion

Robin Fretwell Wilson

If there is one lesson from the controversy over the sterilization and contraception coverage mandate (referred to hereafter as the Mandate) under the new Patient Protection and Affordable Care Act (ACA), it is this: unlike other wars, culture wars are rarely won. Although often overlooked, the "political maelstrom" sparked by the Mandate tapped into deep resistance on two separate grounds.[1] Some objected to contraceptive coverage and sterilization services alike because they believe that all sexual intercourse should have the potential for creating life—a view not widely shared by faith groups or the American public.[2] Others balked specifically at coverage of "abortion-inducing drugs and devices," like emergency contraceptives (ECs).[3] The essence of this objection is that such drugs and devices "are designed to destroy human life after conception," making provision of them an "abortion on demand"—or, worse, "murder because it is the killing of an innocent person."[4] This ground for resistance resonates with far more Americans. Decades after *Roe v. Wade,* many still believe that abortion is "wrong," both within faith communities and outside them.[5]

Few would describe this country's persistent divide over abortion as a settled issue that either side had "won." Just contrast the 1.2 million abortions annually with the steady stream of state legislation to evince respect for fetal life—or, as family planning advocates would say, to erect more and higher hurdles to a woman's access to abortion.[6] But in one crucial respect, the ongoing clash over abortion had reached an equilibrium.

For nearly 40 years, abortion objectors could count on two iron-clad guarantees: first, that no one would ever have to assist with an abortion if doing so were "contrary to his religious beliefs or moral convictions"[7]; and second, that federal tax dollars would not "be expended . . . [for] abortion" except when exceedingly good justifications exist—like saving the woman's life.[8] These guarantees—made in the Church Amendment months after *Roe v. Wade* in 1973 and in the Hyde Amendment three years later in 1976—appeared unassailable. Indeed, far from being under constant retreat, Congress expanded conscience guarantees in successive pieces of legislation since 1973, in Congresses under both Democratic and Republican leadership—acts that were signed into law by presidents from both parties.[9] In addition, Congress has renewed the Hyde Amendment every year since 1976, with strong bipartisan support.[10] Thus, even when abortion itself remained a deeply partisan, contested issue, conscience protections were not.[11]

This remained true until the last few years, when health care institutions and the government exerted significant—some would say unprecedented—pressure on religious objectors to perform *all* requested services or provide *any* mandated benefit, even when doing so would force them to violate deeply held religious beliefs.[12] No one could miss the full-scale clash that erupted between the Obama administration and religious groups over the Mandate, which requires coverage of the full range of FDA-approved contraceptive methods in all plans—public or private, self-insured or commercial.[13] Less noticed, but equally disturbing, were other flash points over abortion and ECs around the country. In lawsuits filed in 2009 and 2011, nurses at two different teaching hospitals say they were coerced into assisting with or training for abortions—over their stated objections and despite an unqualified right to refuse under the Church Amendment.[14] A Louisiana nurse says she was forced to dispense ECs, prompting Louisiana to enact a new state "conscience" law. Like these private actors, a number of states have sought to expand access to EC by directing all providers to dispense ECs, notwithstanding deeply held religious beliefs.[15]

This chapter chronicles these clashes, illustrating the sharp departure from the live-and-let-live regime surrounding abortion objections since *Roe v. Wade*. This chapter first shows that religious objectors are not shielded from legal mandates that conflict with their faith as a matter of U.S. constitutional right, meaning that objectors generally must secure protections in the political process. It then sketches just how quickly seemingly unassailable conscience protections have come under pressure from the federal government, in the form of the Mandate, and from health care providers and state governments. Although these flash points are dissimilar in important ways, together they have left religious objectors feeling that they are under assault.[16]

With advance planning, clashes over contested services can frequently be avoided—without sacrificing access to needed services or respect for objectors. Indeed, across the clashes described here, the concerns of religious objectors have been largely vindicated, albeit after protracted and contentious fights in the political arena and sometimes the courts.

This chapter then turns to one crucial ground on which some family planning advocates and women's rights groups urge policymakers to push back against greater accommodations for religious objectors. These groups say that authorizing refusals to dispense ECs such as Plan B and *ella* condones a scientifically unsupported idea—namely, that Plan B and *ella* "frequently function to destroy fertilized eggs, which [is tantamount to] abortion on demand."[17] This chapter shows that there are two competing accounts about ECs' mechanism of action, neither of which is completely accurate: family planning advocates say that *all* forms of ECs act *only* as contraceptives, whereas objectors say that all forms of ECs *can act* as abortifacients. However, the second part of the chapter, "Objections to 'Abortion-Inducing' Drugs," shows that the truth appears to be somewhere in the middle. *Some forms* of ECs appear *sometimes* to act after fertilization as "contragestives," meaning they destroy a fertilized egg. Thus, religious objectors can legitimately claim that duties to dispense or pay for ECs place them in the position of not knowing whether they would be facilitating the "destruction of innocent human life."[18] In the final analysis, policymakers have responded to the erupting clash between religion and the state over the deeply divisive question of abortion with significant concessions for religious objectors.

PRESSURE ON ABORTION CONSCIENCE PROTECTIONS

The ACA and the Mandate

The ACA ushered in an era of near-universal access to health care services—a goal that had long eluded policymakers in the United

States.[19] Even before the ACA became law, however, many feared a rollback of the deeply ingrained conscience guarantees in the Church and Hyde Amendments. Recall Representative Bart Stupak, who unsuccessfully proposed an amendment to the ACA to ban the use of any federal funds under the ACA for certain abortions.[20] Representative Stupak asked President Obama for—and received—an Executive Order promising that that there would be strict compliance with the ACA's abortion funding restrictions.[21]

The ACA barred premium tax credits and cost-sharing subsidies for low-income Americans from being used to purchase abortion coverage. Congress also included assurances in the ACA that existing conscience guarantees would not be rolled back. And Congress expressly permitted states and qualified health plans to provide no abortion coverage.[22]

Given these assurances, many were surprised that the Mandate required coverage of ECs like Plan B and *ella*.[23] The earliest proposed rules did not exempt religious objectors, prompting a slew of criticism that the Mandate would "impinge upon [their] religious freedom."[24] Later proposals would exempt faith-based employers that see their mission as inculcating religious values and that serve and hire primarily from their own faith.[25] As one commentator quipped, however, "not even Jesus and the apostles would qualify for" that accommodation as drafted.[26] More to the point, that cramped definition provided no refuge for religiously affiliated universities, hospitals, and social services agencies like Catholic Charities or the Salvation Army.

Even supporters of the ACA found this definition to be too restrictive. The Catholic Health Association, which had supported the ACA, explained: "The impact of being told we do not fit into the new definition of religious employer and therefore cannot operate our ministries following our consciences has jolted us. . . . From President Thomas Jefferson to President Barack Obama, we have been promised a respect for appropriate religious freedom."[27]

Many different faith groups, from Catholics to Muslims to evangelical Protestants, said that the Mandate placed the bulk of religious employers "in the untenable position of having to choose between violating the law and violating their consciences."[28] Objectors cited their religious beliefs that sex should be procreative or that "a person is created at conception . . . [making] abortion . . . murder because it is the killing of an innocent person."[29]

The claim of religious groups to a special right to be exempted from the Mandate was met by equally vigorous claims that "all women, regardless of their employer, should be able to access the birth control coverage benefit."[30] Women's rights groups like the National Women's Law Center praised the Obama administration for establishing "a major milestone in protecting women's health [because] . . . [c]ontraception is critical preventive health care."[31] Others decried the inclusion of even a limited exemption for churches, and encouraged the Obama administration to hold the line against broader exemptions.[32]

Religious objectors had to fend for themselves in the political process because they are not shielded against the burdens of generally applicable laws as a matter of federal constitutional right, as the U.S. Supreme Court specifically noted in *Employment Division v. Smith*. (*Smith* was left in place by the Supreme Court's decision in *Hosanna-Tabor Evangelical Lutheran Church and School v. Equal Employment Opportunity Commission*, which held that a ministerial exception, based on the First Amendment's Religion Clauses, bars a suit brought under the Americans with Disabilities Act on behalf of a teacher-minister against a church.[33]) Objectors may receive more robust protections under the federal Religious Freedom Restoration Act, which has become the backbone for the 93 suits challenging the Mandate.[34]

As those suits wound their way through the courts, religious objectors also turned to the political process—with surprising success. Responding to growing rancor over the Mandate, the president in 2012 proffered an accommodation for religious employers. The president explained: "[I]f a woman's employer is a charity or a hospital that has a religious objection to providing contraceptive services as part of their health plan, the insurance company—not the hospital, not the charity—will be required to reach out and offer the woman contraceptive care free of charge without co-pays, without hassle."[35]

The president's proposal encountered stiff resistance. Five hundred scholars, university presidents, religious leaders, and others, led by Archbishop of New York Cardinal Timothy Dolan, labeled that accommodation "unacceptable," accusing the White House of hiding a "grave violation" of religious liberty behind a "cheap accounting trick."[36]

The Obama administration proceeded nonetheless to implement the president's vision. Although it extended no help to for-profit employers, who must still comply with the Mandate, the administration's final regulations relaxed the test to obtain a religious exemption, requiring only that the organization be a faith-based body. Employees of an objecting organization would receive contraceptive coverage from an insurer through separate add-on contraceptive coverage—at no cost to the religious organization and no cost to the employee.[37] The insurer that provides the add-on coverage either absorbs the cost entirely (for group insurance purchased in the marketplace) or pays itself back from monies it would otherwise owe the federal government for running a federally facilitated exchange (for self-insured plans).[38]

Some early critics were mollified. The Catholic Health Association said that "HHS has now established an accommodation that will allow our ministries to continue offering health insurance plans for their employees as they have always done," and expressed gratitude "for the respect and concern demonstrated by all parties in this dialogue."[39] As of this writing, however, not a single litigant has dropped its suit.[40] Why? As Yuval Levin cleverly noted, "Somehow these religious employers are supposed to imagine that they're not giving their workers access to abortive and contraceptive coverage. If religious people thought about their religious obligations the way government lawyers think about the law, this might just work. But they don't."[41]

Despite the continuing discontent, nonprofit religious objectors secured significant accommodations through the political process. They do not directly pay for the objected-to coverage; instead, that coverage comes from a third-party insurer. We see this pattern—of first demanding that objectors set aside religious convictions, then working with them to resolve the tension between the demands of their faith and the needs of others—in the private marketplace as well, as the next section of this chapter demonstrates.

Before turning to other clashes, it is worth noting that Obama administration's two overarching goals—of "respecting religious beliefs and increasing access to important preventive services"—could have been accomplished without encroaching on the religious liberty of employers, thus avoiding the protracted, contentious saga that ultimately unfolded.[42] The Obama administration could have ensured near-universal access by significantly expanding government programs such as Title X that now provide contraceptives to lower-income women.

This solution to what is a very real access issue facing many financially strapped women would have been in keeping with the ACA. The ACA sought to expand the access of *all* lower-income Americans to all health care services, not just contraceptive coverage, by requiring states to extend Medicaid eligibility to "adults with incomes at or below 138% of the federal poverty level."[43] The U.S. Supreme Court ultimately struck down the ACA's Medicaid expansion scheme in June 2012 as exceeding Congress's authority under the Spending Clause.[44] But at the time the Obama administration first proposed the Mandate in January of 2012, the Medicaid expansion scheme had not been invalidated. Following the ACA's model of expanded access to publicly provided services may have been controversial in itself, but it would have avoided the collision over forced payment by one individual of contraceptives and "abortion-inducing drugs" for another.

Significantly, expanded subsidies would have addressed the access concerns animating the Mandate. Birth control pills cost from $160 to $600 a year, and IUDs cost even more.[45] Taxpayers already subsidize contraceptives for many lower income women. In fact, of the 37 million women in "need" of publicly funded contraceptive services and supplies—defined by the Guttmacher Institute as any woman whose income is less than 250 percent of the federal poverty level or who is under 20 years of age—taxpayers provided that coverage for 9 million such women, to the tune of $1.80 billion in 2010: 75 percent of the funds came from Medicaid, 12.0 percent from state appropriations, and 10.0 percent from Title X, while Maternal and Child Health block grants, social services grants, and Temporary Assistance for Needy Families together accounted for 3 percent of all funding.[46] If taxpayers paid for "free" contraceptives for all women in need (37 million), 28 million more would need to be covered, about four times the current number. Of course, aggregate costs for that *average* coverage would almost certainly drop because the government would get a good deal based on volume. But even assuming the same cost per unit, coverage of all women of childbearing age would require an expenditure of $7.4 billion—roughly equivalent to what we spent in 2010 for one month of war in Afghanistan.[47] Moreover, any expenditures would be offset by savings in government-supported health care plans like Medicaid, as well as in savings for Temporary Assistance for Needy Families (TANF) and other payments to needy families, since the number of families would grow at a smaller rate.[48]

One can imagine that providing contraceptives for *every* woman of childbearing age at no cost to the woman would draw fire, especially since wealthier women, who do not need a subsidy, would also benefit. To avoid subsidizing those who do not need a subsidy, the Obama administration could have taken a more focused tack, expanding Title X's family planning services to women with modest incomes. The administration could have, for example, expanded this important safety net to reach women with significantly higher income thresholds—say, for example, 400 percent of poverty, where the ACA's subsidies for premium tax credits and cost-sharing subsidies cut off.[49] Because those most in need represent a fraction of all women of childbearing age, the cost to the public of providing "free" contraceptive coverage to this more circumscribed group would be considerably less.

Whether free coverage for all or free coverage for the neediest, a government subsidy would have given lower-income women access without forcing objecting nonprofit institutions like Notre Dame and for-profit companies like Hobby Lobby to choose between "violating the law [and] violating their consciences." Many have rightly asked how the Obama administration failed to anticipate the deep, sustained blowback over the Mandate. In hindsight, it seems as if the government gained little by precipitating a needless clash over the contours of what the government can rightly demand of religious employers.[50] It would have been far better to have sought a creative solution from the beginning that would balance access to needed services with respect for religious liberty. As the next section notes, creative solutions can protect access without surrendering religious liberty.

Coercion by Health Care Providers

The struggle over the contours of the Mandate is hardly the only clash unfolding over abortion, sterilization, and ECs today. Recently, major medical centers have "revers[ed] a long-standing policy exempting employees who refuse[d] [to help with abortion patients] [for] religious or moral objections."[51] Like religious objectors to the Mandate, providers initially coerced into facilitating abortions have managed to wring important concessions from their employers after protracted litigation and the intervention of federal authorities.

In 2011, a dozen nurses sued the University of Medicine and Dentistry of New Jersey (UMDNJ) in federal court, alleging that they were forced, under threat of professional discipline or dismissal, to assist with abortions in violation of their moral or religious convictions. The nurses alleged that in 2006 UMDNJ changed its policy of assigning only willing same-day surgery unit nurses to participate in abortion procedures. Instead, hospital staff "repeatedly [told the nurses] . . . that they must assist abortions or . . . be terminated . . . [and even though transfer was theoretically possible] no such jobs exist[ed] anyway, so that . . . objection . . . could only lead to . . . termination." When a nurse "reiterated her religious objections to training in or assisting abortions . . . [a staff member] responded that UMDNJ has 'no regard for religious beliefs' of nurses who object, that 'everyone on this floor is required when assigned to do terminations of pregnancy,' that nurses 'are trained to care for patients' elective procedures,' and that 'no patients can be refused by any nurse.'"[52] Two years earlier, in 2009, Cathy Cenzon-DeCarlo, an operating room nurse at New York's Mount Sinai Hospital, brought suit against Mount Sinai, claiming she was coerced into assisting with a late-term, 22-week abortion in violation of the Church Amendment.[53] Cenzon-DeCarlo alleged that, although Mount Sinai staffed around her religious objection to assisting with abortions for 5 years, on May 24, 2009, her superior threatened not only to terminate her if she did not help with an abortion, but also to report her to the nursing board for "patient abandonment." The patient needed a Category 2 abortion, requiring "surgery within 6 hours." Cenzon-DeCarlo alleges that her direct supervisor was available and able to assist with that abortion. Under pressure, Cenzon-DeCarlo ultimately acceded to assisting with the late-term abortion.[54]

At the core of the collision between Cenzon-DeCarlo and Mount Sinai was whether Cenzon-DeCarlo's services could have been performed by anyone else. Maura Carpo, Mount Sinai's clinical nurse manager, whose responsibilities included "facilitating the flow" of daily surgeries, stated in an affidavit that Cenzon-DeCarlo's supervisor offered to allow Cenzon-DeCarlo to leave the operating room during the abortion procedure. Cenzon-DeCarlo would, however, have had "to perform her pre-operative job duties because [the hospital] had not been able to locate a replacement for [her] and the physician made clear that the patient's life was at risk."[55] Cenzon-DeCarlo said her supervisor was able to assist. Thus, Cenzon-DeCarlo's case raises both a factual claim—namely, whether another willing provider was available—as well as a claim of legal entitlement to step aside from a service when assisting with it would violate one's religious beliefs.

In each case, the hospitals' policy reversal—first allowing religious objectors to step aside, then coercing them to participate—must have come as a shock. As noted earlier, the Church Amendment provides an absolute, unqualified ground for objecting to assisting with an abortion or sterilization if it "would be contrary to one's religious beliefs or moral convictions." New Jersey and New York both provide conscientious objectors with an absolute exemption from participating in abortions under state law, as twenty states do. Forty-seven states provide some kind of conscience protection.[56]

In both cases, the objecting providers were vindicated, although the suits took very different paths to that outcome. In the UMDNJ case, *Danquah v. University of Medicine and Dentistry of New Jersey*, the nurses requested and received a temporary restraining order in November of 2011.[57] On December 22, 2011, the parties "memorialized" their agreement with the district court judge that—except when the mother's life is at risk and there are no other non-objecting staff available to assist—nurses with conscientious objections will not have to assist with abortions. In the rare emergency in which no other willing provider is available, "the only involvement of the objecting [nurses] would be to care for the patient until such time as a non-objecting person can get there to take over the care." The parties agreed to these terms despite the fact that the New Jersey law provides that "[n]o person shall be required to perform or assist in the performance of an abortion or sterilization." Thus, the parties' settlement converted the absolute and unqualified exemption under state and federal law into a right qualified by hardship to the patient. U.S. District Court Judge Linares "retain[ed] jurisdiction of this matter to ensure that the terms of the agreement are in fact followed."[58]

Although an accommodation qualified by hardship to the public—like that fashioned in *Danquah*—may not seem like much of a victory, it gives significant protection to religious liberty. Employers can generally take steps to anticipate and avoid collisions between religious liberty and patient access, such as requiring objectors to object in writing, as Cenzon-DeCarlo did.[59] And employers can avoid collisions through thoughtful staffing arrangements, as Mount Sinai seems to have done for 5 years before requiring Canzon-DeCarlo to assist.

Moreover, emergencies for which there is no other individual provider are likely to be rare, especially at large institutions.[60] Thus, when employers take concrete affirmative steps, religious liberty accommodations need not come at the expense of patient access.

The New York case, *Cenzon-DeCarlo v. The Mount Sinai Hospital, et al.*, followed a tortured course in the courts, only to be resolved through an administrative complaint to the federal Department of Health and Human Services (HHS), which enforces the Church Amendment. In the federal district court that first heard the Cenzon-DeCarlo case, the court dismissed Cenzon-DeCarlo's suit, concluding—correctly—that the Church Amendment did not confer a private right of action permitting objectors to enforce the amendment directly. The U.S. Court of Appeals for the Second Circuit affirmed the decision.[61]

Shut out of federal court, Cenzon-DeCarlo filed suit in state court but, crucially, also asked HHS to investigate—yielding a much more sympathetic result. In a settlement with HHS, Mount Sinai revised its policy to unequivocally declare the "legal right of any individual to refuse to participation" in abortion procedures, regardless of its emergency or elective status. Mount Sinai adopted a process for "alternative coverage" so that, should a staff member choose not to participate, the hospital would then consult a list of willing providers.[62] Finally, Mount Sinai agreed to comply with federal conscience protections, train employees about them, and implement a Human Resource policy prohibiting employment discrimination based on one's objection to assisting in abortion procedures.[63]

Pressure by the States

Collisions occur not just over traditional surgical abortion but over "abortion-inducing drugs" too. Consider the dispute between Toni Lemly, a licensed practical nurse, and St. Tammany Parish Hospital.[64] In August 2003, the hospital hired Lemly full-time as an immunization coordinator in its Community Wellness Center. Soon after, the center began offering a family planning clinic on its premises on Thursdays and Fridays. Before opening the clinic, the hospital told Lemly she would have to administer ECs. Lemly vigorously objected, sending an email to the center's director, citing her "deep seeded belief in [the] Supreme Holy God . . . [and that] . . . He is the Creator, Giver, and Taker of life." She noted that she could not "interfere with His plan . . . [and] . . . give pills to take a life He creates." The next day, the hospital presented Lemly with three alternatives: work part-time at the center Monday through Wednesday, apply for a transfer to a different nursing position, or work Monday through Wednesday at the center and two days in a different department. Lemly found none of the proposals suitable. Switching to part-time status would result in a loss of benefits, and Lemly lacked the requisite qualifications for the open positions. Lemly then proposed alternatives of her own so that she could "continue to work full time at the center and continue to give immunizations on Fridays in the morning and afternoon. On Thursdays, [she] proposed that she would remain productive by 1) pulling and making charts for immunization appointments; 2) calling . . . patients and scheduling appointments; and 3) working the front desk as needed." The hospital rejected the proposal because "there was insufficient work unrelated to Family Planning to keep plaintiff busy on Thursdays and Fridays" and reduced her to part-time status.[65]

Lemly then sued the hospital under a state nondiscrimination law and under a nondiscrimination provision in the hospital's contract with the Louisiana Department of Health and Hospitals. A federal court granted the hospital's motion for summary judgment on the contract claim, but remanded to state court for determination of whether the hospital violated the state nondiscrimination law.[66] The state trial court denied the hospital's motion for summary judgment, and the hospital appealed the ruling. The Louisiana Supreme Court affirmed denial of summary judgment to the hospital on the state discrimination issue.[67] Following the Louisiana Supreme Court's ruling, the Louisiana legislature enacted a new conscience protection law. Like the *Danquah* settlement, that legislation provides that a "person has the right not to participate in, and no person shall be required to participate in any health care service that violates his conscience *to the extent that patient access to health care is not compromised.*"[68]

Today, the United States is a classic statutory "checkerboard," with some states giving conscience protections to dispensing ECs, as Louisiana did, and others denying it. Eleven states allow individual providers to refuse to provide ECs, while nine states allow medical institutions to refuse to provide ECs. Often, the professional who objects to dispensing the EC is a pharmacist. Six states explicitly authorize pharmacists to refuse, and six other states have broad refusal clauses that would appear to encompass pharmacists.[69] By contrast, five states place an affirmative obligation on pharmacists or pharmacies to provide ECs. Additionally, "12 states and [D.C.] require emergency rooms to dispense [ECs] on request to assault victims."[70]

Legislators faced with claims like Lemly's necessarily must balance two equally compelling values: respect for conscience and access to needed services.[71] In this regard, accommodations for institutional providers pose a special challenge, because institutions sometimes control large swaths of the market. Moreover, people who present at the emergency rooms of large-market-share institutions often have no choice about where to go. Thus, an absolute, unfettered right for institutions to refuse to provide a contested service could threaten significantly the public's ability to access the service—especially if there are no other willing institutions nearby.[72]

Some of the understandable concerns about granting institutional accommodations stem precisely from market concentration. Catholic hospitals comprise 17 percent of all hospital admissions nationally.[73] Compounding this, many Catholic hospitals possess monopoly power in their relevant communities. Indeed, ninety-one counties in the United States are served exclusively by a Catholic hospital, a number that is likely to grow as Catholic hospitals merge with non-Catholic hospitals.[74]

In my view, respect for conscience should never allow a provider to be in a "blocking position," where the provider's refusal will mean that the patient cannot access the service without considerable hardship—something that is far more likely to occur with a large regional hospital than with an individual provider.[75] Indeed, if the primary goods that legislators balance are patient access and religious liberty, this balance should favor individual exemptions.[76]

Ironically, however, the market power that raises the specter of reduced access has favored the granting of institutional protections if the objector would close the facility rather than comply.[77] While legislators should take threats of exit by religious providers very seriously, they need to ask hard questions about how likely it might be that the objector will choose to accede to civil strictures rather than actually exiting the market.[78] Legislators should determine whether there is a scarcity of other providers, and ascertain the market share of the possible exiting organization, the likelihood that the exiting organization would sell the facility rather than shuttering it, the likelihood of a private buyer or the government acquiring the facility in advance of any shutdown, and the probable timeframe for any transition.

Affirmative obligations to provide ECs in every setting—even when patient access is not threatened—simply overreach, however. As noted above, religious liberty accommodations need not imperil patient access. An accommodation qualified by hardship to the public can preserve both the public's need for access and the religious objector's ability to step aside.[79] This is especially true with ECs, because women have a 72-to-120-hour window during which an EC can prevent pregnancy after unprotected sex.[80]

None of this means, however, that patients have not experienced real difficulty finding ECs; they have.[81] A careful examination of these very real and frustrating experiences shows that they stem principally from a lack of information (that is, the patient has no idea how to find a person who is willing to provide an EC to her), rather than from a lack of access (as when no accessible health care provider will provide an EC to her). Solving a patient's information problem will go a long way toward solving the access problem.[82] Armed with good information, patients in need of ECs should be able to readily find them through willing providers, given the extensive network of abortion providers across the United States. Indeed, the Mandate's inclusion of ECs makes it far more likely that they will be stocked in a given pharmacy, further reducing hurdles to access.

What Is Common across These Contexts?

Although the three contexts differ in important ways, in each context religious groups and individuals have asked for a way to both honor their religious convictions regarding human life and comply with the law. For many policymakers, however, respect for conscience is only the beginning of the analysis. Claims for accommodation have met with a lot of pushback on a number of grounds—not the least of which is whether the conscience objection has any basis in reality, a claim taken up in the next section.[83]

OBJECTIONS TO "ABORTION-INDUCING" DRUGS

Some groups resist accommodations, saying that accommodations legitimize a scientifically unfounded idea—specifically, the claim made by objectors that giving access to an EC is providing "abortion on demand."[84] In 2012, the American College of Obstetricians and Gynecologists (ACOG) said of Plan B and *ella* that "[a] common misconception is that [an EC] causes an abortion. Inhibition or delay of ovulation is the principal mechanism of action. Review of evidence suggests that [an EC] cannot prevent implantation of a fertilized egg."[85]

ACOG is not alone in this view. A *New York Times* editorial lamented that "belief that [Plan B] might be an abortifacient stems from speculative language that the [FDA] approved for its original label, which listed a number of physiological processes by which the pill might prevent pregnancy, including preventing fertilized eggs from implanting in the womb. . . . There was no evidence to support that view at the time, and there is none to support it now."[86]

Precisely because some advocates say ECs never act after fertilization to prevent implantation, they also maintain that objectors have no medically sound basis for refusing to dispense or pay for ECs. Factually, however, the contention that ECs "cannot prevent implantation of a fertilized egg" is simply more complicated than it appears.[87]

What Is Pregnancy?

There is no real disagreement that an abortifacient acts to end a pregnancy. The crux of the inquiry is when pregnancy—and perhaps even life—begins.

Some say that pregnancy begins when implantation is completed, and they contend that this position has "long been clear" in the medical community.[88] Planned Parenthood insists that, "[a]ccording to the general medical definitions of pregnancy that have been endorsed by many organizations—including ACOG and HHS—pregnancy begins when a pre-embryo completes implantation into the lining of the uterus."[89]

Notwithstanding this claim, a quick review of leading medical authorities on human development and embryology demonstrates a split on precisely when pregnancy begins. A 2010 article in the journal *Pharmacotherapy* notes that "[o]pinions differ regarding which specific event constitutes the beginning of life or pregnancy. In the scientific community, there are proponents for implantation and for the completion of fertilization to mark the beginning of pregnancy."[90]

Others mark pregnancy from "conception," but even this term is unclear, with some sources indicating that conception begins with "the implantation of the blastocyst in the endometrium," and others saying conception is the "instant that a spermatozoon enters an ovum and forms a viable zygote."[91] O'Rahilly and Müller's book *Developmental States in Human Embryos* explains that "for precise timing, the words 'gestation,' 'pregnancy,' and 'conception' should be avoided because fertilization is not universally accepted as the commencement: some authors use implantation."[92]

Definitions of pregnancy in state law reflect this lack of consensus. "Some of these laws say that pregnancy begins at fertilization, others at implantation. Several use the term 'conception,' which is often used synonymously with fertilization. . . ."[93] As one commentator writes, not only is the moment of pregnancy contested, but fertilization itself and even the "onset of life" remains contested:

> Indeed, many textbooks devoted to the topic of human embryology, as well as the legal codes of a number of countries and states within the USA, define the completion of fertilization and beginning of life in this manner. Yet this is not the only point at which life is said to begin. Recently, it has been asserted that the life and moral status of the embryo begin at the eight-cell stage, because zygotic transcription (the active utilization of embryonic genes) commences at this time; and prior to this moment, whatever is happening in the "fertilized egg" is being driven by maternal factors. Some push the onset of life to even later, to the formation of specific structures or the onset of specific developmental processes.[94]

Obviously, how one defines pregnancy or the onset of life determines whether a given drug or device may act to induce an abortion in his or her view. As Leung, Levine, and Soon note, "For people who define pregnancy as beginning at implantation, an abortifacient is an agent that interferes with subsequent processes. . . . For those who consider pregnancy to begin with the completion of fertilization, an abortifacient it an agent that interferes with any postfertilization event, including implantation."[95]

Some commentators muddy the debate more than clarify it by saying a drug is or is not abortion-inducing without unpacking what they mean by that term. For example, the Alliance Defending

Freedom states that the Mandate "[p]rovides 'free' coverage for early-abortion pills, contraceptives, sterilizations, and 'education and counseling.'"[96] On the other side of the debate, Planned Parenthood asserts that "[e]mergency contraception prevents pregnancy and helps a woman prevent the need for abortion."[97]

Avoiding a Battle of Terms

Given the morass surrounding the terms "pregnancy," "abortifacient," and "conception," it is more constructive to describe the mechanism of action of any given form of EC in less loaded, descriptive terms like *pre-fertilization, post-fertilization, pre-implantation,* and *post-implantation*—although these terms themselves may pose questions at the boundaries.[98]

Returning to the core inquiry, religious objectors say ECs can "prevent a human embryo . . . from implanting in the wall of the uterus, thereby causing the death of the embryo."[99] ACOG flatly disputes this, saying neither Plan B nor *ella* can "prevent implantation of a fertilized egg."[100]

Religious objectors did not manufacture from whole cloth the concern that Plan B and *ella* may act after fertilization to prevent implantation. They read it on the FDA-approved labels for each drug. The label for Plan B One-Step states that "[i]t works mainly by stopping the release of an egg from the ovary. It is possible that Plan B One-Step may also work by . . . preventing attachment (implantation) to the uterus (womb)."[101] The label for *ella*, approved in 2010, is nearly identical: *ella* says it "mainly works by stopping the release of an egg from the ovary [but] it is possible that *ella* may also work by preventing attachment (implantation) to the uterus."[102] Although the *New York Times* dismisses clear statements like these as "speculative language that the [FDA] approved for its original label," the FDA's website describes ECs' mechanism of action in just these terms. It says that both Plan B and *ella* "may prevent attachment (implantation)."[103] Religious objectors fighting the Mandate have not been blind to the FDA's statements; the FDA's own statements figure prominently in objectors' lawsuits.[104]

Factually, the evidence leading to this labeling stretches back to Plan B's approval. For example, studies published in 2002 said "emergency methods of contraception. . . . exert their negative effect on fertility by . . . creating unfavorable conditions for the implantation or for the establishment of a pregnancy."[105] In 2004, Charles Lockwood, a member of the scientific advisory committee to the FDA that held hearings about whether to make Plan B available over the counter, and now vice president for health sciences at Ohio State University, explained that "[m]any on the FDA panel perceived that a contragestive effect [i.e., an effect after fertilization occurs] was possible and we recommended that the package labeling should describe the drug's potential mechanism of action so that women could make an informed choice about its use and avoid inadvertently violating their own moral or religious beliefs."[106]

Dr. Lockwood noted that in 2002, one group of investigators had concluded that EC works in part "by alteration of the endometrial surface and, therefore, receptivity" of the implanting embryo.

Like Dr. Lockwood, a 2006 editorial in the journal *Contraception* noted ECs "can prevent pregnancy by delaying or inhibiting ovulation. Some of these methods have other established mechanisms of action, and it is possible that *all* may act after fertilization. The preponderance of research, however, shows that ECs do not have a *major* postfertilization mechanism of action."[107]

As late as 2010, an article in *Pharmacotherapy* entitled "Mechanisms of Actions of Hormonal Emergency Contraceptives" concluded as follows:

> [D]isruption of ovulation is supported by the strongest clinical evidence. Although anovulation (or dysfunctional ovulation) can explain the effectiveness of emergency contraceptives, it does not preclude other effects. It is possible that multiple mechanisms account for the total effect of emergency contraceptives. The available data are insufficient to verify theoretical contributions of an alteration in sperm activity, postovulatory hormonal changes, or markers of endometrial receptivity. Further investigations are needed to clarify these questions.[108]

The government's own explanations in regulations approving the sale of Plan B and *ella* as ECs reiterate the same mechanisms of action. The FDA said ECs act "by delaying or inhibiting ovulation, and/or altering tubal transport of sperm and/or ova (thereby inhibiting fertilization), and/or altering the endometrium (thereby inhibiting implantation)."[109]

Despite the FDA's medical descriptions, the Obama administration largely bypasses the concern about how drugs required by the Mandate likely work. The Final Rules granting a religious accommodation simply say the rules "do not violate federal restrictions relating to abortion" because no covered drug or device is an "abortifacient."[110] The White House blog emphasizes that "drugs that cause abortion are not covered by [the Mandate]. . . . Drugs like RU486 are not covered by this policy, and nothing about this policy changes the President's firm commitment to maintaining strict limitations on Federal funding for abortions."[111]

As the following section explains, a significant literature has amassed on Plan B since its approval in 1999, while a burgeoning literature examines *ella*, approved in 2010. Together, the literature shows two drugs that appear to work by very different mechanisms.

Two Very Different Types of Drugs

Despite persistent concerns about a post-fertilization effect since the approval of both EC drugs, the only way that Plan B has ever been demonstrated to operate is as a contraceptive—meaning that it works to prevent fertilization entirely. Specifically, Plan B works to delay ovulation so no egg is released to meet the sperm.[112] While studies of Plan B's contraceptive mechanism of action are now seen as dispositive, study authors acknowledge that post-fertilization effects can never be definitively ruled out.[113]

The evidence about the newer emergency contraceptive, *ella*, is shaping up differently. While Plan B is effective for up to 72 hours after unprotected sex, *ella* works over 120 hours after unprotected sex and is much more effective in preventing pregnancy than is Plan B.[114] For instance, *ella* prevented 85 percent of expected pregnancies as compared with Plan B's 69 percent in one study.[115]

Although *ella* clearly also works to prevent the release of an egg from the ovary and therefore fertilization—as Plan B does[116]—a number of authorities believe that *ella's* enhanced effectiveness stems in part from post-fertilization mechanisms of action. A 2011 article in the *Annals of Pharmacotherapy* concluded that if a woman happens to take *ella* in the five days after unprotected sex—and *after* the egg has already been fertilized—*ella's* "mechanism of action is much more accurately described as contragestive, since only gestation (implantation and growth) of the embryo [fertilized egg] is prevented" during that time frame. Indeed, this contragestive effect likely accounts for *ella's* "enhanced effectiveness. . . . compared with [Plan B]."[117]

Other authorities believe that with *ella*, "there is a unique circumstance and time period in which [*ella*] would have a direct abortifacient effect"—defined to mean "loss of the embryo before or after implantation . . . rather than a contraceptive effect." This would occur when "unprotected intercourse occurs within the fertility window (i.e., less than 120 hours [5 days] before ovulation or not more than 24 hours after ovulation) and [*ella*] is taken after fertilization." Professor Miech, an Associate Professor Emeritus of Molecular Pharmacology, Physiology, and Biotechnology at Brown University, believes that *ella* "blocks the immunotolerance effects of progesterone on the maternal innate immune system, resulting in the immunorejection of an embryo attempting to implant."[118] As with Plan B, evidence of *ella's* precise mechanisms of action may evolve as new studies accumulate.[119]

Does the Mechanism of Action Even Matter?

Even if these authorities are correct—that *ella* may act after fertilization to destroy a fertilized egg, at least sometimes—some would still dismiss the objector's objections. In 2007, for example, ACOG opposed exemptions from the duty to fill prescriptions for ECs for pharmacies and pharmacists, saying that "provider refusals to dispense [ECs] based on unsupported beliefs about its primary mechanism of action should not be justified."[120] In essence, this position says you, the objector, cannot know which way the drug will act, so you cannot legitimately object because it may not act in this way.

An objector would counter that an exemption is warranted not because they positively knew that by dispensing or paying for ECs they might facilitate the destruction of a life, but because they could not positively know they were not. Ultimately, then, this is really a question about who gets to decide in instances of uncertainty.

To be sure of the mechanism of action would require "each study participant to undergo laboratory examination and possibly sonographic examination to determine whether ovulation had already occurred."[121] No one, least of all the makers of EC, wants to do such studies. Moreover, as one obstetrician/gynecologist (Ob/Gyn) has noted, to be sure that ECs were acting only to prevent fertilization and not at a later stage—either before or after implantation—would require "historical knowledge of the woman's menstrual cycles, ultrasound examination, and [certain] hormone urge testing."[122] Surely, nobody wants to permit such intimate questions in order to put to rest the conscience of health care providers.

Many supporters of women's access to ECs discount the concerns of religious objectors, saying that they are far outside the mainstream. In other words, objectors are "wing nuts" if they consider the act of destroying a handful of cells to be tantamount to an abortion. But a significant segment of women see the issue just as objectors do: that using a birth control method that acts after fertilization is wrong.[123]

For example, in a 2001 study of California health care providers, including gynecologists, providers reported that "the majority of women . . . want to be informed . . . about mechanisms of action taking place after fertilization and implantation, regardless of their religiosity or whether they believed that human life begins at fertilization or implantation."[124] Of course, patients may consider information a good in itself, so that the desire to be informed may not stem directly from concerns about a possible post-fertilization effects. Helpfully, other studies more directly examine how women view EC.

For example, a 2005 study of women ages eighteen to fifty seen in Utah and Oklahoma family practices and Ob/Gyn clinics probed whether women in fact have reservations about using drugs that may act after fertilization. Researchers found that 53 percent said they would not use a birth control method that acts after fertilization, and 74 percent said they would not use a method that acts after implantation. When specifically asked if they would change their birth control method if told that "there was a remote possibility" it acted after fertilization, 44 percent of women "would stop using it," while 69 percent "would stop using it" if there was a "remote possibility" of it acting after implantation.[125]

It is possible that choices presented in a vacuum might look very different to a woman who suddenly finds herself in need of an EC. For study participants, however, qualms about these drugs directly reflect their view of when life begins. Forty-eight percent of the women "reported the personal belief that human life begins at fertilization."[126] For them, these methods mean that a life is being ended.[127]

A 2008 anonymous survey over 8 weeks of women being seen at two academic family medicine clinics in the southeastern United States found similar results. "[N]early one-half (47%) of respondents believed that pregnancy begins with fertilization; [and 38%] of respondents stated that they would use [an EC] only if they believed it worked before fertilization or implantation." Researchers tested whether a number of demographic factors predicted these responses, and found it tracked only with lower income: "[w]omen with incomes of less than $40,000 were more likely to believe that life begins at the joining of sperm and egg than women with higher incomes." Strength of religious beliefs did not influence whether a woman believed that life begins at fertilization.[128]

There may be legitimate concerns about how representative these samples are. Yet studies of women's attitudes in Europe, Mexico, and Spain document some women's concerns about using drugs that act after fertilization.[129]

WHERE DOES THIS LEAVE US?

Of course, when claims of faith are involved, the requirement that the rest of society agree with the objector's belief in order for the objector to receive protection would leave almost nothing of religious freedom. As Justice Douglas noted, writing for the Court in *United States v. Ballard*, "Heresy trials are foreign to our Constitution. Men may believe what they cannot prove. They may not be put to the proof of their religious doctrines or beliefs."[130] The U.S. Supreme Court reiterated this principle in its 1981 decision in *Thomas v. Review Board of Indiana Employment Security Division*, explaining that "religious beliefs need not be acceptable, logical, consistent, or comprehensible to others in order to merit First Amendment protection."[131]

Yet, with objections to facilitating surgical abortions or supplying "abortion-inducing drugs," objectors find themselves well within the mainstream of Americans in their opposition to traditional abortion—and their belief that destroying a fertilized egg is morally fraught. Those commonplace intuitions likely account for the conscience guarantees that abortion objectors have enjoyed since 1973, in the face of pressure from health care facilities and governments that sometimes seek to secure patient access at the expense of religious liberty.

As our 40-year experience with abortion conscience clauses shows, it is possible to combine access to needed services with respect for religious liberty. With the Mandate—as with much-needed access to abortion and EC—however, there were better ways forward. We could have avoided a needless moral clash while achieving the Obama administration's two stated goals of "respecting religious beliefs and increasing access to important preventive services" by expanding preexisting programs.[132] While the Obama administration has provided significant accommodations, some groups are still left fending for their religious liberties in the court systems.

As battles continue, there is no doubt that solutions will require creativity and flexibility on both sides. Indeed, protracted public debate and litigation over the Mandate, ECs, and abortion generally have pushed the Obama administration, state legislatures, and health care facilities to find just such creative solutions.

Acknowledgments

I benefitted immensely from the opportunity to present a forerunner of this chapter at the University of Oklahoma School of Law Constitutional Symposium, "Religious Freedom in America: Constitutional Traditions and New Horizons," April 2, 2012, as well as at panel discussions and workshops at The Brookings Institute, Georgetown University Law Center, Oxford University's Magdalen College, Southern Methodist University School of Law, and the Berkley Center for Religion, Peace, and World Affairs at Georgetown University. I am especially indebted to Josh Fairfield, David Gamage, Kent Greenawalt, David Hyman, Tim Jost, Anthony Kreis, Doug Laycock, and Tim MacDonnell for insightful, helpful comments, and to John Eller, Cameron Flynn, and Ron Fuller for their expert, diligent research support. I have signed the amicus curiae brief in *Stormans, Inc. et al. v. Mary Selecky and Judith Billings et al.*, Case No. 07-CV-05374-RBL (2012), which is before the U.S. Court of Appeals for the Ninth Circuit.

NOTES

1. Timothy Stoltzfus Jost, "Analysis of the Obama Administration's Updated Contraception Rule" (blog post), http://law.wlu.edu/faculty/faculty documents/jost/contraception.pdf.

2. *Eternal Word Television Network, Inc., v. Sebelius*, Complaint, Case No. 2:12-cv-00501-SLB (N.D. Ala., Feb. 9, 2012), http://www.becketfund. org/wp-content/uploads/2012/02/EWTN-Complaint-file-stamped.pdf; "The Birth Control Pill: 50 Years Later," CBS News Poll, May 7, 2010, http:// www.cbsnews.com/htdocs/pdf/poll_Birth_Control_Pill_050710.pdf?tag=co ntentMain;contentBody.

3. This chapter uses the term emergency contraceptive (abbreviated EC) to denote all drugs taken after unprotected sex to avoid pregnancy, whatever the mechanism of action.

4. Complaint, The QC Group, Inc., http://www.becketfund.org/wp-content/uploads/2013/08/1-Verified-Complaint-for-Declaratory-and-Injunctive-Relief-7-2-13.pdf; Complaint, Sharpe Holdings, Inc., ¶ 7, http://www .becketfund. org/wp-content/uploads/2013/04/Sharpe-Holdings-complaint.pdf; CatholicVote.org, "Catholic Entrepreneur and Family File Suit against Federal Employer Mandate," news release, October 8, 2012, http://www.catholicvote. org/discuss/wp-content/uploads/2012/10/autocampressreleaseoct8.pdf; Sevil Omer and Stephanie Simon, "Franciscan University Drops Student Health Insurance Plan Over Birth Control Mandate, Costs," NBC News, http://usnews.msnbc.msn.com/_news/2012/05/15/11720706-franciscan-university-drops-student-health-insurance-plan-over-birth-control-mandate-costs; Complaint, The QC Group, Inc., ¶ 3, http://www.becketfund.org/wp-content/uploads/2013/08/1-Verified-Complaint-for-Declaratory-and-Injunctive-Relief-7-2-13.pdf.

5. Congregation for the Doctrine of the Faith, "Instruction Dignitas Personae on Certain Bioethical Questions," § 23, September 8, 2008, http:// www.vatican.va/roman_curia/congregations/cfaith/documents/rc_con_cfaith_doc_20081208_dignitas-personae_en.html; Pontifical Council for the Family, "Vademecum for Confessors Concerning Some Aspects of the Morality of Conjugal Life," February 12, 1997, http://www.vatican.va/roman_curia/pontifical_councils/family/documents/rc_pc_family_doc_12021997_vademecum_en.html.

6. Rachel K. Jones and Kathryn Kooistra, "Abortion Incidence and Access to Services in the United States, 2008," *Perspectives on Sexual and Reproductive Health* 43, no. 1 (March 2011): 41; Planned Parenthood of Southeastern Pennsylvania v. Casey, 505 U.S. 833 (1992); Guttmacher Institute, State Center, "Laws Affecting Reproductive Health and Rights: 2011 State Policy Review," http://www.guttmacher.org/statecenter/updates/2011/statetrends42011. html; Erik Eckholm and Kim Severson, "Virginia Senate Passes Ultrasound Bill as Other States Take Notice," *New York Times*, February 28, 2012, http://www.nytimes.com/2012/02/29/us/virginia-senate-passes-revised-ultrasound-bill.html?pagewanted=all; Pamela M. Prah, "Abortion Ultrasound Debate Intensifies," *StateLine*, March 8, 2012, http://www.stateline.org/live/printable/story?contentId=637350; Rachel Benson Gold and Elizabeth Nash, "Troubling Trend: More States Hostile to Abortion Rights as Middle Ground

Shrinks," *Guttmacher Policy Review* 15, no. 1 (Winter 2012), http://www.guttmacher.org/pubs/gpr/15/1/gpr150114.html.

7. Pub. L. 93-45, §401 codified at 42 U.S.C. §300a-7(b)(1), http://www.hhs.gov/ocr/civilrights/understanding/ConscienceProtect/42usc300a7.pdf.

8. Pub. L. 111-8, 123 Stat. 524 §202, http://www.gpo.gov/fdsys/pkg/PLAW-111publ8/pdf/PLAW-111publ8.pdf; Robin Fretwell Wilson, "Matters of Conscience: Lessons for Same-Sex Marriage from the Health Care Context," in *Same-Sex Marriage and Religious Liberty: Emerging Conflicts*, eds. Douglas Laycock, Anthony R. Picarello, Jr., and Robin Fretwell Wilson (Lanham, MD: Rowman and Littlefield, 2008), 77; Robin Fretwell Wilson, *Demagoguing Abortion: Evaluating Competing Charges About the ACA's Violation of the Hyde Amendment* (unpublished manuscript). Since 1998, the Hyde Amendment has remained the same; it restricts the use of federal funding for abortion services, "except in cases of rape or incest, or when the life of the woman would be endangered." Omnibus Appropriations Act, 2009, Pub. L. 111-8, 123 Stat. 524.

9. 42 U.S.C. § 300a-7(c)(2); 42 U.S.C. § 300a-7(d); Danforth Amendment of 1988 within the Civil Rights Restoration Act, Pub. L. 100-259, http://www.govtrack.us/congress/bills/100/s557; Coats-Snowe Amendment to the 1996 Omnibus Consolidated Rescissions and Appropriations Act of 1996, Pub. L. 104-1344, http://www.govtrack.us/congress/bills/104/hr3019; Weldon Amendment in the Consolidated Appropriations Act of 2005, Pub. L. 108-447, http://www.govtrack.us/congress/bills/108/hr4818.

10. Pub. L. 94-439, 1976, http://thomas.loc.gov/cgi-bin/bdquery/z?d094:HR14232:|TOM:/bss/d094query.html; *Whose Choice? How the Hyde Amendment Harms Poor Women* (New York: Center for Reproductive Rights), 19, http://reproductiverights.org/sites/crr.civicactions.net/files/documents/Hyde_Report_FINAL_nospreads.pdf.

11. In the General Social Survey of 2008, 57.5% of respondents did not "support abortion for any reason," while 39.7% did. See Association of Religion Data Archives (ARDA), "Support Abortion for Any Reason," http://www.thearda.com/QuickStats/qs_110.asp. Among self-identified "liberals," support for unrestricted abortion is 59.4%, for "moderates" it is 41.4%, and for "conservatives" it is 23.8%; see ARDA, "Support Abortion for Any Reason (Demographic Patterns)," http://www.thearda.com/QuickStats/qs_110_p.asp; see also ARDA, "General Social Survey 2008 Cross-Section and Panel Combined," http://www.thearda.com/archive/files/Codebooks/GSS08PAN_CB.asp (using self-identification of political ideology).

12. Letter on behalf of the U.S. Conference of Catholic Bishops by Anthony R, Picarello, Jr., and Michael F. Moses, "RE: Notice of Proposed Rulemaking on Preventive Services" (March 20, 2013), http://www.usccb.org/about/general-counsel/rulemaking/upload/2013-NPRM-Comments-3-20-final.pdf.

13. CRS Report No. R42069, Private Health Insurance Market Reforms in the Patient Protection and Affordable Care Act (ACA).

14. See the subsection in this chapter entitled "Coercion by Health Care Providers" (within the section "Pressure on Abortion Conscience Protections"); see also n. 11 (describing conscience protections).

15. See the subsection below entitled "Pressure by the States" (within the section "Pressure on Abortion Conscience Protections").

16. Reince Priebus, "Obama's Assault on Religious Liberty," *Politico,* February 8, 2012, http://www.politico.com/news/stories/0212/72617.html; Barbara Bradley Hagerty, "Has Obama Waged A War On Religion?" *NPR* (January 8, 2012), http://www.npr.org/2012/01/08/144835720/has-obama-waged-a-war-on-religion .

17. Complaint, Sharpe Holdings, Inc. v. Sebelius, ¶ 7, Case No. 2:12-cv-00092, http://www.becketfund.orgs/wp-content/uploads/2013/04/Sharpe-Holdings-complaint.pdf.

18. Ibid.

19. On June 28, 2012, in *National Federation of Independent Business v. Sebelius,* 132 S. Ct. 2566, 2608, the U.S. Supreme Court upheld the ACA's individual mandate as a constitutional exercise of Congress's taxing power, while striking down a portion of the ACA's Medicaid expansion as exceeding Congress's authority under the Spending Clause.; Barry R. Furrow et al., *Health Care Reform: Supplementary Materials* (Eagan, MN: West, 2012).

20. 155 Cong. Rec. H11819 (November 19, 2009), http://www.gpo.gov/fdsys/pkg/CREC-2009-11-19/pdf/CREC-2009-11-19-pt1-PgS11819.pdf. The proposed amendment by Rep. Stupak and Rep. Pitts passed in the House by 240–194, but was not included in the Senate version of the bill; ultimately the proposed amendment was not included in the ACA when Rep. Stupak and other supporters agreed to support the ACA in exchange for Executive Order 13535.

21. Executive Order 13535, "Ensuring Enforcement and Implementation of Abortion Restrictions in the Patient Protection and Affordable Care Act," section 2 (March 24, 2010); Mimi Hall, "Both Sides of Abortion Issue Quick to Dismiss Order," *USA Today,* March 25, 2010, http://www.usatoday.com/news/washington/2010-03-24-abortion_N.htm.

22. Memorandum to the Senate Committee of Health, Education, Labor and Pensions, from Mark Newsom and Jon O. Shimabukuro, Congressional Research Service, regarding "High Risk Pools Under PPACA and the Coverage of Elective Abortion Services," July 23, 2010; 42 U.S.C.A. § 18023(c)(2)(A); 42 U.S.C.A. § 18023 (c)(3); 42 U.S.C.A. § 18023(b)(4); 42 U.S.C.A. § 18023(a)(1); 42 U.S.C.A. § 18023(b)(1)(A).

23. 42 U.S.C.A. § 300gg-13; U.S. Department of Health and Human Services, "A Statement by U.S. Department of Health and Human Services Secretary Kathleen Sebelius" (January 20, 2012), http://www.hhs.gov/news/

press/2012pres/01/20120120a.html; Health Resources and Services Administration, U.S. Department of Health and Human Services, "Women's Preventive Services: Required Health Plan Coverage Guidelines," http://www.hrsa.gov/womensguidelines/; Timothy Stoltzfus Jost, "Analysis of the Obama Administration's Updated Contraception Rule," http://law.wlu.edu/faculty/facultydocuments/jost/contraception.pdf.

24. "Interim Final Rules for Group Health Plans and Health Insurance Issuers Relating to Coverage of Preventive Services Under the Patient Protection and Affordable Care Act," 75 FR 41726 (July 19, 2010); 76 FR at 46621 (August 3, 2012); 76 FR at 46623.

25. "Group Health Plans and Health Insurance Issuers Relating to Coverage of Preventive Services Under the Patient Protection and Affordable Care Act," 76 FR 46621 (August 3, 2011).

26. Stan Lloyd, letter to editor, "ACA needs moral objection exemption," *Cincinnati.com* (July 2, 2012), http://cincinnati.com/blogs/letters/2012/07/02/aca-needs-moral-objection-exemption/.

27. Carol Keehan, "Something Has to be Fixed," *Catholic Health World* (February 15, 2012), http://www.chausa.org/publications/catholic-health-world/article/february-15-2012/something-has-to-be-fixed.

28. Religious objections have come not only from Catholics, but also from representatives of numerous Muslim, mainline Christian, and "evangelical Christian" universities; Timothy Dolan et al., "Unacceptable," February 28, 2012, http://www.becketfund.org/wp-content/uploads/2012/02/Unacceptable-2-28-12pm.pdf.; Matthew Larotonda, "Catholic Churches Distribute Letter Opposing Obama Healthcare Rule," *ABC News*, January 29, 2012, http://abcnews.go.com/blogs/politics/2012/01/catholic-churches-distribute-letter-opposing-obama-healthcare-rule/.

29. Complaint, The QC Group, Inc., ¶ 3, http://www.becketfund.org/wp-content/uploads/2013/08/1-Verified-Complaint-for-Declaratory-and-Injunctive-Relief-7-2-13.pdf; Cathleen Kaveny, "Catholic Kosher: Is The Ban on Contraception Just an Identity Marker," *Commonweal*, May 21, 2012, http://www.commonwealmagazine.org/catholic-kosher. See also "Live-Blogging from Georgetown," *Mirror of Justice*, September 21, 2012, http://mirrorofjustice.blogs.com/mirrorofjustice/2012/09/live-blogging-from-georgetown.html#comments.; Eternal Word Television Network, Inc., v. Sebelius, Case No. 2:12-cv-00501-SLB (N.D. Ala., Feb. 9, 2012), http://www.becketfund.org/wp-content/uploads/2012/02/EWTN-Complaint-file-stamped.pdf.

30. Planned Parenthood Federation, "Planned Parenthood Applauds HHS for Ensuring Access to Affordable Birth Control," January 20, 2012, http://www.plannedparenthood.org/about-us/newsroom/press-releases/planned-parenthood-applauds-hhs-ensuring-access-affordable-birth-control-38582.htm.

31. National Women's Law Center, "HHS Decision on Contraceptive Coverage a Major Milestone," January 20, 2012, http://www.nwlc.org/press-release/hhs-decision-contraceptive-coverage-important-milestone.

32. J. Lester Feder, "On Contraception, Obama May Please Nobody," *Politico*, December 8, 2011.

33. A live debate is under way about how broadly or narrowly to read *Hosanna-Tabor.* See Larry Sager, "Draft from the New Religious Institutionalism," DePaul University, September 26–27, 2013.

34. 42 U.S.C. § 2000bb et seq.; To see the statuses of the ongoing lawsuits, see "HHS Mandate Information Central," *The Becket Fund for Religious Liberty*, http://www.becketfund.org/hhsinformationcentral/.

35. See Richard Wolf, "Obama Tweaks Birth Control Rule," *USA Today*, February 10, 2012, http://content.usatoday.com/communities/theoval/post /2012/02/source-obama-to-change-birth-control-rule/1. See also n. 1.

36. "Unacceptable," Statement of Apr. 11, 2012, http://www.becketfund. org/wp-content/uploads/2012/04/Unacceptable-4-11.pdf; Wolf, "Obama Tweaks," (see n. 35); "Catholic Group Backs Obama Birth Control Policy," *Boston Globe*, February 10, 2012, http://www.boston.com/news/nation/washington/articles /2012/02/10/catholic_group_backs_obama_birth_control_policy/.

37. "Coverage of Certain Preventive Services Under the Affordable Care Act," 78 FR 8456-01, 8461, 8462, 8465 (February 6, 2013).

38. "Coverage of Certain Preventive Services Under the Affordable Care Act," 78 FR 39869 (2013).

39. Sister Carol Keehan, "Catholic Health Association Is Fine with the Final HHS Rule As It Is UPDATED," *Patheos*, July 9, 2013, http://www. patheos.com/blogs/yimcatholic/2013/07/catholic-health-association-is-fine-with-the-final-hhs-rule-as-it-is.html.

40. Eric Rassbach, counsel of record for dozens of litigants, said the "final rule . . . still makes our nonprofit clients the gatekeepers to abortion and provides no protection to religious businesses." The Becket Fund for Religious Liberty, "Final HHS Rule Fails to Protect Constitutional Rights of Millions of Americans," June 28, 2013, http://www.becketfund.org/becket-welcomes-opportunity-to-study-final-rule-on-hhs-mandate/; "Religious liberty advocates criticize HHS mandate's final rules; bishops pledge statement," *Catholic World News*, July 1, 2013, http://www.catholicculture.org/news/headlines/index. cfm?storyid=18304; Statement of Cardinal Timothy Dolan, Responding to June 28 Final Rule on HHS Mandate, cited at http://dioscg.org/wordpress /?p=7744.

41. Yuval Levin, "A New Round of Intolerance," *National Review Online*, February 1, 2013, http://www.nationalreview.com/corner/339566/new-round-intolerance-yuval-levin.

42. Cecilia Muñoz, "Health Reform, Preventive Services, and Religious Institutions," *The White House Blog*, February 1, 2012, http://www.whitehouse.gov/ blog/2012/02/01/health-reform-preventive-services-and-religious-institutions.

43. The Kaiser Commission on Medicaid and the Uninsured, "Issue Brief: Analyzing the Impact of State Medicaid Expansion Decisions," (July 2013): 1,

http://kaiserfamilyfoundation.files.wordpress.com/2013/07/8458-analyzing-the-impact-of-state-medicaid-expansion-decisions2.pdf.

44. *National Federation of Independent Business v. Sebelius*, 132 S. Ct. 2566, 2608 (2012).

45. "How Much Does Birth Control Cost?" Alpha Consumer, *U.S. News & World Report*, August 27, 2010, http://money.usnews.com/money/blogs/alpha-consumer/2010/08/27/how-much-does-birth-control-cost.

46. Guttmacher Institute, "Facts Sheet: Publicly Funded Contraceptive Services in the United States," March 2014, http://www.guttmacher.org/pubs/fb_contraceptive_serv.pdf.

47. As a comparison, in 2013, the authorized monthly expenditure on the war in Afghanistan was $7.2 billion. See "Cost of the Afghanistan War: By the Numbers," *Friends Committee on National Legislation*, June 6, 2013, http://fcnl.org/issues/afghanistan/Cost_of_the_Afghanistan_War_By_the_Numbers_13_FEB13.pdf.

48. 78 FR 39869 (2013).

49. See CSR Report No. R42663, Health Insurance Exchanges Under the Patient Protection and Affordable Care Act (ACA), January 31, 2013, 34, https://www.fas.org/sgp/crs/misc/R42663.pdf.

50. Sarah Kliff, "The Birth Control Blowback," *The Washington Post*, January 30, 2012, http://www.washingtonpost.com/blogs/wonkblog/post/the-birth-control-blowback/2012/01/30/gIQA52jNcQ_blog.html.

51. Rob Stein, "New Jersey Nurses Charge Religious Discrimination over Hospital Abortion Policy," *The Washington Post*, November 27, 2011, http://www.washingtonpost.com/national/health-science/new-jersey-nurses-charge-religious-discrimination-over-hospital-abortion-policy/2011/11/15/gIQAydgm2N_story.html.

52. Verified Complaint at 2, 7–9, 14–15, Danquah v. Univ. of Med. & Dentistry of N.J., No. 2:11-cv-06377-JLL-MAH (D.N.J. Oct. 31, 2011), http://www.lifenews.com/wp-content/uploads/2011/11/newjerseynursesabortion.pdf; Transcript of Proceedings, Danquah v. Univ. of Med. and Dentistry of N.J., No. 11-6377 (D.N.J. Dec. 22, 2011).

53. Memorandum in Support of Motion for Preliminary Injunction at 1, *Cenzon-DeCarlo v. Mount Sinai Hosp.*, 2010 WL 169485 (E.D. N.Y. 2010) (No. 09-3120), http://www.telladf.org/UserDocs/Cenzon-DeCarloPIbrief.pdf.

54. First Amended Verified Complaint ¶¶ 64–67, *Cenzon-DeCarlo v. Mount Sinai Hosp.*, 2010 WL 169485 (E.D.N.Y. 2010) (No. 09-3120); Thaddeus M. Baklinski, "NY Catholic Nurse Forced to Participate in Abortion Describes Ordeal,"*LifeSitenews.com*, July 28, 2009, http://www.lifesitenews.com/ldn/2009/jul/09072806.html.

55. *Cf. Danquah v. Univ. of Med. & Dentistry of N.J.*, No. 11-6377-JLL, at *2 (D.N.J. Nov. 3, 2011), http://www.adfmedia.org/files/DanquahTRO.pdf; Carpo Aff. at ¶ 1–2, 10, 11, Cenzon-DeCarlo v. Mount Sinai Hosp., No. 10237-10 (N.Y. Sup. Ct., Kings Cnty. Feb. 7, 2011).

56. N.J. Stat. Ann. 2A:65A-1; N.Y. Civ. Rights Law § 79-i; "Matters of Conscience," Appendix, Category 4.

57. *Danquah v. Univ. of Med. & Dentistry of N.J.*, No. 11-6377-JLL, at *2 (D.N.J. Nov. 3, 2011), http://www.adfmedia.org/files/DanquahTRO.pdf.

58. Transcript of Proceedings, *Danquah v. Univ. of Med. and Dentistry of N.J.*, No. 11-6377 (D. N. J. Dec. 22, 2011), at 5–6.

59. Robin Fretwell Wilson, "The Calculus of Accommodation: Contraception, Abortion, Same-Sex Marriage, and other Clashes Between Religion and the State," *Boston College Law Review* 53 (October 2, 2012), 1417, http://papers.ssrn.com/s013/papers.cfm?abstract_id=2155867; Robin Fretwell Wilson, "Insubstantial Burdens: The Case for Government Employee Exemptions to Same-Sex Marriage Laws," *Northwestern Journal of Law and Social Policy* 5, no. 2 (2010): 318, http://papers.ssrn.com/s013/papers.cfm?abstract_id=2027942; Wilson, "Matters of Conscience," 77 (see n. 8); Robin Fretwell Wilson, "The Limits of Conscience: Moral Clashes over Deeply Divisive Healthcare Procedures," *American Journal of Law & Medicine* 34 (2008): 41; Nathan J. Diament et al., "Comments Submitted to the U.S. Department of Health and Human Services with Regard to the Proposed Rescission of the 'Conscience Regulation' Relating to Healthcare Workers and Certain Healthcare Services" [RIN: 0991-AB49], April 7, 2009, http://www.ouradio.org/images/uploads/HHS_Conscience_Regulation_Comments.pdf.

60. How rare a collision will be depends on a number of factors, including the number of likely objectors and willing providers, hours of service, staffing arrangements, and how often the public seeks a given service. Wilson, "Insubstantial Burdens" (see n. 59).

61. Robin Fretwell Wilson, "Empowering Private Protection of Conscience," *Ava Maria Law Review* 9, no. 1 (Fall 2010): 101, 104; *Cenzon-DeCarlo v. Mount Sinai Hosp.*, 626 F.3d 695, 699 (2d Cir. 2010); *Cenzon-DeCarlo v. The Mount Sinai Hospital, et al.*, Docket Nos. 2011-02282 and 2011-07705 (N.Y. App. Div., Apr. 12, 2010). Cenzon-DeCarlo then filed separate state court claims that were dismissed in part and settled in part through summary judgment for the hospital: *Cenzon-DeCarlo v. Mount Sinai Hosp.*, 962 N.Y.S. 2d 845 (Sup. Ct. 2010). Cenzon-DeCarlo appealed the decision, but the appellate court affirmed the decision: *Cenzon-DeCarlo v. Mount Sinai Hosp.*, 101 A.D.3d 924 (2012). The Court of Appeals of New York denied a subsequent motion for leave to appeal: *Cenzon-DeCarlo v. Mount Sinai Hosp.*, 21 N.Y.3d 858 (2013).

62. *Nursing Clinical and Administrative Manual.* (New York: The Mount Sinai Hospital, n.d.), http://www.adfmedia.org/files/MtSinaiPolicy.pdf.

63. Department of Health and Human Services, Letter, Ref. No. 10-109676 (February 1, 2013), http://www.adfmedia.org/files/Cenzon-DeCarlo HHSfindings.pdf.

64. *Lemly v. St. Tammany Parish Hosp.*, 614 F. Supp. 2d 727 (E.D. La. 2008).

65. Ibid.

66. *Lemly*, 614 F. Supp, 2d at 730, 733; La. Rev. Stat. Ann. § 23:332 (2012).

67. *Lemly v. St. Tammany Parish Hosp.*, 8 So. 3d 588, 588 (2009).

68. La. Rev. Stat. Ann. § 40:1299-35-9 (2009) (emphasis added).

69. Guttmacher Institute, "State Policies in Brief: Refusing to Provide Health Services," October 1, 2012, http://www.guttmacher.org/statecenter/spibs/spib_RPHS.pdf.

70. Guttmacher Institute, "State Policies in Brief: Emergency Contraception," October 9, 2012, http://www.guttmacher.org/statecenter/spibs/spib_EC.pdf.

71. Some assert a third value: patient choice. Patients only have a meaningful choice, they say, when institutions can choose *not* to provide a specific contested service. Just think of the patient who seeks a provider with common values—for instance a pro-life reproductive specialist. See Matt Bowman and Christopher Schandevel, "The Harmony Between Professional Conscience Rights and Patients' Right of Access," *Social Science Research Network* (February 2, 2012), http://papers.ssrn.com/s013/papers.cfm?abstract_id=1998363.

72. Wilson, "Insubstantial Burdens" (see n. 59); Wilson, "Limits of Conscience" (see n. 59).

73. Guttmacher Institute, "Advocates Work to Preserve Reproductive Health Care Access When Hospitals Merge," April 2000, http://www.guttmacher.org/pubs/tgr/03/2/gr030203.pdf.

74. Liz Bucar and Catholics for a Free Choice, "Caution: Catholic Health Restrictions May be Hazardous to Your Health," *Merger Trends* 2 (1999), http://www.catholicsforchoice.org/topics/healthcare/documents/1998cautioncatholichealthrestrictions.pdf; Reed Abelson, "Catholic Hospitals Expand, Religious Strings Attached," *New York Times*, February 20, 2012, http://www.nytimes.com/2012/02/21/health/policy/growth-of-catholic-hospitals-may-limit-access-to-reproductive-care.html?pagewanted=all.

75. Cameron Flynn and Robin Fretwell Wilson, "Institutional Conscience and Access to Services: Can We Have Both?" *Virtual Mentor* 15, no. 3 (March 2013), http://virtualmentor.ama-assn.org/2013/03/pfor1-1303.html.

76. Robert K. Vischer, *Conscience and the Common Good: Reclaiming the Space Between Person and State* (New York: Cambridge University Press, 2010); Wilson, "Limits of Conscience" (see n. 59).

77. See the subsection in this chapter entitled "Two Very Different Types of Drugs" (within the section "Objections to 'Abortion-Inducing' Drugs").

78. With adoption services, legislators considering a religious exemption might consider a variety of factors, such as the impact an exemption (or denial of one) would have on children awaiting adoption, and same-sex couples seeking to adopt. Among other questions, legislators should also ask whether other providers of adoption services would readily serve gay couples seeking to

adopt; whether information-forcing rules could direct prospective parents to willing providers; and, if the state rejects religious accommodations, whether objecting agencies would exit the market, and if so, how many children would they have placed and how many of these children would be picked up by other agencies after their exit. See Robin Fretwell Wilson, "Essay: A Matter of Conviction: Moral Clashes Over Same-Sex Adoption," *BYU Journal of Public Law* 22 (2008): 475, 479–83.

79. Wilson, "Calculus of Accommodation" (see n. 59); HHS Letter (see n. 63).

80. See the subsection in this chapter entitled "What Is Pregnancy?" (within the section "Objections to 'Abortion-Inducing' Drugs").

81. Wilson, "Limits of Conscience" (see n. 59).

82. HHS Letter (see n. 63). Of course, this is more difficult when a patient presents to an objecting facility during an emergency situation.

83. Wilson, "Calculus of Accommodation" (see n. 59).

84. Complaint, Sharpe Holdings, Inc., ¶ 7, http://www.becketfund.org/wp-content/uploads/2013/04/Sharpe-Holdings-complaint.pdf; "Catholic Entrepreneur and Family File Suit" (see n. 4); Omer and Simon, "Franciscan University" (see n. 4).

85. The American College of Obstetricians and Gynecologists, Committee on Heath Care for Underserved Women, "Access to Emergency Contraception," *Committee Opinion* 542 (November 2012), http://www.acog.org/Resources_And_Publications/Committee_Opinions/Committee_on_Health_Care_for_Underserved_Women/Access_to_Emergency_Contraception.

86. Editorial, "How Morning-After Pills Really Work," *New York Times*, June 8, 2012, http://www.nytimes.com/2012/06/09/opinion/how-morning-after-pills-really-work.html.

87. See n. 84.

88. Rachel Benson Gold, "The Implications of Defining When a Woman is Pregnant," *The Guttmacher Report on Public Policy* 8, no. 2 (May 2005), http://www.guttmacher.org/pubs/tgr/08/2/gr080207.html.

89. "The Difference Between Emergency Contraception and Medication Abortion," *Planned Parenthood*, http://www.plannedparenthood.org/resources/research-papers/difference-between-emergency-contraception-medication-abortion-6138.htm (accessed September 3, 2013). 90. Vivian W. Y. Leung, Marc Levine, and Judith A. Soon, "Mechanisms of Action of Hormonal Emergency Contraceptives," *Pharmacotherapy* 30, no. 2 (2010): 158, 160.

91. *Stedman's Medical Dictionary*, 27th ed. (Baltimore: Lippincott Williams & Wilkins, 2006); Walter L. Larimore et al., letter to the editor, "In Response: Does Pregnancy Begin at Fertilization?" *Family Medicine* 36, no. 10 (November–December 2004), 690, http://www.stfm.org/fmhub/fm2004/November/Walter690.pdf.

92. Ronan O'Rahilly and Fabiola Müller, *Developmental Stages in Human Embryos* (Washington, DC: Carnegie Institute of Washington, 1987), 5; see also Larimore, letter to the editor (n. 91).

93. Gold, "The Implications of Defining" (see n. 88).

94. Maureen L. Condic, "When Does Human Life Begin? A Scientific Perspective," 1 *The Westchester Institute for Ethics & The Human Person* 1, no. 1 (October 2008).

95. Leung, Levine, and Soon, "Mechanisms of Action" (see n. 90); Larimore, letter to the editor (see n. 91); Gabriela Noé et al., "Contraceptive Efficacy of Emergency with Levonorgestrel Given Before or After Ovulation," *Contraception* 81, no. 5 (May 2010): 414, 418–19.

96. "ObamaCare and Its Mandates Fact Sheet," *Alliance Defending Freedom* (August 8, 2012), http://www.alliancedefendingfreedom.org/content/docs/facts/ObamaCare-and-its-Mandates.pdf.

97. "The difference between Emergency Contraception," *Planned Parenthood* (see n. 89).

98. Condic, "Human Life" (see n. 94)

99. *CCU v. Sebelius*, Complaint, ¶ 30, Aug. 6, 2013, http://www.becketfund.org/wp-content/uploads/2013/08/CCU.pdf.

100. See n. 82.

101. U.S. Food and Drug Administration, "Plan B One-Step Prescribing Information," 7 (2009), http://www.accessdata.fda.gov/drugsatfda_docs/label/2009/021998lbl.pdf.

102. Watson Medical Communications, *ella* label, "Highlights of Prescribing Information," http://www.accessdata.fda.gov/drugsatfda_docs/label/2010/022474s000lbl.pdf.

103. "Birth Control: Medicines to Help You." *U.S. Food and Drug Administration* (August 2013), http://www.fda.gov/ForConsumers/ByAudience/ForWomen/FreePublications/ucm313215.htm.

104. Complaint, Sharpe Holdings, ¶ 81, http://www.becketfund.org/wp-content/uploads/2013/04/Sharpe-Holdings-complaint.pdf; FDA, "Birth Control Guide," http://www.fda.gov/forconsumers/byaudience/forwomen/freepublications/ucm313215.htm.

105. G. Ugocsai et al., "Scanning Electron Microscopic (SEM) Changes of the Endometrium in Women Taking High Doses of Levonorgestrel as Emergency Postcoital Contraception," *Contraception* 66, no. 6 (2002): 433, 433.

106. Charles J. Lockwood, "Editorial: OTC Emergency Contraception: The Right Choice," *Contemporary OB/GYN* (January 2004), http://www.americanbusinessmedia.com/images/abm/pdfs/events/neal_library/Contemporary%20OBGYN--Class%20B%20Cat%203--1.pdf.

107. James Trussell, "Editorial: Mechanism of Action of Emergency Contraceptive Pills," *Contraception* 74 (2006): 87–89 (emphasis added).

108. Leung, Levine, and Soon, "Mechanisms of Action," 158, 166 (see n. 90).

109. "Prescription Drug Products; Certain Combined Oral Contraceptives for Use as Postcoital Emergency Contraception," *Federal Register* 62, no. 37 (February 25, 1997): 8610–12, http://www.gpo.gov/fdsys/pkg/FR-1997-02-25/pdf/97-4663.pdf.

110. "Prescription Drug Products," *Federal Register* (see n. 109); 45 CFR 46.202(f); 78 FR 39869 (2013).

111. The White House Blog, "Health Reform, Preventive Services, and Religious Institutions," http://www.whitehouse.gov/blog/2012/02/01/health-reform-preventive-services-and-religious-institutions.

112. See James Trussell, Elizabeth G. Raymond, & Kelly Cleland, "Emergency Contraception: A Last Chance to Prevent Unintended Pregnancy" (unpublished manuscript, February 2014), 5–6, http://ec.princeton.edu/questions/ec-review.pdf; Noé et al., "Contraceptive Efficacy," 414, 419, 420 (see n. 95).

113. James Trusell, "Editorial: Mechanism of Action of Emergency Contraceptive Pills," *Contraception* 74 (2006): 87; Noé et al., "Contraceptive Efficacy," 414 (see n. 95).

114. U.S. Food and Drug Administration, Plan B One-Step Prescribing Information (see n. 101); Watson Medical Communications, *ella* label (see n. 102).

115. Kristina Gemzell-Danielsson and Chun-Xia Meng, "Emergency Contraception: Potential Role of Ulipristal Acetate," 2 *International Journal of Women's Health* 2 (April 17, 2010): 57, 59, https://www.dovepress.com/emergency-contraception-potential-role-of-ulipristal-acetate-peer-reviewed-article-IJWH-recommendation1.

116. Ibid.

117. Jeffry Keenan, "Ulipristal Acetate: Contraceptive or Contragestive?" *The Annals of Pharmacotherapy* 45 (June 2011): 813, 814.

118. Ralph P. Miech, "Immunopharmacology of Ulipristal as an Emergency Contraceptive," *International Journal of Women's Health* 3 (2011): 391, 392, http://www.ncbi.nlm.nih.gov/pmc/articles/PMC3225469/. See also Pelin Batur, "Emergency contraception: Separating fact from fiction," *Cleveland Clinic Journal of Medicine* 79, no. 11 (November 2012): 771, 771, http://www.ccjm.org/content/79/11/771.full.pdf+html.

119. Popular reporting on *ella* emphasizes both the findings about *ella's* possible mechanisms of action and the uncertainty remaining about those mechanisms. Rob Stein, "5-Day-After Contraceptive Wins FDA Approval," *Washington Post*, August 14, 2010; Pam Belluck, "Abortion Qualms on Morning-After Pill May be Unfounded," *New York Times*, June 5, 2012, http://www.nytimes.com/2012/06/06/health/research/morning-after-pills-dont-block-implantation-science-suggests.html?pagewanted=all.

120. Committee on Ethics of the American College of Obstetricians and Gynecologists, "The Limits of Conscientious Refusal in Reproductive Medicine," *ACOG Committee Opinion* 385 (November 2007), http://www.acog.org

/Resources_And_Publications/Committee_Opinions/Committee_on_Ethics /The_Limits_of_Conscientious_Refusal_in_Reproductive_Medicine. Some conscience clauses key protection to the reasonability of the belief; see, for example, Kan. Stat. Ann. § 65-443 (West 2012).

121. Keenan, "Ulipristal Acetate" (see n. 117).

122. Keenan, "Ulipristal Acetate" (see n. 117).

123. Cristina Lopez-del Burgo et al., "Knowledge and Beliefs about Mechanism of Action of Birth Control Methods Among European Women," *Contraception* 85 (2012): 69.

124. C.A. Sherman, S.M. Harvey, L.J. Beckman, and D.B. Petitti, "Emergency Contraception: Knowledge and Attitudes of Health Care Providers in a Health Maintenance Organization," *Women's Health Issues* 11, no. 6 (November– December 2001): 448, http://www.ncbi.nlm.nih.gov/pubmed/11566288.

125. H.M. Dye, et al., "Women and Post-Fertilization Effects of Birth Control: Consistency of Beliefs, Intentions and Reported Use," *BMC Women's Health* 5 (2005): 11.

126. Ibid.

127. In 2000, when asked, "Which best describes your view of when life begins?," 47% of Americans said that life beings at conception. *Harris Interactive Poll, 2000.* See also J.W. Campbell III, S.C. Busby, and T.E. Steyer, "Attitudes and Beliefs About Emergency Contraception Among Patients at Academic Family Medicine Clinics," *Annals of Family Medicine* 6, suppl. 1 (2008): S23. ("Additionally, the topic of EC involves moral implications for patients concerning their beliefs about the beginning of life. A public opinion poll of more than 15,000 people showed that almost 50% of the population believe that life begins at conception, or when the sperm and egg join.")

128. Campbell et al., "Attitudes and Beliefs" (see n. 127).

129. Lopez-del Burgo et al., "Knowledge and Beliefs" (see n. 123).

130. United States v. Ballard, 322 U.S. 78, 86–87 (1944).

131. 450 U.S. 707, 714.

132. Muñoz, "Health Reform" (see n. 42).

7   In This Enlightened Age and Land of Equal Liberty

Implications of Equality for Religion and Marriage

Harry F. Tepker, Jr.

Our nation's earliest principles of religious liberty were principles of equality. They are the root of an evolving, maturing aspiration that government must deny no person the equal protection of the laws. Such principles formed a basis of an instinct expressed by Thomas Jefferson in his First Inaugural Address that even majority rule has limits. Americans, Jefferson said, "will bear in mind this sacred principle, that though the will of the majority is in all cases to prevail, that will to be rightful must be reasonable; that the minority possess their equal rights, which equal law must protect, and to violate would be oppression."[1] That instinct was transformed into principles, such as the contested claim of Justice John Paul Stevens that the duty of government to be rational or reasonable "includes elements of legitimacy and neutrality that must always characterize the performance of the sovereign's duty to govern impartially."[2]

MADISON'S "MORE EXTREME NOTIONS" OF SEPARATION

The idea that America was conceived in liberty and dedicated to equality is, of course, not new, as anyone who memorized the Gettysburg Address in elementary school might remember. But some early understandings may have been lost and forgotten.

To begin with only one example, Justice Clarence Thomas thinks James Madison is an extremist with views of religious liberty that have little to do with the Establishment Clause. Specifically, though

170

Madison did believe in "the separation of church and state," Justice Thomas does not[3]—or at least he frequently writes to criticize prevailing doctrines of church–state separation. In a prominent pledge of allegiance case,[4] Justice Clarence Thomas offered this startling argument: simply, Thomas claimed Madison's words do not deserve prominence. Although "more extreme notions of the separation of church and state [might] be attribut[able] to Madison, many of them clearly stem from 'arguments reflecting the concepts of natural law, natural rights, and the social contract between government and a civil society,' rather than the principle of nonestablishment in the Constitution."[5] Justice Thomas believes states ought to have more room to promote, teach, and endorse religious doctrine. Madison's words give Justice Thomas discomfort: government lacks authority over the religion of individuals, the community, and "we, the people." Madison seems to conclude that government endorsement of religion, government definition of the sacred, and government by rules derived solely from religious dictates are wrong, discriminatory, destructive of liberty, and beyond the rightful scope of secular authority. It is difficult, even impossible, to allow displays of the Ten Commandments and sacred text,[6] religious ceremony in graduation ceremonies,[7] and formal legal expression of commitments to God on behalf of majorities[8] if Madison's words are taken seriously.

Put another way, Madison's "extreme" ideas should not count as evidence of the Constitution's disestablishment principle. As is often true with ambiguous constitutional text, our contemporary understandings of the Framers' hopes and expectations are distorted by "reading the mystery novel backwards."[9] We know too much of what the Framers should have been considering to guide us in today's disputes. Still, it is an unusual departure from originalist methodology to strike evidence of Madison's thinking as irrelevant and immaterial.

This chapter focuses on one aspect of Justice Thomas's error. He may be quite correct when he notes that Madison derived his principles from other ideas, such as natural rights, equality, and the rightful content of the social contract. He is not correct to infer that, "therefore," Madison's inspirations are irrelevant to nonestablishment or a broader religious liberty. Justice Thomas supplements his attack on Madison's utility with a highly unique claim that the First Amendment—or at least the Establishment Clause—is a states' rights provision and contains no content that can be incorporated through the Fourteenth Amendment and applied to the states; only the Free

Exercise Clause can be incorporated.[10] Justice Thomas has persuaded few: despite some sound and fury, there is considerable practical agreement about elements of separation.[11]

Less studied is Madison's view that religious liberty derives from the principle that "[e]quality . . . ought to be the basis of every law."[12] As relentless criticism of "separation" as an organizing principle of religious liberty has increased,[13] some scholars have turned to ethical conceptions of equality to defend cherished decisions promoting religious liberty. For example, Professor Martha Nussbaum draws an important lesson from the early history of religious liberty in the young American republic: "Above all, . . . the mixture of civil with religious jurisdictions threatened an equality of standing in the public realm that was enormously precious to all Americans. Separation, to the extent that the framers urged it, was not a way of belittling religion, it was a way of respecting human beings."[14]

The *Memorial and Remonstrance against Religious Assessments*[15] is the most extensive and sophisticated expression of Madison's defense of—and passion for—religious liberty. Famously and influentially, Madison claimed a person's duty to God is "precedent both in order of time and degree of obligation, to the claims of Civil Society."[16] So, Madison reasons, "The Religion . . . of every man must be left to the conviction and conscience of every man; and it is the right of every man to exercise it as these may dictate. . . . It is the duty of every man to render to the Creator such homage, and such only, as he believes to be acceptable to him."[17] Madison also argues that

If "all men are by nature equally free and independent," all men are to be considered as entering into Society on equal conditions; as relinquishing no more, and therefore retaining no less, one than another, of their natural rights. Above all are they to be considered as retaining an "equal title to the free exercise of Religion according to the dictates of Conscience." Whilst we assert for ourselves a freedom to embrace, to profess and to observe the Religion which we believe to be of divine origin, we cannot deny an equal freedom to those whose minds have not yet yielded to the evidence which has convinced us. If this freedom be abused, it is an offence against God.[18]

The *Memorial and Remonstrance* was an anonymous attack on Patrick Henry's bill for mandatory taxation of the citizenry to benefit churches.[19] Madison was building on and defending the work of friend and ally Thomas Jefferson and the historic bill for Religious Freedom in Virginia. "[No] man . . . shall be enforced, restrained, molested, or burthened in his body or goods, nor shall otherwise suffer, on account of his religious opinions or belief; but [expression of religious views] shall in no wise diminish, enlarge, or affect their civil capacities."[20]

Jefferson offered justifications for his vision of equal liberty. "Our civil rights have no dependence on our religious opinions, any more than our opinions in physics or geometry. . . ."[21] Jefferson argued that there should be no impairment of standing in the community or civil rights or protection of the laws because of religion—a right for believers and nonbelievers.

Jefferson was proud of his bill, which he listed among his achievements on his tombstone (which did not mention that he was the third president of the United States). But it was Madison who, using Henry's bill as the moment, passed Jefferson's bill. The Madisonian–Jeffersonian principles are broad, sweeping, idealistic, and an early example of an antidiscrimination principle. The bill and its principles are one beginning of America's search for constitutional principles protecting religious liberty.[22]

The Jefferson and Madison invocations of equality were not merely the rhetoric of the moment. This analysis emerges in the first few years after Jefferson's claim in the Declaration of Independence that "all men are created equal." Later, in 1789, when keeping a campaign promise to introduce a bill of rights in Congress, Madison reminded his colleagues that many states, in their own bills of rights, often did "no more than state the perfect equality of mankind; this to be sure is an absolute truth, yet it is not absolutely necessary to be inserted at the head of a constitution."[23] It is difficult for modern scholars and subsequent generations to understand what Madison and Jefferson meant. They were, after all, slave owners. They were representatives and advocates of their state's slave-owning interests, including preservation of state power to enact positive law sanctioning slavery instead of the presumptions of liberty recognized by English common law.[24] What could they have been thinking?

For one thing, both seem to have concluded that all human beings were born free and equal in their right to worship God—or not—according to their own sense of duty. Government might enact laws that modified the status and opportunities of human beings, but not the "equal rights of conscience."

The arguments of Madison and Jefferson are a beginning for understanding a root principle. America's conception of equality was not—and never has been—an equality of wealth, power, talent, or property.[25] The Declaration dedicates the nation to a concept of equality of rights, including the inalienable right described by Jefferson's graceful phrase, the "pursuit of happiness," the nation's original "mystery passage."[26] Historians and political theorists have debated what Jefferson meant. Pauline Maier argues that Jefferson drew from George Mason, who drafted Virginia's Declaration of Rights, which used more complicated terms: "the enjoyment of life and liberty, with the means of acquiring and possessing property, and pursuing and obtaining happiness and safety."[27] Maier adds: "For Jefferson and his contemporaries, happiness no doubt demanded safety or security, which would have been in keeping with the biblical phrase one colonist after another used to describe the good life: to be at peace under their vine and fig tree with none to make them afraid. (Micah 4:4)." She draws upon the analysis of another scholar, Ronald Hamowy: "When Jefferson spoke of an inalienable right to the pursuit of happiness, he meant that men may act as they choose in their search for ease, comfort, felicity and grace, either by owning property or not, by accumulating wealth or distributing it, by opting for material success or asceticism, in a word by determining the path to their own earthly and heavenly salvation as they alone see fit."[28]

So the basic civil rights and civil capacities of all free and independent human beings are ways and means of the pursuit of happiness, and include the rights to which Jefferson refers in his draft of his bill to establish religious freedom in Virginia.

REASONS TO REJOICE

Critics of a casual overemphasis on Madison and Jefferson as the alpha and omega of original understanding of religious freedom[29] have a point: the two Virginians adopted theories in advance of general understandings. Still, the Virginians were influential, and not as "extreme" as Justice Thomas suggests. Consider two statements from the first of Virginia's leading citizens, General George Washington.[30] President Washington, in his first term, offered an assessment of America's policies, aspirations, and opinions:

The Citizens of the United States of America have a right to applaud themselves for having given to mankind examples of an enlarged and liberal policy: a policy worthy of imitation. All possess alike liberty of conscience and immunities of citizenship. It is now no more that toleration is spoken of, as if it was by the indulgence of one class of people, that another enjoyed the exercise of their inherent natural rights. For happily the Government of the United States, which gives to bigotry no sanction, to persecution no assistance requires only that they who live under its protection should demean themselves as good citizens, in giving it on all occasions their effectual support.[31]

When Washington wrote this assessment, the First Amendment had been proposed, but not ratified. In his second term, after ratification, the first president again expressed his understanding:

We have abundant reason to rejoice that in this land the light of truth and reason has triumphed over the power of bigotry and superstition and that every person may here worship God according to the dictates of his own heart. In this enlightened Age & in this Land of equal liberty it is our boast, that a man's religious tenets, will not forfeit his protection of the Laws, nor deprive him of the right of attaining & holding the highest offices that are known in the United States.[32]

Students of American history might judge the "father of our country" harshly for his boasts. Truth and reason? Just when did the power of bigotry and superstition decline? Ever? But the president's statement may be better understood as his sense of what would be or could be achieved, if the people lived up to the First Amendment, the Bill of Rights, and the separate additional protections of the nation's state constitutions. He echoes the essence of the Jefferson and Madison positions, and as the prominent leader of America, he offers an additional reliable—perhaps more reliable—symbol of an aspiration supported by a national consensus. But Washington's statements could be critiqued by Justice Thomas in exactly the same way he dismissed Madison's " more extreme" views. Washington was talking not only of the duty not to make laws respecting establishments of religion; he was talking about a broader commitment to civic equality without regard to religion.

For still more evidence of original understandings, consider an exchange between two famous friends, rivals, and presidents: John Adams and Thomas Jefferson. The Virginian expressed both optimism and confidence in a letter to Adams, when he offered "sincere congratulations" on the recent decision of Connecticut to create a new constitution, which provided for religious freedom. In Jefferson's view, it was "the resurrection of Connecticut to light and liberality." He thought the state's decision was part of a pattern that showed "a protestant popedom is no longer to disgrace the American history and character."[33] The more skeptical and wiser Adams basically agreed with Jefferson about what was best constitutional policy, but feared passionate true believers remained all too ready to impose their religious will on others—by harsh means.

> Oh! Lord! Do you think that Protestant Popedom is annihilated in America? Do you recollect, or have you ever attended to the ecclesiastical strifes in Maryland, Pennsylvania, New York, and every part of New England?
>
> What a mercy it is that these people cannot whip, and crop, and pillory, and roast as yet in the United States! If they could, they would.[34]

Adams and Jefferson paid attention to state constitutions because the basic human rights commitments were defined by the states, not the federal government. Importantly, when the states wrote their own fundamental law addressing the individual's rights of worship, they frequently borrowed from Jefferson or Madison. For only one example, the constitution of Arkansas, adopted in 1836, says plainly, "the civil rights, privileges, or capacities of any citizen shall in nowise be diminished or enlarged, on account of his religion."[35] The American understandings were, indeed, broader than the words of the Establishment Clause.

EQUAL LIBERTY AND THE
BIRTH OF THE FOURTEENTH AMENDMENT

Original thinking is not enough. A link to constitutional text is essential. This paper assumes, for purposes of argument, Justice Thomas has a point about the nation's original understanding of the Establishment

Clause. Even if the Justice were correct, the antidiscrimination principle underlying the original understandings of "equal liberty" bear upon the Fourteenth Amendment, and the Equal Protection Clause. When Abraham Lincoln, lawyer and political candidate, pointed to a link between the Declaration of Independence and the Constitution, he offered a political, moral, and philosophical argument. He did not make the mistake of assuming that a natural rights ideology could govern judges' interpretations of the federal constitution.[36] He explained that what he believed was a philosophical commitment of the nation:

> [The] authors of [the Declaration of Independence] intended to include all men, but they did not intend to declare all men equal in all respects. They did not mean to say all were equal in color, size, intellect, moral developments, or social capacity. They defined with tolerable distinctness, in what respects they did consider all men created equal—equal in "certain inalienable rights, among which are life, liberty, and the pursuit of happiness." This they said, and this meant. They did not mean to assert the obvious untruth, that all were then actually enjoying that equality, nor yet, that they were about to confer it immediately upon them. In fact they had no power to confer such a boon. They meant simply to declare the right, so that the enforcement of it might follow as fast as circumstances should permit. They meant to set up a standard maxim for free society, which should be familiar to all, and revered by all; constantly looked to, constantly labored for, and even though never perfectly attained, constantly approximated, and thereby constantly spreading and deepening its influence, and augmenting the happiness and value of life to all people of all colors everywhere.[37]

Before 1868, there was little or nothing in the Constitution to support Lincoln's view. Nor was there anything to link the ideals of the Declaration and the natural rights of human beings. But the Fourteenth Amendment was a way the nation kept Lincoln's promise at Gettysburg, that "this nation under God shall have a new birth of freedom."[38] When Lincoln and abolitionists had attacked slavery, they emphasized "natural rights," not citizenship rights or political rights.[39] Lincoln focused on the direct contradiction between slavery and the "inalienable" and "natural" right of each human being to consume the fruits of his or her own labor. But there was—and is—more to the rights at stake. Abolitionists argued that the "peculiar institution" separated lovers; it tore children from their families; it destroyed all of the ways and means of survival. These themes were dramatized in *Uncle Tom's Cabin*[40] and the antebellum writings of Frederick Douglass.[41] Eloquently, these human rights advocates argued that equality of right—as derived from the Declaration—was offended when human beings could not read, could not learn, could not revere God and study the Scriptures, could not marry, could not form families, could not enter into contracts or hold property, could not gain access to the courts or protection from the law. This was not a new list of "natural rights" or basic "civil rights." What was new was that Americans came to understand, over time, that these rights of human beings extended to all. Religiously inspired exercise of religious freedom is part of this story; so is religiously influenced concepts of the rights of man, the equality of right secured by the Declaration, and a denunciation of the tyrannical notion that one group of human beings was ineligible for these rights, solely because of the color of their skin.

For now, we need not review familiar controversies about whether the Fourteenth Amendment "incorporated" the Bill of Rights or all forms of race discrimination, including segregation. It is useful to focus on the narrowest view of original intent: At a minimum, Congress sought to abolish the "Black Codes" adopted by southern states after they reorganized recognized state governments.[42] The Civil Rights Act of 1866[43] sought to guarantee certain specified rights, including "the same right to make and enforce contracts."[44] The primary purpose of the Fourteenth Amendment was to ensure that the Civil Rights Act of 1866 was constitutional.[45] All, regardless of race, were to have equal civil rights and capacities to enter into contracts, hold property, and make decisions to form families and relationships. This was the accepted consensus: all human beings were born free to chart a path in life in pursuit of happiness.

IMPLICATIONS FOR A CULTURE WAR: TENTATIVE THOUGHTS

Do these forgotten aspects of original understanding constitute a "usable past"[46] to guide justices in their interpretive duties? If originalism requires justices to guess about what James Madison would have thought about specific modern controversies, history offers little help, and almost all modern doctrine is mere invention. But originalism is often defended as more sophisticated than a clumsy guessing process searching for the Framers' specific state of mind.[47] Originalism requires only an authentic "underlying premise . . . fairly discoverable in the Constitution"[48] to justify invalidating the work of the political branches. In context, the duty of government to be neutral and fair has deep, authentic, meaningful roots in American jurisprudential history.

Recovery of forgotten equality themes in original understandings of religious liberty may offer distinct advantages for interpretation of the Constitution and the Equal Protection Clause. As explained, the concept of equal civil rights has historic antecedents stronger than the dubious fictions of "substantive due process," which as Judge Richard Posner has written, "stinks in the nostrils of modern liberals and modern conservatives alike, because of its association with Dred Scott's case and with *Lochner* and the other freedom of contract cases, because of its formlessness, . . . and because it makes a poor match with the right to notice and hearing that is the procedural content of the clause."[49]

A related benefit is that the Jefferson–Madison equality themes have a history, influence, and legitimacy superior to oft-criticized, open-ended, vague, and aspirational "mystery passages" authored by justices, often without precedent or annotation. Such passages are offered to justify discoveries of new "fundamental rights" protected by a determined judiciary's "close scrutiny," as opposed to ordinary "liberty interests" which receive little protection because courts only expect reasonable regulations.

Consider, for example, *Lawrence v. Texas*,[50] in which Justice Anthony Kennedy wrote: "Liberty presumes an autonomy of self that includes freedom of thought, belief, expression, and certain intimate conduct. The instant case involves liberty of the person both in its spatial and more transcendent dimensions."[51] He added, unhelpfully for judges in search of manageability and clarity, "Our obligation is to define the liberty of all, not to mandate our own moral code."[52] He cited and quoted a case and passages from his own co-authored opinion on abortion,[53] including the often-mocked "sweet mystery of life" passage.[54] Justice Kennedy argued that the anatomy of liberty must extend beyond enumerated rights. Liberty includes unenumerated but fundamental personal decisions relating to marriage, procreation, contraception, family relationships, child rearing, and education. The broader concept of liberty "involve[es] the most intimate and personal choices a person may make in a lifetime, choices central to personal dignity and autonomy, . . . central to the liberty protected by the Fourteenth Amendment. At the heart of liberty is the right to define one's own concept of existence, of meaning, of the universe, and of the mystery of human life. Beliefs about these matters could not define the attributes of personhood were they formed under compulsion of the State."[55] To state the problem most kindly, such passages persuade those already persuaded, and few others. The broad, eloquent aspirational tone is difficult to explain or apply as a principle of law.[56] All of this was offered to refute, but may have corroborated, Justice White's warnings and worries in *Bowers v. Hardwick*[57] that justices should not discover new fundamental rights based on "judge-made constitutional law having little or no cognizable roots in the language or design of the Constitution."[58]

In *Lawrence*, Justice Sandra Day O'Connor turned away from "substantive due process." She thought it mattered not one bit whether sodomy or sexual intimacy was a "fundamental right." She thought the better approach was whether all persons were treated the same, equally. Her formulation of the issue was "whether, under the Equal Protection Clause, moral disapproval is a legitimate state interest to justify by itself a statute that bans homosexual sodomy, but not heterosexual sodomy." She focused on the discriminatory line drawn by Texas law. Her rationale was more precise: "Moral disapproval of this group, like a bare desire to harm the group, is an interest that is insufficient to satisfy rational basis review under the Equal Protection Clause."[59] As this paper suggests, Justice O'Connor had more support in history and jurisprudence than she cited.

Perhaps the most prominent battle on the current agenda bears the label "marriage equality." A more precise formulation of the issue might be "whether two adults of the same gender with capacity to consent may make enforceable mutual promises to share lives, property, family and homes in 'pursuit of happiness.'"

Judges and scholars should search for an answer that does not require further stretching of the concept of "due process" for newer, broader lists of "fundamental rights." Also, they should avoid declarations that morality is not enough to justify an ordinary law.[60] They should avoid confusing rationales that use the deferential tests of the Court to strike down traditions or deeply held moral views as hysterical or irrational.[61] Also, the debate should not turn on what James Madison thought about homosexuality.[62]

To see the beginning of a path to a justice of equal rights, four propositions must be addressed.

1. Marriage—or the right to make enforceable life-sharing promises—is a form of contract protected by federal constitutional traditions. Avoiding "substantive due process" inquiries, it is not essential to reaffirm the truth of *Loving v. Virginia*:[63] "The freedom to marry has long been recognized as one of the vital personal rights essential to the orderly pursuit of happiness by free men." Marriage is both a contract and traditionally treated as a "civil right" or, to use the more archaic phrase from Jefferson's bill, a "civil capacity." So a theory of equal contract rights points toward a theory of equal marriage rights, subject to litigating the semantics of marriage.

2. Public policy is a basis for government rules that some contracts cannot be made and enforced, but religion alone cannot be the sole basis for denying the obligation of a contract. Government must always have a secular purpose for its law.[64] The principle articulated as part of Establishment Clause jurisprudence has equal force when evaluating discrimination.

3. The discrimination against same-sex unions is derived from religious teachings. The line between "traditional marriage" and same-sex unions does not reflect a more general nonreligious morality, as easily seen in the rhetoric of those who can recognize only "traditional marriage" as part of God's plan.[65]

It is no proper function of government to assume authority for defining or promoting the sacred. Churches have a right to preach virtue and to condemn sin, to advise individual human beings on the proper way to pursue happiness; and we all should hope never to live in a community which fails to acknowledge and respect such rights. But it is not government's mission, function, purpose, or legitimate power to confound sin with crime, as one of the great religious teachers of early America said—not long after he persuaded James Madison to "flip-flop" and to embrace a bill of rights. Elder John Leland of the Baptist Church made the point in a famous remark, often quoted, too often forgotten:

> What leads legislators into this error, is confounding sins and crimes together—making no difference between moral evil and state

rebellion: not considering that a man may be infected with
moral evil, and yet be guilty of no crime, punishable by law. If a
man worships one God, three Gods, twenty Gods, or no God—
if he pays adoration one day in a week, seven days or no day—
wherein does he injure the life, liberty or property of another?
Let any or all these actions be supposed to be religious evils of
an enormous size, yet they are not crimes to be punished by laws
of state, which extend no further, in justice, than to punish the
man who works ill to his neighbor.[66]

**4. Equality of right was designed to benefit those who believe
and those who do not.** It is designed to protect conscientious religious worship but also conscientious refusals to adhere to religious
dictates. Professor Nussbaum, a distinguished, eloquent, and scholarly advocate of marriage equality, has concluded that the Free
Exercise Clause is not a persuasive basis for enforcing same-sex
unions.[67] But her analysis depends on a view that the only persuasive claim can be made by the individual of conscientious religious
scruples, and there is no burden on a right to worship or practice
of religion.[68] On the other hand, it seems clear that Madison's principles and Jefferson's bill were designed to protect nonbelieving
nonadherents as well.

The language from Justice O'Connor in *Lawrence*, quoted above,
may be borrowed, adapted, and narrowed. The issue is "whether, under
the Equal Protection Clause, [religious] disapproval is a legitimate
state interest to justify by itself a [public policy] statute that [bars
enforceability of mutual life-sharing promises made by two persons
of the same gender to each other], but not heterosexual [marital
unions]." As applied, the principles lead to a more precise rationale:
"[Religious] disapproval of [homosexuals and homosexual acts], like
a [religious motive] to harm [any] group, is . . . insufficient [as a
public policy] to . . . the Equal Protection Clause."

Governments may not deny same sex couples access to courts
to enforce life-sharing promises for sectarian, ecclesiastical, or
essentially religious reasons. When so denied, they are denied equal
protection—as originally understood. The fact that the couples
choose—or feel they must seek —happiness outside the forms of
religious sanctions or dictates is not a legitimate justification for
discrimination. Put another way, no American government has legitimate power to hurl a class of human beings not adhering to religious

dogma, rites, or forms away from the community. Government may not exile nonadherents to a life of loneliness, isolation, or civic powerlessness. Washington's boasts for our "land of equal liberty" are meaningless if government may condemn nonadherents into a civic and civil exile, stripped of equal dignity and civil rights.

The Equal Protection Clause was a mechanism for America to embrace the natural rights discussed by Jefferson and Madison, and later by Lincoln and allies in an era of civil war, national reconstruction, a constitutional refounding, and reformation. The implications of "equal liberty," born of specific understandings of religious freedom, but extended by experience, inform the meaning of the Fourteenth Amendment. The roots are real and authentic: the roots trace back to the Framers' thinking about direct relationships between God and individual human beings, liberty to adhere to religious dogma as well as liberty to dissent and act based on personal rejection of such religious dogma. The interrelationships between these ethical and egalitarian aspirations are a fundamental core of the American constitutional heritage.

NOTES

The title of this chapter comes from George Washington, *Letter to the "New Church" in Baltimore* (January 27, 1793), reprinted in George Washington, *Writings*, ed. John Rhodehamel (New York: Library of America, 1997), 834. The author thanks Anna Imose, his research assistant, for her work and suggestions.

1. Thomas Jefferson, First Inaugural Address, March 4, 1801, reprinted in Thomas Jefferson, *Writings*, ed. Merrill Peterson (New York: Library of America, 1984), 492–93.

2. City of Cleburne v. Cleburne Living Center, 473 U.S. 432, 452 (1985) (Stevens, J., concurring).

3. Martha C. Nussbaum, *Liberty of Conscience: In Defense of America's Tradition of Religious Equality* (New York: Basic Books, 2008), 105–108 (comparing the understandings of Justice Thomas and Madison).

4. Elk Grove Unified School District v. Newdow, 542 U.S. 1, (2004) (Thomas, J., concurring).

5. Ibid.

6. *McCreary County v. ACLU of Kentucky*, 545 U.S. 844 (2005).

7. *Lee v. Weisman*, 505 U.S. 577 (1992).

8. *Green v. Haskell County Board of Commissioners*, 568 F.3d 784 (10th Cir. 2009).

9. John P. Roche, "The Founding Fathers: A Reform Caucus in Action," *American Political Science Review* 55 (December, 1961): 799, 815:

> Probably, our greatest difficulty is that we know more about what the framers should have meant than they . . . did. We are intimately acquainted with the problems that their Constitution should have been designed to master; in short, we have read the mystery novel backwards. . . .
>
> [W]hen we move to the question of extrapolated intentions, we enter the realm of spiritualism. When men in our own time . . . launch into talmudic exegsis [to discover the Framers'] intentions, . . . they are engaging in a historical Extra-Sensory Perception.

10. Elk Grove Unified School District v. Newdow, 542 U.S. at 49–52 (Thomas, J., concurring).

11. See, for example, Michael W. McConnell, "Five Reasons to Reject the Claim That Religious Arguments Should Be Excluded from Democratic Deliberation," 1999 Utah L. Rev. 639, 640–41:

> To be sure, some aspects of what can be called "separation" are essential, and essentially uncontroversial. The government should not control the institutions of the church; nor should churches have any institutional role, as such, in government. No citizen is entitled to special privileges on account of membership in a favored denomination; nor may there be special disabilities for anyone else. Moreover, the original conception of separation—that government be strictly limited so as not to invade the province of religion—remains the best means of preserving religious freedom. Government protects religious freedom best by leaving religiously sensitive matters to the private sphere.

12. James Madison, "Memorial and Remonstrance Against Religious Assessments," June 20, 1785, reprinted in James Madison, *Writings*, ed. Jack N. Rakove (New York: Library of America, 1999), 31.

13. Compare, for example, William W. Van Alstyne, "Trends in the Supreme Court: Mr. Jefferson's Crumbling Wall—A Comment on Lynch v. Donnelly," *Duke Law Journal* 1984 (1984): 770–87, criticizing Supreme Court decisions undermining Jefferson's separation principles, with Philip Hamburger, *Separation of Church and State* (Cambridge, MA: Harvard University Press, 2002), arguing separation is "without constitutional foundation" and distinct from disestablishment objectives of the First Amendment.

14. Nussbaum, *Liberty Of Conscience*, 114; see also, for example, Christopher L. Eisgruber and Lawrence S. Sager, *Religious Freedom and the Constitution* (Cambridge, MA: Harvard University Press, 2007), promoting an ethical theory of "equal liberty" that "insists in the name of equality that no members of the political community ought to be devalued on account of the spiritual foundations

of their important commitments and projects," p. 4, but also "we do not wish to lean heavily on the historical case in favor of Equal Liberty," p. 72.

15. Madison, "Memorial and Remonstrance."

16. Ibid.

17. Ibid.

18. Ibid.

19. For recent accounts of the work of Madison and Jefferson in Virginia's progress toward religious freedom, see Andrew Burstein and Nancy Isenberg, *Madison and Jefferson* (New York: Random House, 2010), 117–18; Nussbaum, *Liberty Of Conscience*, 72–114; Christopher L. Eisgruber and Sager, *Religious Freedom*, 72–73.

20. Thomas Jefferson, A Bill for Establishing Religious Freedom (June 12, 1779), reprinted in Thomas Jefferson, *Writings*, ed. Merrill Peterson (New York: Library of America, 1984), 346.

21. Ibid.

22. Nussbaum, *Liberty of Conscience*, 90–97.

23. James Madison, address to U.S. House of Representatives proposing a Bill of Rights, June 8, 1789, reprinted in James Madison, *Writings*, ed. Jack N. Rakove (New York: Library of America, 1999), 445.

24. *Somersett v. Stewart*, 20 State Tr 1, Lofft 1 (King's Bench 1772). This famous English slavery case is often cited in favor of a legal or constitutional presumption that a human being is born free.

25. See Lincoln's discussion of the meaning of equality in the Declaration, text accompanying n. 36 and n. 40.

26. The term "mystery passage" has become a familiar jab at the explanations of Justice Kennedy for some controversial decisions. As discussed below at note 54, it is a reference to opinions in *Planned Parenthood v. Casey*, 505 U.S. 833 (1992), and *Lawrence v. Texas*, 539 U.S. 558 (2003).

27. Pauline Maier, *American Scripture: Making the Declaration of Independence* (New York: Knopf, 1997), 134, analyzing the Virginia Declaration of Rights, art. I (1776).

28. Ronald Hamowy, "Jefferson and the Scottish Enlightenment: A Critique of Garry Wills's Inventing America: Jefferson's Declaration of Independence," *William & Mary Quarterly*, 3d ser., 36 (1979): 503–23, 517, 519; Maier, *American Scripture*, 134 n. 79.

29. Hamburger, *Separation*, 482 (see n. 13): "in the history of separation, Jefferson is but a passing figure"; Hamburger, 356–59: assessing motives for nineteenth century advocates elevating Madison and separation as an explanation for American conception of religious liberty.

30. Some scholars see evidence that Washington's views are similar to a modern theory of "nonpreferentialism." See, for example, Nussbaum, *Liberty of Conscience*, 112.

31. George Washington, letter to the Hebrew Congregation of Newport, RI, August 18, 1790 , reprinted in George Washington, *Writings*, ed. John Rhodehamel (New York: Library of America, 1997), 767.

32. George Washington, letter to the "New Church" of Baltimore, MD, January 27, 1793, reprinted in George Washington, *Writings*, ed. John Rhodehamel (New York: Library of America, 1997), 834.

33. Thomas Jefferson, letter to John Adams, May 5, 1817, in Lester J. Cappon, ed., *The Adams–Jefferson Letters* (Chapel Hill: University of North Carolina Press, 1959), 512.

34. John Adams, letter to Thomas Jefferson, May 18, 1817, in Lester J. Cappon, ed., *The Adams–Jefferson Letters* (Chapel Hill: University of North Carolina Press, 1959), 515.

35. Ark. Const. of 1836, art. 2, § 4.

36. Robert Cover, *Justice Accused: Antislavery and the Judicial Process* (New Haven: Yale University Press, 1975), 27: "But those giants who managed the awesome transition from revolutionaries to 'constitutionaries' . . . were seldom, if ever, guilty of confusing law with natural right. These men, before 1776, used nature to take the measure of law and to judge their own obligations of obedience, but not as a source of rules for decision."

37. Abraham Lincoln, speech on the Dred Scott decision, June 26, 1857. As Republican senate candidate, Lincoln reaffirmed his position by quoting his own earlier remarks in the seventh and final debate with Stephen A. Douglas. Seventh Lincoln-Douglas debate: Lincoln's reply, Alton, IL, October 15, 1858, in Abraham Lincoln, *Speeches and Writings 1832–1858*, ed. Don E. Fehrenbacher (New York: Library of America 1989), 794.

38. Abraham Lincoln, The Gettysburg Address, November 19, 1863, in Abraham Lincoln, *Speeches and Writings 1832–1858*, ed. Don E. Fehrenbacher (New York: Library of America 1989), 536.

39. James Oakes, "Natural Rights, Citizenship Rights, States' Rights and Black Rights: Another Look at Lincoln and Race," in *Our Lincoln: New Perspectives on Lincoln and His World*, ed. Eric Foner (New York: W.W. Norton, 2008).

40. Harriet Beecher Stowe, *Uncle Tom's Cabin* (Boston: John P. Jewett & Co., 1852).

41. Frederick Douglass, *My Bondage and My Freedom* (New York: Miller, Orton & Mulligan, 1855); *A Narrative of the Life of Frederick Douglass, An American Slave* (Boston: Anti-Slavery Office,1845).

42. Raoul Berger, *Government by Judiciary: The Transformation of the Fourteenth Amendment*, 2nd ed. (Indianapolis: Liberty Fund, 1997), 34–35, 65, 66.

43. Civil Rights Act of April 9, 1866, ch. 21, 14 Stat. 27.

44. Ibid.; Berger, *Government by Judiciary*, 33 (see n. 42).

45. Berger, *Government by Judiciary*, 30. "Today, it is generally accepted that the Fourteenth Amendment was understood to provide a constitutional basis for protecting the rights set out in the Civil Rights Act of 1866."

McDonald v. City of Chicago, 561 U.S. 3025 (2010), slip op. at 28 (Alito, J., for the Court).

46. Henry Steele Commager, *The Search for a Usable Past and Other Essays in Historiography* (New York: Knopf, 1967).

47. Judge Robert Bork offered a rebuttal to criticisms by Justice William Brennan that Bork's view was "arrogant," in part because it "demands that Justice discern exactly what the Framers thought about the question under consideration." Bork offered in defense a more flexible and realistic view: "Of course the view described by Justice Brennan is arrogant, or would be, if anybody took such a position." Robert H. Bork, *The Tempting of America: The Political Seduction of the Law* (New York: Free Press, 1990), 162 (discussing and refuting William Brennan, Speech to the Text and Teaching Symposium, Georgetown University, October 12, 1985).

48. John Hart Ely, *Democracy and Distrust: A Theory of Judicial Review* (Cambridge, MA: Harvard University Press, 1980), 1–2.

49. Richard A. Posner, *Overcoming Law* (Cambridge, MA: Harvard University Press, 1995), 179–80.

50. 539 U.S. 558 (2003).

51. Ibid.

52. Ibid.

53. Planned Parenthood of Southeastern Pa. v. Casey, 505 U.S. 833 (1992).

54. Lawrence v. Texas, 539 U.S. at 588. In *Lawrence*, Justice Scalia offered biting and mocking criticisms of Justice Kennedy's "dictum of its famed sweet-mystery-of-life passage." He argued: "I have never heard of a law that attempted to restrict one's 'right to define' certain concepts; and if the passage calls into question the government's power to regulate *actions based on* one's self-defined 'concept of existence, etc.,' it is the passage that ate the rule of law."

55. 539 U.S. at 574 (quoting Planned Parenthood, 505 U.S. at 881)

56. Justice Kennedy is frequently criticized for his "airy and vague rhetoric": Jeffrey Toobin, *The Oath: The Obama White House and the Supreme Court* (New York: Doubleday, 2012), 67. But he is not alone as a Supreme Court justice who yields to the temptation to be just a little bit vague in pursuit of persuasive prose. The majority opinion in *Griswold v. Connecticut*, 381 U.S. 479 (1965), the decision announcing a constitutional right of privacy, is often a target of criticism for its nonlegal approach to penumbras. Justice Louis Brandeis also authored "mystery" passages of his own that speculated about Framers' intent, with little historical authentication. For example, in *Whitney v. California*, 274 U.S. 357 (1927), a case about free speech rights of aspiring "revolutionaries," Justice Brandeis offered a nutshell history of the Framers' thinking on "the secret of happiness": "Those who won our independence believed that the final end of the State was to make men free to develop their faculties, and that, in its government, the deliberative forces should prevail over the arbitrary. They valued liberty both as an end, and as a means. They believed liberty to

be the secret of happiness, and courage to be the secret of liberty" (274 U.S. at 375). In another case, *Olmstead v. United States*, 277 U.S. 438 (1928), Justice Brandeis included another argument linking constitutional liberty to man's "spiritual" nature:

> The makers of our Constitution undertook to secure conditions favorable to the pursuit of happiness. They recognized the significance of man's spiritual nature, of his feelings and of his intellect. They knew that only a part of the pain, pleasure and satisfaction of life are to be found in material things. They sought to protect Americans in their beliefs, their thoughts, their emotions and their sensations. The conferred, as against the government, the right to be let alone—the most comprehensive of rights and the right most valued by civilized men. (277 U.S. at 478)

Americans had certain assumptions, sometimes cultural presuppositions, underlying their belief in "rights" as expressed in a lesser known essay by James Madison (James Madison, "Property," March 29, 1792, reprinted in James Madison, *Writings*, ed. Jack N. Rakove (New York: Library of America, 1999), 515. Madison includes broad, idealistic, and aspirational explanations of "property" that go far beyond personal possessions and real estate:

> [Property] in its particular application means "that dominion which one man claims and exercises over the external things of the world, in exclusion of every other individual."
>
> In its larger and juster meaning, it embraces every thing to which a man may attach a value and have a right; and *which leaves to every one else the like advantage.*
>
> **** [A] man has a property in his opinions and the free communication of them.
>
> He has a property of peculiar value in his religious opinions, and in the profession and practice dictated by them.
>
> He has a property very dear to him in the safety and liberty of his person.
>
> He has an equal property in the free use of his faculties and free choice of the objects on which to employ them.
>
> In a word, as a man is said to have a right to his property, he may be equally said to have a property in his rights.
> ****
>
> Government is instituted to protect property of every sort; as well that which lies in the various rights of individuals, as that which the term particularly expresses. This being the end of government, that alone is a *just* government, which *impartially* secures to every man, whatever is his *own*.
> ****
>
> More sparingly should this praise be allowed to a government, where a man's religious rights are violated by penalties, or fettered by

tests, or taxed by a hierarchy. Conscience is the most sacred of all property; other property depending in part on positive law, the exercise of that, being a natural and unalienable right. To guard a man's house as his castle, to pay public and enforce private debts with the most exact faith, can give no title to invade a man's conscience which is more sacred than his castle, or to withhold from it that debt of protection, for which the public faith is pledged, by the very nature and original conditions of the social pact.

57. 478 U.S. 186 (1986)

58. Ibid., 194.

59. *Lawrence v. Texas*, 539 U.S. 582–83 (O'Connor, J., concurring). To explain her older and narrower rationale, Justice O'Connor quoted Justice Robert Jackson (*Lawrence*, 585, quoting Railway Express Agency, Inc. v. New York, 336 U. S. 106, 112–13 [1949]) in his concurring opinion:

The framers of the Constitution knew, and we should not forget today, that there is no more effective practical guaranty against arbitrary and unreasonable government than to require that the principles of law which officials would impose upon a minority be imposed generally. Conversely, nothing opens the door to arbitrary action so effectively as to allow those officials to pick and choose only a few to whom they will apply legislation and thus to escape the political retribution that might be visited upon them if larger numbers were affected.

A law branding one class of persons as criminal solely based on the State's moral disapproval of that class and the conduct associated with that class runs contrary to the values of the Constitution and the Equal Protection Clause, under any standard of review.

60. Compare *Bowers v. Hardwick*, 478 U.S., 196 ("The law . . . is constantly based on notions of morality, and if all laws representing essentially moral choices are to be invalidated under the Due Process Clause, the courts will be very busy indeed.") with *Lawrence*, 505 U.S. at 599 (Scalia, J., dissenting). The majority opinion in *Lawrence* "effectively decrees the end of all morals legislation" because it holds "the promotion of majoritarian sexual morality is not even a *legitimate* state interest."

61. Compare *Romer v. Evans*, 517 U.S. 620, 634 (1996) (Colorado's law raises "the inevitable inference that the disadvantage imposed is born of animosity toward the class of persons affected") with *id.*, at 645 (Scalia, J., dissenting) ("The Court's portrayal of Coloradans as a society fallen victim to pointless, hate-filled 'gay-bashing' is so false as to be comical").

62. Ollman v. Evans, 750 F.2d 970, 995–96 (D.C. Cir. 1984) (Bork, J.), application of the First Amendment to a libel suit: "It is the task of the judge in this generation to discern how the framers' values, defined in the context of

the world they knew, apply to the world we know. The world changes in which unchanging values find their application. . . . [T]he ultimate constitutional consideration, is the constitutional freedom that is given into our keeping. A judge who refuses to see new threats to an established constitutional value, and hence creates a crabbed interpretation that robs a provision of its full, fair and reasonable meaning, fails in his judicial duty."

63. *Loving v. Virginia*, 388 U.S. 1 (1967). *Loving* may help demonstrate that a superficial equal treatment does not satisfy equal protection. All were allowed the right to marry within their race; all were denied the marry outside their race. Still, the individual was denied the equal right to marry the person loved.

64. *McCreary County v. ACLU of Kentucky*, 545 U.S. 844 (2005):

> The touchstone for our analysis is the principle that the "First Amendment mandates governmental neutrality between religion and religion, and between religion and nonreligion." *Epperson* v. *Arkansas*, 393 U. S. 97, 104 (1968); *Everson* v. *Board of Ed. of Ewing*, 330 U. S. 1, 15–16 (1947); *Wallace, supra*, at 53. When the government acts with the ostensible and predominant purpose of advancing religion, it violates that central Establishment Clause value of official religious neutrality, there being no neutrality when the government's ostensible object is to take sides. *Corporation of Presiding Bishop of Church of Jesus Christ of Latter-day Saints* v. *Amos*, 483 U. S. 327, 335 (1987) ("*Lemon*'s 'purpose' requirement aims at preventing [government] from abandoning neutrality and acting with the intent of promoting a particular point of view in religious matters"). Manifesting a purpose to favor one faith over another, or adherence to religion generally, clashes with the "understanding, reached . . . after decades of religious war, that liberty and social stability demand a religious tolerance that respects the religious views of all citizens. . . ." *Zelman* v. *Simmons-Harris*, 536 U. S. 639, 718 (2002) (Breyer, J., dissenting). By showing a purpose to favor religion, the government "sends the . . . message to . . . nonadherents 'that they are outsiders, not full members of the political community, and an accompanying message to adherents that they are insiders, favored members.'" *Santa Fe Independent School Dist.* v. *Doe*, 530 U. S. 290, 309–10 (2000) (quoting *Lynch* v. *Donnelly*, 465 U. S. 668, 688 (1984) (O'Connor, J., concurring).

Ibid. at 860. Only proof of a sincere, authentic secular purposes will do. Ibid. at 864–65 (Souter, J.); see also *Santa Fe Independent Sch. Dist. v. Doe*, 530 U.S. at 308 (holding "it is nonetheless the duty of the courts to 'distinguis[h] a sham secular purpose from a sincere one'"); *Edwards v. Aguillard*, 482 U.S. 578, 586–87 (1987) ("it is required that the statement of such purpose be sincere and not a sham").

65. In an election in May of 2012, "North Carolinians voted in large numbers . . . for an amendment that would ban same-sex marriages, partnerships and civil unions, becoming the 30th state in the country and the last in the South to include a prohibition on gay marriage in the state constitution." Campbell Robertson, "North Carolina Voters Pass Same-Sex Marriage Ban," *New York Times*, May 8, 2012. A leader of the effort that prevailed at the polls offered a typical summary of the issue as she saw it: "'We are not anti-gay—we are pro-marriage,'Tami Fitzgerald, chairwoman of the executive committee for the pro-amendment Vote for Marriage NC, said at a victory rally in Raleigh. . . . 'And the point, the whole point is simply that you don't rewrite the nature of God's design for marriage based on the demands of a group of adults.'" Ibid. See also, generally, Martha Nussbaum, *From Disgust to Humanity: Sexual Orientation and Constitutional Law* (New York: Oxford University Press, 2010), arguing that "disgust" has been a motivating emotion in opponents of equal rights for lesbian and gay citizens.

66. John Leland [writing under the pen name of "Jack Nipps"], *The Yankee Spy* (Boston, 1794), reprinted in Charles Hyneman and Donald Lutz, *American Political Writing during the Founding Era: 1760–1805*, vol. 2 (Indianapolis, IN: Liberty Press, 1983), 979.

67. Nussbaum, *Liberty of Conscience*, 335, 338. Despite religious motivations of those opposing rights for gays, "it seems difficult to imagine any Free Exercise claim in this area."

68. Ibid.

8   Sikh Americans, Popular Constitutionalism, and Religious Liberty

Rajdeep Singh

On August 5, 2012, as Sikhs in the United States prepared to celebrate the centennial of the first Sikh American gurdwara (Sikh house of worship) in Stockton, California,[1] a gunman with known ties to hate groups entered a gurdwara in Oak Creek, Wisconsin, and murdered six worshippers in one of the worst attacks on an American place of worship since the 1963 bombing of the 16th Street Baptist Church in Birmingham, Alabama.[2] The Stockton Gurdwara Centennial and the Oak Creek massacre are high and low points, respectively, in an unfolding story that is deeply intertwined with American history but remarkably understudied. This essay attempts to outline and contextualize the story of Sikh Americans, a small but conspicuous community, from their migration to the United States at the dawn of the twentieth century to their increasingly visible leadership roles in addressing threats to civil rights and religious liberty in the post-9/11 environment, including successful efforts to pass equal employment opportunity legislation in California and Oregon.

Apart from its relative novelty, the Sikh American story can also meaningfully inform contemporary debates about America's national identity and constitutional heritage. Political discourse in the United States is replete with competing views about whether American nationhood is exclusively tied to the Judeo-Christian tradition. For example, although a 1796 treaty with Tripoli stated that the United States "is not in any sense founded on the Christian religion,"[3] the U.S. Supreme Court in 1892 declared that the United States "is a Christian nation."[4] More recently, President Barack Obama

asserted at a 2009 press conference in Turkey that "we do not consider ourselves a Christian nation or a Jewish nation or a Muslim
nation; we consider ourselves a nation of citizens who are bound
by ideals and a set of values."[5] Virginia congressman J. Randy Forbes,
founder of the Congressional Prayer Caucus, challenged President
Obama's assertion, arguing that "[w]hile America has always welcomed individuals of diverse faiths and nonfaith, we have never
ceased to be a Judeo-Christian nation."[6] What the Sikh American
story shows, and what this essay argues, is that although Sikhs have
not always been welcomed in the United States, the American nation
has nevertheless been shaped and strengthened in profound ways
by Sikhs, who derive inspiration not only from their religious heritage but also America's constitutional heritage. This demonstrates
that America's ideals are not exclusively tied to the Judeo-Christian
tradition; that these ideals resonate with diverse religious communities across the United States; and that a fuller realization of
America's ideals depends on the contributions of all Americans,
regardless of their religion.

THE SIKH HERITAGE

The Sikh religion was founded more than five hundred years ago in
the Punjab region of South Asia by Guru Nanak (1469–1539) and
developed over the course of more than two centuries by nine succes-
sive gurus. The Sikh gurus formally rejected the caste system, religious exclusivity, and gender inequality, emphasizing instead the
oneness of God and humankind.[7] To visibly express their religious
devotion, in adherence to a tradition inaugurated in 1699 by the
tenth guru, Guru Gobind Singh (1666–1708), devout Sikhs formally
initiated into the Sikh religion are known collectively as *Khalsa* and
wear or maintain five religious articles on their bodies—*kesh* (unshorn
hair, signifying acceptance of the body as God created it), *kanga* (wooden
comb, signifying cleanliness), *kara* (steel bracelet, signifying a commitment to living righteously), *kachera* (cotton undershorts, signifying
moral discipline), and *kirpan* (religious sword, signifying a commitment
to upholding justice).[8] Devout Sikhs are also required to keep their
heads covered with the *dastaar* (turban, signifying sovereignty).[9]

    To secure justice, Sikhs are religiously required to resist tyranny,
and many have done so at the cost of their own lives. This is a

tradition inaugurated by the Sikh gurus themselves. One of the most striking examples is that of Guru Tegh Bahadur, the ninth Sikh guru, who is revered for standing up for the religious freedom of Hindus— whose beliefs he did not share—in the face of Mogul repression, an act of defiance resulting in his execution in 1675 by order of the Mogul Emperor Aurangzeb.[10] For more than a century after his execution, Sikhs were repeatedly driven to the brink of extinction by Mogul persecution before rebounding and establishing a sovereign Sikh empire, which was annexed by the British in 1849.[11] During India's freedom struggle against British colonialism, despite comprising less than two percent of India's population, Sikhs constituted a majority of those who were imprisoned, exiled, or executed in the cause of India's independence.[12] Even while their brethren resisted British colonialism, an estimated 100,000 Sikhs served in the British Armed Forces during World War I, comprising around 20 percent of the total number of volunteers from India;[13] over 83,000 Sikh soldiers died and more than 109,000 were wounded in the cause of the Allies during both World Wars,[14] and five Sikhs were awarded the Victoria Cross for gallantry in these conflicts.[15] More recently, after India gained independence from Britain in 1947, thousands of Sikhs participated in civil disobedience movements in favor of greater self-determination, and thousands more lost their lives during a brutal crackdown on Sikh nationalists during the 1980s and 1990s.[16]

Although the visible constituents of Sikh identity are often viewed with confusion and consternation by those unfamiliar with or inimical toward Sikhs, the Sikh identity is a source of cohesion and self-definition for the faithful. Much in the way a soldier wears a uniform as a declaration of his or her membership in a military organization, devout Sikhs wear a uniform signifying a commitment to the ideals of the Sikh gurus, including a religious commandment to secure the well-being of all people, regardless of who they are and what they believe. This religious imperative is imparted to Sikh children at gurdwaras worldwide, much in the way American students recite the Pledge of Allegiance in their schools and recall daily America's guarantee of "liberty and justice for all." Notwithstanding the hardships they have faced throughout history, Sikhs today are a thriving community of more than 25 million worldwide,[17] with no signs of abandoning their activist spirit or commitment to defending human rights for themselves and others.

SIKH AMERICANS, FROM 1900 TO SEPTEMBER 10, 2001

Despite being among the most visible people in the United States, owing to their distinctive appearance, Sikh Americans collectively number no more than a half-million.[18] Although many Americans learned about Sikhs for the first time in the context of post-9/11 hate crimes and discrimination, Sikhs have lived in the United States for more than a century, overcoming major obstacles along the way. What follows is a brief summary of Sikh American history before September 11, 2001.

On April 6, 1899, the *San Francisco Chronicle* reported on the arrival of four Sikhs to the city, describing them as "the most picturesque group that has been seen on the Pacific Mail dock for many a day."[19] According to anthropologist Bruce La Brack, Sikhs began migrating more steadily to the United States during the first decade of the twentieth century but were not always welcomed by their fellow Americans:

> [T]heir darker complexion, distinctive turbans, non-Christian faiths, food preferences, and cultural traditions marked them as strangers and foreigners. Whatever the reality of their situations, they were openly and actively discriminated against, and broadly stereotyped by the media [and] were widely held to be culturally unassimilable and socially undesirable as citizens.[20]

These inhospitable attitudes occasionally led to violence. For example, on September 4, 1907, a mob attacked a community of predominantly Sikh laborers (who were dubbed as "Hindus," despite their Sikh heritage), ultimately driving them out of the town of Bellingham, Washington.[21] Although the *Bellingham Herald* condemned the violence in an editorial the following day, the very same editorial reinforced bigoted attitudes about the victims:

> The Hindu is not a good citizen. It would require centuries to assimilate him, and this country need not take the trouble. Our racial burdens are already heavy enough to bear. . . . Our cloak of brotherly love is not large enough to include him as a member of the body politic. His ways are not our ways; he is not adaptable, and will not in many generations make a good American citizen. Moreover he is not even a good workman[.][22]

The following year, another riot erupted in Marysville, California, aimed at expelling immigrants from South Asia.[23] Expressing xenophobic sentiment at the time, an August 1910 cartoon in the *San Francisco Call* depicted Uncle Sam attempting to dispose of a turbaned immigrant, accusing immigrants from South Asia of "incompetence" and "indolence."[24]

During this period in American history, xenophobic attitudes also found expression at the highest levels of American government. For example, Congress attempted to halt Asian immigration through legislation such as the Chinese Exclusion Act of 1882,[25] the Geary Act of 1892,[26] and the Immigration Acts of 1917 and 1924.[27] In 1923, the U.S. Supreme Court held that Bhagat Singh Thind—a Sikh who immigrated to the United States in 1913, enlisted in the U.S. Army during World War I, and applied to become a naturalized citizen[28]—was ineligible for citizenship because he was not a "white person" under federal law operative at the time; according to Justice George Sutherland, who wrote the Court's opinion, "[i]t may be true that the blond Scandinavian and the brown Hindu have a common ancestor in the dim reaches of antiquity, but the average man knows perfectly well that there are unmistakable and profound differences between them today[.]"[29]

Anti-Asian bigotry, codified in restrictive immigration policies, affected the demographics of the first Sikh American communities. According to Professor Brack, "fewer [than] ten thousand [South Asians] ever came to the United States in the first half of the 20th century, and only sixteen percent of those remained by mid-century. [And] at mid-century there were fewer than 1600 Indians, mostly Sikhs, remaining in the entire United States."[30] It was not until Congress effectively abolished anti-Asian immigration restrictions through the Immigration and Nationality Act of 1965 that the population of Sikh Americans began to grow substantially.[31]

As the Sikh American population increased during the second half of the twentieth century, and as Americans adopted the Sikh religion, so too did visible challenges to their civil rights, particularly in the context of equal employment opportunity. In responding to these challenges, Sikh Americans saw mixed results. In 1974, a U.S. Army court in New Jersey spared a Sikh soldier imprisonment and a less than honorable discharge from the service for wearing a turban and maintaining uncut hair while on duty; one month earlier, two other Army privates who had converted to Sikhism had been imprisoned and discharged for doing the same.[32] In 1981, the Army revised its appearance regulations in a manner that severely restricted the ability of Sikhs to serve in the Army.[33] The same year, a federal court in Georgia ruled in *EEOC v. Sambo's of Georgia* that a national restaurant chain could lawfully deny a manager position to a bearded Sikh applicant; although the plaintiff kept his beard neatly tied and was previously employed at a rival restaurant chain, the court concluded that a religious accommodation would diminish the "clean cut" image of the restaurant, increase the risk of noncompliance with sanitation regulations, and undermine employee morale and efficiency.[34] In 1988, a Maryland Sikh filed a high-profile complaint against Domino's Pizza after the restaurant denied him a job on account of his religiously mandated beard; a settlement in the case was reached more than a decade later when the company finally allowed employees to keep beards, ostensibly because of their increasing fashionableness.[35] Whatever the motivations behind the settlement, it diminished the implicit assertion by the Sambo's court a few years earlier that Sikhs are unclean, unsanitary, and unable to foster morale and efficiency in the workplace.

While Sikh Americans confronted these civil rights challenges at home, significant community resources were committed to creating awareness about the escalating conflict between Sikh nationalists and the government of India and the deteriorating human rights situation in Punjab. From 1988 until 2001, the overwhelming majority of references to Sikhs in the U.S. Congress, according to the Congressional Record, concerned these issues. One of the few exceptions was the introduction of a bill in 1990 by former Illinois Congressman Dennis Hastert that would have permitted Sikhs to serve in the U.S. Armed Forces with their religious articles intact; the bill never emerged from the committee to which it was referred.[36]

SIKH AMERICANS, FROM SEPTEMBER 11, 2001, TO THE PRESENT

The September 11, 2001, terrorist attacks on the United States marked a turning point in the Sikh American story. Although Sikhs in the United States had already encountered violence and discrimination during the twentieth century, the community never made serious efforts to educate the public about their religious traditions or invest in advocacy organizations that could comprehensively respond to domestic challenges. As a consequence, the horrific nature of the 9/11 attacks, coupled with pervasive images of turbaned terrorist masterminds in the mass media, made Sikhs vulnerable to conflation, stereotyping, and violence. During the first week after 9/11, American newspapers documented more than 40 hate crimes and backlash incidents targeting Sikhs.[37] One of the targets was Mr. Balbir Singh Sodhi, who was shot and killed outside his gas station in Mesa, Arizona, on September 15, 2001; his assailant bragged about wanting to "kill the ragheads responsible for September 11."[38]

It was in this context that a group of volunteers formed the Sikh Coalition, which would eventually become the nation's largest Sikh civil rights organization. During the first three months after 9/11, the Sikh Coalition documented more than 300 hate crimes and backlash incidents targeting Sikhs, including school bullying, racial and religious profiling, and job discrimination. The new organization appealed to the federal government for assistance, and laid the groundwork for advocacy that continues unabated to this day. On October 18, 2001, the U.S. Senate passed a resolution condemning bigotry and violence against Sikh Americans, and declaring that the civil rights and liberties of all Americans, including Sikhs, should be protected in the post-9/11 environment.[39] In November 2001, the U.S. Department of Transportation issued a guidance document to air carriers and airport security personnel reminding them to refrain from racial and religious profiling; according to the agency, the guidance was a response to "a rash of improper and insensitive searches and other improper treatment of Sikh and Arab Americans by airport and air carrier security personnel."[40] On December 11, 2001, the Sikh Coalition testified before the U.S. Equal Employment Opportunity Commission (EEOC) and persuaded the agency to publish guidance documents on the rights of individuals vulnerable to post-9/11 job discrimination.[41]

In the years after the murder of Mr. Balbir Singh Sodhi, the Sikh American community for the first time in its history invested in organizations devoted to systematically addressing domestic civil rights challenges, including hate crimes, school bullying, racial and religious profiling, and job discrimination. Collectively, these challenges diminish the quality of life of Sikhs and create an environment that, at its worst, can have a chilling effect on the willingness and ability of Sikhs to maintain their identity. Recognizing the gravity of these challenges, Sikh Americans have responded by pursuing leadership roles in the cause of promoting civil rights and religious liberty for all Americans and have made considerable progress.

Hate Crimes

Hate crimes remain a persistent problem for the Sikh American community. A survey of Sikh Americans published in 2006 by Harvard University revealed that eighty-three percent of respondents either personally experienced or knew someone who experienced a hate crime or incident on account of their religion.[42] A grassroots survey of Sikhs in New York City published by the Sikh Coalition in 2008 revealed that nine percent of respondents had experienced physical assaults because of their religion since 9/11.[43] A similar survey of Sikhs in the San Francisco Bay Area published by the Sikh Coalition in 2010 revealed that ten percent of respondents had experienced bias-based assaults or property damage because of their religion since 9/11.[44] According to the Federal Bureau of Investigation's (FBI's) hate crime statistics, there were at least 6,628 hate crimes reported in the United States in 2010.[45] A 2005 report by the Bureau of Justice Statistics suggested that the true number of hate crimes in the United States may be 15 times higher than that which is currently reported.[46] Even so, given the relatively small Sikh American population, the rates at which Sikhs experience hate crimes are staggeringly high, suggesting that Sikhs may be hundreds of times more likely than their fellow Americans to experience hate crimes during their lives.

   Although Sikhs are acutely susceptible to hate crimes, there was no official mechanism for tracking hate crimes against Sikhs. To remedy this, the Sikh Coalition wrote to Attorney General Eric Holder in January 2011 to request that the FBI begin tracking hate crimes against Sikhs, as the agency does for other religious communities, to improve data quality and resource allocation.[47] The request foreshadowed the suspected hate-motivated murder of two elderly Sikhs in Elk Grove, California;[48] an assault on a Sikh cab driver in Sacramento, California;[49] an assault on a Sikh transit worker in New York City;[50] an assault on a Sikh cab driver in Seattle, Washington;[51] the suspected hate-motivated shooting of a Sikh business owner in Port Orange, Florida;[52] an assault on a Sikh octogenarian in Fresno, California;[53] and the massacre of six Wisconsin Sikhs at the Oak Creek Gurdwara.[54]

In the course of more than two years, the Sikh Coalition's request was endorsed by 135 bipartisan members of the United States Senate[55] and House of Representatives,[56] as well as the Community Relations Service and Civil Rights Division of the U.S. Department of Justice.[57] In June 2013, U.S. Attorney General Eric Holder finally announced that the FBI would begin tracking hate crimes against Sikhs as well as Hindus, Arabs, Buddhists, Mormons, Jehovah's Witnesses, and Orthodox Christians.[58] Although this expansion of federal hate crime tracking met a longstanding demand for recognition by the Sikh American community, its significance lies in the fact that the policy change also benefitted the followers of other faith traditions.

In response to the Oak Creek massacre in August 2012, the Sikh Coalition rallied more than 150 organizations to demand a hearing on hate crimes and hate groups in the U.S. Senate.[59] The Subcommittee on the Constitution, Civil Rights, and Human Rights of the Senate Judiciary Committee acceded to the request, and organized a hearing on September 19, 2012, on hate crimes and the threat of domestic extremism.[60] Over 400 people attended the hearing.[61] Mr. Harpreet Singh Saini, whose mother lost her life during the Oak Creek massacre, testified before the Subcommittee about the need to track hate crimes against Sikhs and reduce violence and bigotry in the United States.[62] In the course of doing so, Saini became the first Sikh to testify before the U.S. Senate. Speaking about his faith and the faith of his late mother, he said:

> We ache for our loved ones. We have lost so much. But I want people to know that our heads are held high. My mother was a devout Sikh. Like all Sikhs, she was bound to live in *Chardi Kala*—a state of high spirits and optimism. She was also taught as a Sikh to neither have fear of anyone nor strike fear in anyone. So despite what happened, we will not live in a state of fear, nor will we make anyone fearful. Like my Mother, my brother and I are working every day to be in a state of high spirits and optimism . . . I want to build a world where all people can live, work, and worship in America in peace.[63]

Notably, Saini also addressed the common misconception that Sikhs are targeted for violence only because they are mistaken for Muslims: "So many have asked Sikhs to simply blame Muslims for attacks against our community or just say 'We are not Muslim.' But we won't blame anyone else. An attack on one of us is an attack on all of us."[64] This was the same attitude of interfaith solidarity underlying the Sikh Coalition's decision to repudiate Congressman Peter King for organizing hearings in 2011 that focused narrowly on radicalization in the American Muslim community rather than domestic extremism more generally.[65]

School Bullying

School bullying is the most widespread problem affecting Sikh Americans today. A Sikh Coalition community survey published in 2007 revealed that sixty-two percent of turban-wearing Sikh students in the Queens borough of New York City experienced bullying, and that forty-two percent of them had been hit or involuntarily touched because of their turbans.[66] A similar survey published in 2010 found that seventy-four percent of turbaned Sikh boys in the San Francisco Bay Area had suffered bias-based bullying and harassment.[67] A more recent survey of Sikh children in metropolitan areas near Fresno, California; Indianapolis, Indiana; Seattle, Washington; and Boston, Massachusetts found that a majority of respondents experienced bullying because of their religion.[68] By comparison, according to a U.S. Department of Education study, approximately twenty-eight percent of twelve- to eighteen-year-old students reported having been bullied at school during the school year in 2009.[69]

A spate of high-profile bullying incidents between 2007 and 2008 in New York and New Jersey led to a significant development in the history of Sikh American advocacy: the passage of the first civil rights law for which Sikh Americans were the catalysts. In May 2007, a Sikh boy had his hair forcibly cut by a bully.[70] In June 2008, a Sikh girl also had her hair forcibly cut by a bully.[71] That same month, another Sikh student sustained a facial fracture after being punched in the face with a set of keys by a student who was attempting to remove his turban.[72] A month earlier, another Sikh student had his turban set on fire by a fellow student.[73] In response to these incidents, the Sikh Coalition conducted media outreach and organized public protests to create awareness about the issue, ultimately persuading local government officials to enact an anti-bullying regulation in New York City: Chancellor's Regulation A-832. The new regulation established an annual diversity training program entitled *Respect for All* and a procedure for preventing and addressing student-to-student bias-based harassment in New York City public schools.[74] More recently, the Sikh Coalition has conducted follow-up studies to improve implementation of the new regulation.[75] In addition, the Sikh Coalition has called for the inclusion of religion as a protected category under Title VI of the Civil Rights Act of 1964; its absence as a protected category narrows the jurisdiction of the federal government to address bias-based bullying and harassment in American public schools.[76]

Racial and Religious Profiling

Sikh travelers began encountering heightened scrutiny at American airports in the immediate aftermath of the 9/11 attacks, sometimes to the extent of being forced to remove their turbans without cause in full public view at security checkpoints as a condition of boarding airplanes.[77] For Sikhs, forcible turban removal of this nature is akin to a strip search and a substantial burden on the free exercise of religion. Notwithstanding this, only days after the 9/11 attacks, former Louisiana Congressman John Cooksey declared, "[i]f I see someone come in and he's got a diaper on his head and a fan belt around that diaper on his head, that guy needs to be pulled over and checked."[78] In November 2001, the Department of Transportation (DOT) restored confidence among Sikh travelers by issuing policy guidance in opposing racial and religious profiling and setting forth search guidelines for religious headcoverings.[79] The new guidelines made removal of religious head coverings a last resort in cases where an alarm was triggered, and categorically stated that "selecting a man for additional screening solely because he is wearing a turban, as some Sikh men and women do, is unlawful discrimination."[80]

After several years of relative stability, Sikh travelers suddenly began encountering extra scrutiny again at American airports in August 2007, including removal or pat-downs of their turbans after passing through metal detectors without incident.[81] By this time, jurisdiction over airport security screening had passed from the DOT to the newly constituted U.S. Department of Homeland Security (DHS) and its sub-agency, the Transportation Security Administration (TSA).[82] In response to opposition from Sikh advocacy organizations, the TSA revised its policies in October 2007 in a manner that made turban removal a last resort in the event of an unresolved alarm.[83]

Around this time, the Community Relations Service at the U.S. Department of Justice, in collaboration with the Sikh American Legal Defense and Education Fund, also released *On Common Ground*,[84] a training video on Sikh cultural awareness for law enforcement officials that has also been used by the TSA to train thousands of airport screeners.[85] Notwithstanding these measures, Sikhs continue to face disparate screening at American airports.

According to the TSA, air travelers who wear religious head coverings, including Sikh turbans, are subject to the "possibility of additional security screening, which may include a pat-down search of the head covering."[86] Additional screening is justified, according to the TSA, "if the security officer cannot reasonably determine that the head area is free of a detectable threat item,"[87] even after a traveler passes through a screening device without incident. In practice, however, instead of being subject to the "possibility" of random additional screening, Sikh travelers who wear turbans have been advised by TSA personnel that such screening is mandatory, resulting in one hundred percent additional/secondary screening rates of Sikhs at most U.S. airports—a phenomenon suggestive of racial and religious profiling. Significantly, although the U.S. Department of Justice in 2003 issued an official policy statement on profiling, entitled *Guidance Regarding the Use of Race by Federal Law Enforcement Agencies*, it did not include religion as a protected category.[88]

In response to these challenges, the Sikh Coalition presented its concerns to Congress at a 2011 hearing on racial profiling and the use of suspect classifications in law enforcement, marking the first time a Sikh testified in the U.S. House of Representatives.[89] Mindful that the Sikh community is not the only one with grievances against the TSA, the Sikh Coalition has also spearheaded public interest campaigns on behalf of all travelers with a view toward promoting accountability at the TSA. For example, in May 2012, the Sikh Coalition launched a free mobile phone application called FlyRights, which allows any traveler to file official complaints of mistreatment and discrimination with the DHS and TSA directly from their iPhone and Android phones.[90] Despite the novelty of FlyRights and the enthusiasm it generated in the media, time will tell whether the American public *writ large* will begin to demand that the federal government meaningfully address the problems of racial and religious profiling.

Job Discrimination

Sikh Americans continue to face barriers to equal employment opportunity. According to Sikh Coalition community surveys, nine percent of Sikhs in New York City[91] and twelve percent of Sikhs in the San Francisco Bay Area[92] believe they have experienced bias-based discrimination in the workplace. Job discrimination against Sikh Americans manifests itself either as refusal to accommodate Sikh religious articles or relegation of Sikhs to positions that preclude contact with customers or the general public.

Although discrimination occurs in both the public and private sectors, public sector discrimination against Sikh job applicants and employees is particularly corrosive to civil rights, because it amounts to government-approved discrimination and creates a low benchmark for private sector employers. In March 2003, the Sikh Coalition filed a federal lawsuit against the New York Police Department (NYPD) on behalf of Mr. Amric Singh Rathour, a Sikh traffic officer who was terminated after refusing to remove his turban and beard.[93] Ironically, the press conference announcing the lawsuit featured presentations by devout Sikh law enforcement officers from Canada and the United Kingdom.[94] After the New York Attorney General's office expressed its intent to join the lawsuit,[95] the NYPD settled the lawsuit in July 2004 and reinstated Rathour and another Sikh who was previously precluded from working as a traffic officer.[96]

In July 2005, the Sikh Coalition and the Center for Constitutional Rights filed a lawsuit against the New York Metropolitan Transportation Authority (MTA) on behalf of Mr. Kevin Harrington, a Sikh train operator.[97] Harrington and his fellow Sikh transit workers had been told to either brand their turbans with the MTA logo or else work out of public view,[98] even though other workers were permitted to wear nonreligious head coverings, such as baseball caps, in public view.[99] Ironically, prior to the lawsuit, Harrington was honored by the MTA for his heroism on September 11, 2001; as the attacks unfolded, he reversed his train out of lower Manhattan and led passengers to safety—while wearing an unbranded turban.[100] The lawsuit dragged on for almost seven years, even after the intervention of the U.S. Department of Justice, but the MTA ultimately settled in 2012, allowing transit workers to wear religious head coverings in public as long as they are colored blue to match the MTA uniform.[101]

THE EMERGENCE OF SIKH AMERICAN LEADERSHIP
FOR WORKPLACE RELIGIOUS FREEDOM

AB 1964—California Workplace Religious Freedom Act

Although Sikh plaintiffs like Amric Singh Rathour and Kevin Har-rington enjoyed successful outcomes through litigation, lawsuits are expensive and time-consuming endeavors, and absolute success is not always guaranteed. In other words, what makes Sikhs and other religious minorities particularly vulnerable to job discrimination are weaknesses in federal workplace religious freedom laws, which give employers no incentive to accommodate religious observers. Title VII of the U.S. Civil Rights Act of 1964, as amended, requires an employer to reasonably accommodate the religious practices of an employee unless doing so would impose an undue hardship on the conduct of the employer's business.[102] According to the U.S. Supreme Court in *Trans World Airlines, Inc. v. Hardison,* an undue hard-ship to an employer in the context of religious accommodation merely means anything more than a *de minimis* cost or inconve-nience.[103] For employers, this is not a heavy burden of proof. Accord-ing to some courts, even noneconomic costs are relevant to deter-minations of undue hardship.[104]

This interpretation of Title VII is troubling to religious liberty advocates because it undercuts equal employment opportunity for religious observers. In defining "undue hardship," if the concept of cost is unhinged from economic reality, employers can deny religious accommodations on the basis of armchair assumptions and specu-lation. This is what empowered the employer in *EEOC v. Sambo's of Georgia* to argue that hiring a Sikh would increase the risk of non-compliance with sanitation regulations and undermine employee morale and efficiency,[105] and why American law enforcement agen-cies can deny Sikhs jobs and rest the denial on an unfounded assump-tion that devout Sikhs cannot safely wear protective gas masks.[106] Although health and safety are legitimate concerns for employers and employees alike, many employers may not realize that Sikhs can and often do tie their uncut beards in a manner that allows them to comply with health regulations in the food services industry and safely wear protective gas masks in the uniformed services. Between 2009 and 2010, the Sikh Coalition worked with the U.S. Army to allow three devout Sikh soldiers to serve with their religious articles intact;

to its credit, rather than disqualifying these soldiers *a priori*, the Army allowed them to successfully demonstrate compliance with safety requirements, including requirements relating to protective gas masks, and all have served with distinction.[107]

Although legal conflicts commonly arise when employers make no accommodations for religiously observant job applicants and employees—and in such cases the dispositive question is usually whether an accommodation would result in an undue hardship to the employer—some courts have occasion to consider the extent to which an accommodation favored by an employer can be deemed reasonable under Title VII.[108] In 2002, a federal district court in Illinois held in *Birdi v. United Airlines, Corp.* that an employer satisfied its Title VII obligation to make a reasonable accommodation of a turbaned Sikh employee by offering him positions out of public view, on the ground that such an accommodation technically eliminated the conflict between his religious observance and the company's corporate image policies.[109] In effect, the court decided that as long as the employee was able to wear his turban—albeit out of public view—in accordance with his faith, that was sufficient.

Although the *Birdi* case was merely a federal district court case, it has dangerous precedential value because it permits employers to segregate religious observers from customers and argue that this satisfies the obligation to make reasonable accommodations under Title VII, particularly if religious observers are afforded the same pay and benefits as public-facing employees. Drawing inspiration from the American civil rights movement of the 1950s and 1960s, the Sikh Coalition has argued that this is a modern-day instantiation of the "separate but equal" doctrine, and secured support for its position from the leaders of the Congressional Black Caucus, Congressional Hispanic Caucus, and Congressional Asian Pacific American Caucus.[110] The argument against segregating religiously observant employees from customers in the name of corporate image is that the practice reinforces stereotypes about what American workers should look like. What counts as "professional" or "clean-cut" in the context of corporate image is a function of majoritarian norms, which often do not take religious minorities into account. In other words, there is nothing objective or neutral about a corporate image policy that relegates Sikhs and other religious observers to the back rooms of the workforce. As a practical matter, if such policies prevent religious observers from gaining customer service experience, this thwarts their professional growth; as a legal matter, this undermines the integrative purpose of Title VII.

To address these issues, religious advocacy and civil rights organizations have attempted to strengthen religious accommodation standards under Title VII through federal legislation known as the Workplace Religious Freedom Act (WRFA).[111] If the most recent version of WRFA, first introduced by then senator John Kerry in 2010, is reintroduced in Congress and signed into law, it would allow employers to deny religious accommodations only if such accommodations would impose a "significant difficulty or expense" on the conduct of the employer's business—the same balancing test used in the Americans with Disabilities Act; in addition, owing to a revision to WRFA requested by the Sikh Coalition, the latest version of the bill clarifies that segregating religious observers from customers and the general public cannot be regarded as a "reasonable" accommodation.[112]

In February 2012, mindful of the occasional slowness of the legislative process in the U.S. Congress and the pressing need to address the problem of religious discrimination in the workplace, the Sikh Coalition began working with California Assembly Member Mariko Yamada to draft and introduce a state version of WRFA in the most populous state in the nation and one of the largest economies in the world.[113] Titled AB 1964 as a tribute to the Civil Rights Act of 1964, the final version of the bill ultimately received support from ninety-nine California legislators and was opposed by only ten.[114] On September 8, 2012—just over a month after the Oak Creek massacre, and over 100 years after Sikhs settled in California and encountered discrimination for the first time—AB 1964 was signed into law by California Governor Jerry Brown.[115]

Poignantly, the coalition of individuals and organizations that helped enact AB 1964 reflected the uniqueness of American pluralism. Assembly Member Mariko Yamada, the author of AB 1964, came from a Japanese ancestry family that was detained in internment camps during the Second World War, and understood, in a personal way, the importance of combating discrimination.[116] As sponsors of AB 1964, the Sikh Coalition partnered with advocates from the Muslim, Jewish, and Seventh-Day Adventist communities to build interfaith support for the bill.[117] The California Sikh community itself sent over 3000 petition messages to California lawmakers in support of AB 1964, and testified in large numbers at four separate legislative committee hearings.[118] As of the time of its passage, AB 1964 provides workers in California the strongest protection against religious discrimination anywhere in the nation.

Religious Freedom for Oregon Teachers

AB 1964 was the second instance where Sikh Americans launched a successful legislative campaign at the state level in the cause of workplace religious freedom. In July 2009, as Oregon finalized the passage of its own state WRFA, Sikh advocates publicly took exception to a significant gap in the legislation.[119] Although the underlying bill purported to strengthen religious liberty protections for workers in Oregon, it excluded teachers from the scope of these protections, providing that "a school district, education service district or public charter school does not commit an unlawful employment practice . . . by reason of prohibiting a teacher from wearing religious dress while engaged in the performance of duties as a teacher."[120] As it turned out, Oregon was one of only three states in the country— along with Pennsylvania[121] and Nebraska[122]—with long-standing statutory bans on religious dress for public schools. Oregon law categorically stated that "no teacher in any public school shall wear any religious dress while engaged in the performance of duties as a teacher."[123] Much like the restrictive federal immigration laws of the late nineteenth and early twentieth centuries, Oregon's ban on religious dress for public school teachers originated in the context of bigotry toward racial and religious minorities. According to the *Oregon Blue Book*, a publication of the state of Oregon about its own history,

> the [Ku Klux] Klan, [Federation of Patriotic Societies], and Scottish Rite Masons sponsored a bill, passed in 1922 in the general election, to compel all children to attend public schools. The overtly anti-Catholic measure threatened to close all parochial schools and military academies. The state Supreme Court ruled the law unconstitutional in 1924 and the U.S. Supreme Court concurred in 1925. The Ku Klux Klan found a strange champion in the Oregon legislature. Kaspar K. Kubli, speaker of the House of Representatives, happened to possess winning initials and became a rallying point for efforts to drive through the Alien Property Act of 1923. The law prohibited Japanese from purchasing or leasing land in Oregon. The legislature also passed a

law forbidding wearing of sectarian clothing, namely priestly vestments or nuns' habits, in classrooms.[124]

Although the religious dress ban was aimed at Catholics in conjunction with an effort to close parochial schools, its architects may not have envisioned that it would be formally attacked as unjust not once, but twice, by Sikh Americans.

In 1983, Karta Kaur Khalsa (formerly known as Janet Cooper), a public school teacher and convert to the Sikh religion, was fired for wearing a turban to work in Eugene, Oregon; she filed a lawsuit the following year, and her case reached the Oregon Supreme Court in 1986.[125] In the course of deciding the case against her in *Cooper v. Eugene School District 4J*, the court acknowledged that the ban on religious dress for public school teachers originated in "the period of anti-Catholic intolerance," but declared that the law's recodification in 1965 by the Oregon legislature converted the ban into a benign effort to "maintain the religious neutrality of the public schools, to avoid giving children or their parents the impression that the school, through its teacher, approves and shares the religious commitment of one group and perhaps finds that of others less worthy."[126] After pivoting away from the bigoted origins of the law and recasting it as an effort to preserve religious neutrality, the court upheld its constitutionality under state and federal law, asserting that it protected impressionable children from "conscious or unconscious" religious indoctrination.[127]

Ironically, despite the attempt by the Oregon Supreme Court to uphold the constitutionality of the ban on religious neutrality grounds, the court itself could not remain neutral in the course of delivering its opinion. According to the court,

[religious dress] must be judged from the perspective both of the wearer and of the observer, that it is dress which is worn by reason of its religious importance to the teacher and also conveys to children of the age, background, and sophistication typical of students in the teacher's class a degree of religious commitment beyond the choice to wear common decorations that a person might draw from a religious heritage, such as a necklace with a small cross or Star of David. A teacher does not violate the statute by wearing a garment or a color that unintentionally happens to imply membership in some religious group, nor, for instance, by dressing in clerical garb to assume a role in a classroom historical exercise or a performance of, say, George Bernard Shaw's Saint Joan . . . [or if] a teacher makes an occasional appearance in religious dress, for instance on her way to or from a seasonal ceremony.[128]

Thus, although Khalsa's turban was found to be an affront to religious neutrality in her classroom, the Oregon Supreme Court implied that her case may have been decided differently if she had been a Christian wearing a cross or a Jew wearing a Star of David. Much in the way the U.S. Supreme Court's 1923 decision in the case of Bhagat Singh Thind sought to exclude Sikhs and people of South Asian origin from the mainstream of American society through arbitrary racial distinctions, the *Cooper* court arbitrarily distinguished between the Sikh turban and religious emblems more familiar to it. The *Cooper* decision added insult to injury by suggesting that a turban may have been acceptable as part of an educational or theatrical costume, or if wearing it was merely a seasonal obligation.

When Oregon's religious dress ban was challenged again by Sikh advocates in 2009, they called for its repeal through the legislative process. On February 4, 2010, the Sikh Coalition rallied 16 interfaith and civil rights organizations and issued a joint letter to leaders in the Oregon legislature calling for repeal of the religious dress ban.[129] In pertinent part, the letter read:

> Supporters of the status quo have argued that allowing public school teachers to wear religious dress will disrupt religious neutrality in the classroom and lead to proselytization of students. Both propositions are factually incorrect. The private act of wearing religious dress in adherence to faith is distinguishable from the public act of asserting a proselytizing message. The Establishment Clause of the U.S. Constitution affords sufficient protection against state endorsement of religion; banning all forms of religious dress for teachers is a prohibitively overbroad approach to the issue. This explains why the legislature of North Dakota repealed its ban on religious dress for public school teachers in 1998, and why it is increasingly common to find teachers wearing *yarmulkes* (headcoverings), *hijabs* (headscarves), and *dastaars* (turbans) in public schools throughout our diverse nation.[130]

In addition, after an intervention request by Sikh advocates,[131] the U.S. Department of Justice opened an investigation into the legality of Oregon's religious dress ban.[132] The Oregon House of Representatives responded by introducing HB 3686, a bill to repeal the ban on religious dress for public school teachers.[133]

In its written testimony to the Oregon legislature[134] and a letter to Oregon Governor Ted Kulongoski,[135] the Sikh Coalition enclosed a testimonial from Ajeet Singh, a doctoral candidate at Columbia University and alumnus of Teach for America, a prestigious community service program that places accomplished college graduates in underresourced American schools.[136] Singh, who passed away in July 2010, gave readers a glimpse into his family background and all-American upbringing:

> I was born in a small town in California. I grew up playing on the school soccer team and participated in the spelling bee. Education is what enabled my Sikh parents to go from being born in tiny villages in India to immigrating and achieving the American Dream. I've worked hard and followed their example. But there's one problem: according to an out-of-date Oregon law, I'm different.[137]

Singh then summarized his successful experience as a public school teacher:

> I recently served as a high school history teacher with Teach For America in Brooklyn, New York, where I taught at the Brooklyn Academy for Science and Environment (2007–08) and the Ronald Edmonds Learning Center (2006–07). I am currently pursuing my PhD in History at Columbia University. When I first graduated college, I decided to give back to the country that has given so much to me by becoming a teacher. I chose to work in the toughest schools with the neediest students. My students broke records on the annual New York State Regents examination.[138]

Drawing on his experiences as a teacher, Singh went on to express and explain his support for repealing Oregon's ban on religious dress for public school teachers:

> As a New York City schoolteacher, I taught about the diversity of our world through the state's World History curriculum.

Although I wear a turban in accordance with my religious beliefs, my Sikh identity did not offend my students and did not prevent them from succeeding. I know from experience that there is a clear distinction between educating students and preaching to them. The view of New York policymakers is that children who grow up in a diverse society will become better citizens if they gain exposure to people from different backgrounds. We know that only education can overcome ignorance and promote a more tolerant society. In an increasingly globalized world, we cannot afford to remain blind to diversity. . . . In a country predicated on the motto, *E Pluribus, Unum,* we now can make it so.[139]

On February 10, 2010, the Oregon House of Representatives passed HB 3686 by a fifty-one to eight margin, and the Senate followed suit on February 23, 2010, by a twenty-one to nine margin.[140] With Sikhs and members of other faith communities by his side, Governor Ted Kulongoski made history by repealing Oregon's ban on religious dress for public school teachers on April 1, 2010.[141]

CONCLUSION

The August 5, 2012, massacre of Sikh worshippers at a gurdwara in Oak Creek, Wisconsin, underscored the vulnerability of Sikh Americans to bigotry and violence. Although Sikh Americans continue to experience hate crimes, school bullying, racial and religious profiling, and job discrimination on account of their religion, they have responded—as they have throughout history—with an organized determination to vindicate their rights and the rights of their fellow Americans. One of the most recent signs of the growing determination of the Sikh American community to increase its visibility and participation in American political discourse was the formation in April 2013 of the first-ever American Sikh Congressional Caucus in the U.S. Congress—a bipartisan body comprised of nearly thirty members as of the time of its formation, dedicated to addressing Sikh American civil rights issues.[142] Another sign that the Sikh American community is making its presence felt is the growing support for inclusion of observant Sikh Americans in the U.S. Armed Forces. In December 2013, the U.S. Commission on Civil Rights wrote to the Department of Defense to express concern about the denial of equal opportunity to observant Sikh Americans who wish to serve in the U.S. Armed Forces.[143] As of April 2014, 105 members of the U.S. House of Representatives[144] and 15 U.S. Senators[145] have written to the Department of Defense, requesting that Sikh Americans be given an equal opportunity to serve in the military while observing the requirements of their religion. In April 2014, the Pentagon hosted its first-ever celebration of Vaisakhi, a Sikh religious festival.[146] Despite the hardships they have experienced, Sikh Americans have made significant progress toward a fuller realization of their civil rights, and are poised to consolidate their position as leaders in the cause of protecting civil rights and religious liberty for all Americans. Given that Sikhs were once legally barred from immigrating to or obtaining citizenship in the United States, the progress that Sikh Americans continue to make in the cause of securing religious liberty for all Americans is proof that America benefits from religious pluralism, and that Americans are defined by their shared commitment to constitutional ideals, not the religion they belong to or whether they happen to wear a turban.

NOTES

1. Kevin Parrish, "Sikhs Honor Rich History in Stockton," *The Record*, September 22, 2012, http://www.recordnet.com/apps/pbcs.dll/article?AID=/2012 0922/A_NEWS/209220318/-1/.

2. Joe Heim, "Wade Michael Page Was Steeped in Neo-Nazi 'Hate Music' Movement," *Washington Post*, August 7, 2012, http://www.washingtonpost. com/lifestyle/style/wade-michael-page-was-steeped-in-neo-nazi-hate-music-movement/2012/08/07/b879451e-dfe8–11e1-a19c-fcfa365396c8_story.html.

3. Treaty of Peace and Friendship between the United States of America and the Bey and Subjects of Tripoli of Barbary, *November 4, 1796*, http://avalon .law.yale.edu/18th_century/bar1796t.asp, cited by Louis Fisher and Katy J. Harriger, *American Constitutional Law, Volume Two: Constitutional Rights: Civil Rights and Civil Liberties*, 8th ed. (Durham, NC: Carolina Academic Press, 2009), 556.

4. See Church of the Holy Trinity v. United States, 143 U.S. 457, 471 (1892), cited by Fisher and Harriger, *American Constitutional Law.*

5. White House Office of the Press Secretary, "Joint Press Availability with President Obama and President Gul of Turkey," April 6, 2009, http://www. whitehouse.gov/the-press-office/joint-press-availability-with-president-obama-and-president-gul-turkey.

6. J. Randy Forbes, "Obama Is Wrong When He Says We're Not a Judeo-Christian Nation," *U.S. News & World Report*, May 7, 2009, http://www.usnews.com/opinion/articles/2009/05/07/obama-is-wrong-when-he-says-were-not-a-judeo-christian-nation.

7. See, generally, Nikky-Guninder Kaur Singh, *Sikhism: An Introduction* (London: I.B. Tauris, 2011); Patwant Singh, *The Sikhs* (London: John Murray Publishers, 1999); Eleanor Nesbitt, *Sikhism: A Very Short Introduction* (New York: Oxford University Press, 2005). English translations of the Sikh scripture, *Sri Guru Granth Sahib*, are available at http://www.srigranth.org.

8. See, generally, Kaur Singh, *Sikhism: An Introduction*; Patwant Singh, *The Sikhs*; Nesbitt, *Sikhism: A Very Short Introduction*.

9. See, generally, Kaur Singh, *Sikhism: An Introduction*; Patwant Singh, *The Sikhs*; Nesbitt, *Sikhism: A Very Short Introduction*.

10. Patwant Singh, *The Sikhs*, 47–48.

11. Ibid., 70–174.

12. Ibid., 253–54.

13. Amandeep Singh Madra and Paramjit Singh, *Warrior Saints: Three Centuries of the Sikh Military Tradition* (London: I. B. Tauris, 1999), 110.

14. Ibid., 41, quoting General Sir Frank Messervy, in F.T. Birdwood, foreword to *The Sikh Regiment In The Second World War* (East Sussex, UK: Naval & Military Press,1953).

15. Madra and Singh, *Warrior Saints*, 158.

16. See, generally, Jaskaran Kaur, *Twenty Years of Impunity: The November 1984 Pogroms of Sikhs in India*, 2nd ed. (Portland, OR: Ensaaf, 2006), http://www.ensaaf.org/publications/reports/20years/20years-2nd.pdf; Romesh Silva, Jasmine Marwaha, and Jeff Klingner, "Violent Deaths and Enforced Disappearances During the Counterinsurgency in Punjab, India: A Preliminary Quantitative Analysis," A Joint Report by Benetech's Human Rights Data Analysis Group and Ensaaf, Inc., January 2009, http://www.ensaaf.org/publications/reports/descriptiveanalysis/reportwcover.pdf.

17. Pew Forum on Religion and Public Life, Other Religions, "The Global Religious Landscape: A Report on the Size and Distribution of the World's Major Religious Groups as of 2010," December 18, 2012, http://www.pewforum.org/global-religious-landscape-other.aspx (citing an estimate by the World Religion Database).

18. Pew Research Center, "How Many U.S. Sikhs?," August 6, 2012, http://www.pewresearch.org/2012/08/06/ask-the-expert-how-many-us-sikhs.

19. "Sikhs Allowed to Land," *San Francisco Chronicle*, April 6, 1899, reproduced in "Echoes of Freedom: South Asian Pioneers in California: 1899–1965," The Library, University of California–Berkeley, 2001, http://www.lib.berkeley.edu/SSEAL/echoes/introduction/chapter0_2.html.

20. Bruce La Brack, "A Century of Sikhs in California: From the Periphery to the Center," July 3, 2011, Sikh Foundation International, http://www.

sikhfoundation.org/sikh-punjabi-language-studies/a-century-of-sikhs-in-california-by-bruce-la-brack.

21. See Mary Lane Gallagher, "1907 Bellingham mob forced East Indian workers from town," *Bellingham Herald*, September 2, 2007, http://www.bellinghamherald.com/2007/09/02/170095/1907-bellingham-mob-forced-east.html; "1907 Bellingham Riots," Special Section, University of Washington, Seattle Civil Rights and Labor History Project, 2007, http://depts.washington.edu/civilr/bham_intro.htm.

22. Editorial, "A Public Disgrace," *Bellingham Herald*, September 5, 1907, reproduced by Woodring College of Education at Western Washington University, http://www.wce.wwu.edu/resources/AACR/documents/east-indian-public-disgrace.shtml.

23. "Hindus Driven Out," *New York Times*, January 28, 1908, reproduced in "Echoes of Freedom: South Asian Pioneers in California: 1899–1965," The Library, University of California–Berkeley, 2001, http://www.lib.berkeley.edu/SSEAL/echoes/chapter4/chapter4_2.html.

24. Cartoon, "A New Problem for Uncle Sam," *San Francisco Call*, August 13, 1910, reproduced in "Echoes of Freedom: South Asian Pioneers in California: 1899–1965," The Library, University of California–Berkeley, 2001, http://www.lib.berkeley.edu/SSEAL/echoes/chapter4/chapter4_1.html.

25. Chinese Exclusion Act, May 6, 1882, reproduced in 2001 by PBS.org, New Perspectives on the West: Archives from the West from 1877–1887, Documents on Anti-Chinese Immigration Policy, http://www.pbs.org/weta/thewest/resources/archives/seven/chinxact.htm#act.

26. Geary Act of 1892, reproduced in 2012 by Chinatown San Francisco, http://www.sanfranciscochinatown.com/history/1892gearyact.html.

27. See U.S. Department of State, Office of the Historian, "Milestones: 1921–1936: The Immigration Act of 1924 (The Johnson-Reed Act)," http://history.state.gov/milestones/1921–1936/ImmigrationAct. The text of the 1917 Immigration Act is available at http://library.uwb.edu/guides/usimmigration/39%20stat%20874.pdf, and the text of the 1924 Immigration Act is available at http://library.uwb.edu/guides/usimmigration/43%20stat%20153.pdf.

28. See "Bhagat Singh Thind," 2000, *Roots in the Sand*, PBS.org, http://www.pbs.org/rootsinthesand/i_bhagat1.html.

29. *United States v. Bhagat Singh Thind*, 261 U.S. 204 (1923).

30. La Brack, "A Century of Sikhs,"(see n. 20).

31. "Echoes of Freedom: South Asian Pioneers in California: 1899–1965," The Library, University of California–Berkeley, 2001, http://www.lib.berkeley.edu/SSEAL/echoes/chapter13/chapter13.html.

32. "Army Judge Acquits Sikh Wearing Turban on Duty," *New York Times*, January 8, 1974.

33. "Religious Exceptions in Army Uniform End," *New York Times*, August 22, 1981.

34. See *EEOC v. Sambo's of Georgia*, 530 F.Supp. 86 (N.D. Ga. 1981).

35. Timothy B. Wheeler, "Domino's Pizza Drops Ban on Facial Hair for Workers," *Baltimore Sun*, January 4, 2000; LOOC, Inc., d/b/a/ *Domino's Pizza, Inc. v. Prabhjot S. Kohli*, 347 Md. 258 (C.A. Md. 1997).

36. See H.R 5672, 101st Congress (1990).

37. South Asian Americans Leading Together, "American Backlash: Terrorists Bring War Home in More Ways Than One," 2001, http://old.911digitalarchive. org/documents/BiasReport.pdf.

38. "We are Not the Enemy: Hate Crimes Against Arabs, Muslims, and Those Perceived to be Perceived to be Arab or Muslim after September 11," *Human Rights Watch* 14, no. 6 (G) (November 2002): 18, http://www.hrw. org/legacy/reports/2002/usahate/usa1102.pdf (quoting Sergeant Mike Goulet of the Mesa, Arizona, police department).

39. S. Con. Res. 74, 107th Congress (2001), http://www.gpo.gov/fdsys/ pkg/BILLS-107sconres74es/pdf/BILLS-107sconres74es.pdf.

40. U.S. Department of Transportation, *Guidance for Screeners and Other Security Personnel* (Washington, DC, 2001), http://airconsumer.ost.dot.gov/ rules/20011116.htm; see also U.S. Department of Transportation, *Answers to Frequently Asked Questions Concerning the Air Travel of People Who Are or May Appear to Be of Arab, Middle Eastern or South Asian Descent and/or Muslim or Sikh* (Washington, DC, 2001), http://www.dot.gov/sites/dot.dev/files/docs/ 20011119.pdf.

41. U.S. Equal Employment Opportunity Commission, "Employment Discrimination in the Aftermath of September 11," remarks of Amardeep Singh, Legal Director, The Sikh Coalition, December 11, 2001, http://www.eeoc. gov/eeoc/meetings/archive/12–11–01-sikh.html; U.S. Equal Employment Opportunity Commission, *Questions and Answers about Employer Responsibilities Concerning the Employment of Muslims, Arabs, South Asians, and Sikhs*, last modified March 21, 2005, http://www.eeoc.gov/facts/backlash-employer.html.

42. June Han, *We Are Americans Too: A Comparative Study of the Effects of 9/11 on South Asian Communities*, Discrimination and National Security Initiative, Pluralism Project, Harvard University (September 2006), 2–3, http:// pluralism.org/affiliates/kaur_sidhu/We_Are_Americans_Too.pdf.

43. *Making Our Voices Heard: A Civil Rights Agenda for New York City's Sikhs* (New York: Sikh Coalition, 2008), 6, http://www.sikhcoalition.org/documents/pdf/RaisingOurVoicesReport.pdf.

44. *Sikh Coalition Bay Area Civil Rights Report 2010* (New York: Sikh Coalition, 2010), 4, http://www.sikhcoalition.org/documents/pdf/Bay_Area_Civil_ Rights_Agenda.pdf.

45. U.S. Department of Justice, Federal Bureau of Investigation, "Hate Crime Statistics 2010: Incidents and Offenses," http://www.fbi.gov/about-us/ cjis/ucr/hate-crime/2010/narratives/hate-crime-2010-incidents-and-offenses.

46. Southern Poverty Law Center, "Report: FBI Hate Crime Statistics Vastly Understate Problem," *Intelligence Report* (Winter 2005), http://www.splcenter

.org/get-informed/intelligence-report/browse-all-issues/2005/winter/hate-crime.

47. See "Hate Crimes and the Threat of Domestic Extremism: Hearing Before the Senate Subcommittee on the Constitution, Civil Rights, and Human Rights of the Senate Committee on the Judiciary," (statement for the record from the Sikh Coalition), 112th Cong. (2012), http://www.sikhcoalition.org/images/documents/statementfortherecordfromthesikhcoalition.pdf.

48. Nick Carbone, "Timeline: A History of Violence Against Sikhs in the Wake of 9/11," *Time*, August 6, 2012, http://newsfeed.time.com/2012/08/06/timeline-a-history-of-violence-against-sikhs-in-the-wake-of-911.

49. Cathy Locke, "Two Men Enter No-Contest Pleas in Attack on Sikh Taxi Driver," *Sacramento Bee*, March 7, 2011, http://blogs.sacbee.com/crime/archives/2011/03/w-sacramento-pd-2.html.

50. John Lauinger, "MTA Employee Loses Three Teeth to Hate Nut's Sucker Punch on a Train Memorial Day," *New York Daily News*, June 5, 2011, http://articles.nydailynews.com/2011-06-05/local/29640761_1_bias-attacks-bias-incident-jiwan-singh.

51. Levi Pulkkinen, "Anti-Muslim Bigot Beat Sikh Cab Driver," *Seattle Post-Intelligencer*, October 28, 2012, http://www.seattlepi.com/local/article/Police-Anti-Muslim-bigot-beat-Sikh-cab-driver-3985421.php.

52. Lyda Longa, "Port Orange Sikh Forgives Attackers, But Wants Them Brought to Justice," *Daytona Beach News Journal*, March 8, 2013, http://www.news-journalonline.com/article/20130308/NEWS/303089971.

53. Stephanie Stone and Mariana Jacob, "Sikh Man Beaten With Steel Pipe in Fresno Hate Crime," KFSN-TV (May 7, 2013), http://abc30.com/archive/9094041.

54. Heim, "Wade Michael Page" (see n. 2).

55. "Feinstein Urges Tracking of Hate Crimes against Sikh, Hindu, and Arab Americans," February 19, 2013, http://www.feinstein.senate.gov/public/index.cfm/press-releases?ID=f4edefd3-d762-4933-b1b4-5dfe1cdc51bd.

56. Crowley, "Over 100 Members of Congress Urge Stronger Action to Protect Sikh, Hindu, and Arab-American Communities from Hate Crimes," March 21, 2013, http://crowley.house.gov/press-release/crowley-over-100-members-congress-urge-stronger-action-protect-sikh-hindu-arab; "American Sikh Caucus Calls on FBI to Track Hate Crimes Targeting Sikhs," May 21, 2013, http://valadao.house.gov/news/documentsingle.aspx?DocumentID= 334901.

57. Annysa Johnson, "Oak Creek community meetings show support for Sikhs," *Milwaukee Journal Sentinel*, December 3, 2012, http://www.jsonline.com/news/milwaukee/oak-creek-community-meetings-show-support-for-sikhs-8m7spi3–181949201.html; U.S. Department of Justice, "A Visit to Oak Creek," *The Justice Blog*, December 12, 2012, http://blogs.justice.gov/main/archives/2593.

58. Attorney General Eric Holder, "Healing Communities and Remembering the Victims of Oak Creek," *The Justice Blog*, August 2, 2013, http://blogs.justice.gov/main/archives/3233.

59. Mike Johnson and Annysa Johnson, "Sikh Coalition, Others Ask Senate Panel for Hate Crime Hearing," *Milwaukee Journal Sentinel*, August 21, 2012, http://www.jsonline.com/news/crime/sikh-coalition-others-ask-senate-panel-for-hate-crime-hearing-r26is42–166934476.html.

60. "Hate Crimes and Domestic Extremism," *C-Span* video, 1:38:53, September 19, 2002, http://www.c-spanvideo.org/program/308281–1.

61. Karen Herzog, "Congressional Hearing Addresses Hate Crimes after Sikh Attack," *Milwaukee Journal-Sentinel*, September 19, 2012, http://www.jsonline.com/features/religion/congressional-hearing-addresses-hate-crimes-extremism-after-sikh-attack-vt6u47u-170379006.html.

62. *Hate Crimes and the Threat of Domestic Extremism: Hearing Before the Senate Subcommittee on the Constitution, Civil Rights, and Human Rights of the Senate Committee on the Judiciary*, 112th Cong. (2012) (testimony of Harpreet Singh Saini), http://media.jsonline.com/documents/Saini.pdf.

63. Ibid.

64. Ibid.

65. "The Extent of Radicalization in the American Muslim Community and That Community's Response: Hearing Before the House Committee on Homeland Security" (statement for the record from the Sikh Coalition), 112th Cong. (2011), http://www.gpo.gov/fdsys/pkg/CHRG-112hhrg72541/pdf/CHRG-112hhrg72541.pdf.

66. Sikh Coalition, *Hatred in the Hallways: A Preliminary Report on Bias Against Sikh Students in New York City's Public Schools* (June 2007), http://www.sikhcoalition.org/documents/pdf/HatredintheHallwaysFinal.pdf.

67. *Sikh Coalition Bay Area Civil Rights Report 2010*, 4 (see n. 44).

68. The Sikh Coalition, *Go Home Terrorist: A Report on the Bullying of Sikh American School Children* (2014), *available at* http://sikhcoalition.org/documents/pdf/go-home-terrorist.pdf.

69. U.S. Department of Education, National Center for Education Statistics, "Indicators of School Crime and Safety: 2011—Key Findings," NCES 2012-002, February 2012, http://nces.ed.gov/programs/crimeindicators/crimeindicators2011/key.asp.

70. "Sikh Boy's Hair Forcibly Cut in Hate Attack," Sikh Coalition, May 25, 2007, http://www.sikhcoalition.org/stay-informed/sikh-coalition-advisories/144.

71. "Sikh Girl's Hair Cut by Fellow Student in New York City School," Sikh Coalition, June 21, 2008, http://www.sikhcoalition.org/advisories/2008/nyc-sikh-girls-hair-cut-by-another-student.

72. "Another Sikh Boy Suffers Hate Assault in New York City School," Sikh Coalition, June 5, 2008, http://www.sikhcoalition.org/advisories/2008/another-sikh-boy-assaulted-in-school.

73. Jeff Diamant, "Sikh Student's Turban Set Ablaze During School Fire Drill," *Star-Ledger*, May 12, 2008, http://www.nj.com/news/index.ssf/2008/05/sikh_students_turban_set_on_fi.html.

74. "New Chancellor's Regulation to Prevent Bias-Based Harassment and Bullying in Schools," Sikh Coalition, September 3, 2008, http://www.sikhcoalition.org/stay-informed/sikh-coalition-advisories/237.

75. Sikh Coalition, "NYC Teachers Doubt Effectiveness of City Anti-Bullying Efforts," February 25, 2011, http://salsa.wiredforchange.com/o/1607/t/0/blastContent.jsp?email_blast_KEY=94106.

76. See *Peer-to-Peer Violence and Bullying: Examining the Federal Response* (Washington, D.C.: U.S. Commission on Civil Rights, September 2011), http://www.usccr.gov/pubs/2011statutory.pdf.

77. Laurie Goodstein, "American Sikhs Contend They Have Become a Focus of Profiling at Airports," *New York Times*, November 10, 2001, http://www.nytimes.com/2001/11/10/national/10SIKH.html.

78. "National Briefing/South: Louisiana: Apology from Congressman," *New York Times*, September 21, 2001, http://www.nytimes.com/2001/09/21/us/national-briefing-south-louisiana-apology-from-congressman.html.

79. U.S. Department of Transportation, *Guidance for Screeners* (see n. 40); see also U.S. Department of Transportation, *Answers to Frequently Asked Questions* (see n. 40).

80. Ibid.

81. Neil MacFarquhar, "Airport Scrutiny of Headgear Raises Bias Claims from Sikhs," *New York Times*, August 30, 2007, http://www.nytimes.com/2007/08/30/us/nationalspecial3/30sikh.html?_r=0.

82. Transportation Security Administration, U.S. Department of Homeland Security, "9/11 and TSA: Message from Administrator John S. Pistole," September 11, 2013, http://www.tsa.gov/about-tsa/september-11-2001-and-tsa.

83. Eileen Sullivan, "TSA revises rule on travelers with turbans," *Associated Press*(October 17,2007),http://usatoday30.usatoday.com/travel/flights/2007-10-16-tsa-turbans_N.htm.

84. U.S. Department of Justice, Community Relations Service, *On Common Ground—Law Enforcement Training Video on Sikhism*, http://www.justice.gov/crs/video/ocg-video.htm.

85. Sikh Coalition, "TSA Develops New Procedure for Screening Turbans at U.S. Airports," October 17, 2007, http://www.sikhcoalition.org/stay-informed/sikh-coalition-advisories/216.

86. Transportation Security Administration, U.S. Department of Homeland Security, "Religious and Cultural Needs," http://www.tsa.gov/traveler-information/religious-and-cultural-needs (latest revisions: 06 December 2012).

87. Ibid.

88. U.S. Department of Justice, Civil Rights Division, "Guidance Regarding the Use of Race by Federal Law Enforcement Agencies," June 2003, http://www.fletc.gov/training/programs/legal-division/downloads-articles-and-faqs/downloads/doj-guidance/racialprofiling.pdf/view.

89. See "Racial Profiling and the Use of Suspect Classifications in Law Enforcement Policy: Hearing Before the House Subcommittee on the Constitution,

Civil Rights, and Civil Liberties of the House Committee On the Judiciary" (statement of Amardeep Singh, Director of Programs, Sikh Coalition), 111th Cong. (2010), http://judiciary.house.gov/_files/hearings/pdf/Singh100617.pdf.

90. Associated Press, "Mobile App Helps Report Unfair Airport Screeners," *Fox News*, April 30, 2012, http://www.foxnews.com/us/2012/04/30/mobile-app-helps-report-unfair-airport-screeners/.

91. *Making Our Voices Heard*, 12 (see n. 43).

92. *Sikh Coalition Bay Area Civil Rights Report* (New York: Sikh Coalition, 2010), 21, http://www.sikhcoalition.org/documents/pdf/Bay_Area_Civil_Rights_Agenda.pdf.

93. "Sikh to Sue Police Over Turban and Beard," *New York Times*, March 4, 2003, http://www.nytimes.com/2003/03/04/nyregion/sikh-to-sue-police over-turban-and-beard.html.

94. Alex Davidson, "Ozone Park Sikh files harassment suit against NYPD," *Times Ledger*, March 6, 2003, http://www.timesledger.com/stories/2003/10/20030306-archive76.html.

95. Susan Saulny, "State Lawyer to Aid Sikh Suing Police in Bias Case," *New York Times*, June 5, 2004, http://www.nytimes.com/2004/06/05/nyregion/state-lawyer-to-aid-sikh-suing-police-in-bias-case.html.

96. James Barron, "Two Sikhs Win Back Jobs Lost by Wearing Turbans," *New York Times*, July 29, 2004, http://www.nytimes.com/2004/07/29/nyregion/two-sikhs-win-back-jobs-lost-by-wearing-turbans.html.

97. Robert Smith, "Sikhs Object to MTA Logo Requirement," *National Public Radio*, July 16, 2005, http://www.npr.org/templates/story/story.php?storyId=4757415.

98. Ted Mann, "MTA Settles Bias Lawsuit," *Wall Street Journal*, May 30, 2012, http://online.wsj.com/article/SB10001424052702303640104577436743688465710.html.

99. Margaret Hartmann, "MTA Allows Muslim Employees to Wear Head Coverings," *New York Magazine*, May 31, 2012, http://nymag.com/daily/intelligencer/2012/05/mta-lets-muslim-employees-wear-head-coverings.html.

100. Ted Mann, "MTA Settles Bias Lawsuit," *Wall Street Journal*, May 30, 2012, http://online.wsj.com/article/SB10001424052702303640104577436743688465710.html.

101. Ibid.

102. See 42 U.S.C. § 2000e(j). Employers have a duty to accommodate an employee's religious practices as long as they can reasonably accommodate the practices and the accommodation does not cause undue hardship on the employer's business.

103. See 432 U.S. 63, 84 (1977). Accommodation of religious beliefs requiring more than a *de minimis* cost to the employer normally results in undue hardship and therefore is not required by current law.

104. See, for example, *EEOC v. The GEO Group Inc.*, No. 09-3093 (3rd Cir. 2010), http://www.ca3.uscourts.gov/opinarch/093093p.pdf

105. See *EEOC v. Sambo's of Georgia*, 530 F.Supp. 86 (N.D. Ga. 1981).

106. Don Thompson, Associated Press, "Bearded man can't be prison guard, Calif. Says," *NBC News*, January 25, 2011, http://www.nbcnews.com/id/41263508/ns/us_news-crime_and_courts.

107. Steve Elliott, "Sikh Soldiers Allowed to Serve, Retain Their Articles of Faith," U.S. Army, March 25, 2010, http://www.army.mil/article/36339/sikh-soldiers-allowed-to-serve-retain-their-articles-of-faith; Steve Elliott, "Second Sikh Doctor Allowed to Wear Articles of Faith; Enlisted Soldier in Training," U.S. Army, September 9, 2010, http://www.army.mil/article/44944; Susanne Kappler, "Keeping Faith: Sikh Soldier Graduates Basic Training," *Ft. Jackson Leader*, November 10, 2010, http://www.army.mil/article/47924/keeping-faith-sikh-soldier-graduates-basic-training.

108. See *Ansonia Bd. of Education v. Philbrook*, 479 U.S. 60 (1986).

109. See *Birdi v. United Airlines*, Corp, No. 99 C 5576, 2002 WL 471999, 2002 U.S. Dist. LEXIS 9864 (N.D. Ill. 2002).

110. See "CAPAC Chair Praises New Workplace Religious Freedom Protections in California," Congressional Asian Pacific American Caucus, September 10, 2012, http://capac-chu.house.gov/press-release/capac-chair-praises-new-workplace-religious-freedom-protections-california.

111. S. 4046, 110th Congress (2010), http://thomas.loc.gov/cgi-bin/query/z?c111:S.4046.IS:.

112. Ibid.

113. California Assembly Bill AB1964, http://leginfo.legislature.ca.gov/faces/billNavClient.xhtml?bill_id=201120120AB1964.

114. Ibid.

115. Patrick McGreevy, "Bill Protects Religious Garb, Grooming in the Workplace," *Los Angeles Times*, September 9, 2012, http://articles.latimes.com/2012/sep/09/local/la-me-workplace-discrimination-20120909.

116. Meeta Kaur and Winty Singh, "This Is What Unity Looks Like: AB1964," *Hyphen Magazine*, August 8, 2012, http://www.hyphenmagazine.com/blog/archive/2012/08/what-unity-looks-ab-1964.

117. California Assembly Bill AB1964, http://leginfo.legislature.ca.gov/faces/billNavClient.xhtml?bill_id=201120120AB1964.

118. Sikh Coalition, "Free Voices. Sikh Voices: Year in Review 2012," http://sikhcoalition.org/images/documents/sc2012_inreview_newsletter.pdf.

119. Harry Esteve, "Sikhs Protest School Exemption in Oregon Religious Freedom Bill," *The Oregonian*, July 15, 2009, http://www.oregonlive.com/politics/index.ssf/2009/07/school_exemption_in_religious.html; William McCall, Associated Press, "Teachers Still Can't Wear Religious Clothing in 3 States," *USA Today*, September 2, 2009, available at http://usatoday30.usatoday.com/news/religion/2009-09-02-religious-dress-teachers_N.htm.

120. Oregon Senate Bill 786 (2009), https://olis.leg.state.or.us/liz/2009R1/Measures/Text/SB786/Enrolled.

121. Public School Code of 1949, P.L 30, No. 14, Sec. 1112 ("[N]o teacher in any public school shall wear in said school or while engaged in the performance of his duty as such teacher any dress, mark, emblem or insignia indicating the fact that such teacher is a member or adherent of any religious order, sect or denomination."), http://www.legis.state.pa.us/WU01/LI/LI/US/HTM/1949/0/0014. .HTM.

122. Nebraska Revised Statute 79–898 ("Any teacher in any public school in this state who wears, in such school or while engaged in the performance of his or her duty, any dress or garb indicating the fact that such teacher is a member or an adherent of any religious order, sect, or denomination, shall be deemed guilty of a misdemeanor, and upon conviction thereof be fined in any sum not exceeding one hundred dollars and the costs of prosecution or shall be committed to the county jail for a period not exceeding thirty days or both."), http://uniweb.legislature.ne.gov/laws/statutes.php?statute=79–898.

123. Oregon Senate Bill 786 (2009) (see n. 119).

124. Oregon Secretary of State, Oregon Blue Book, "Oregon History: Mixed Blessings," (2014), http://bluebook.state.or.us/cultural/history/history24.htm.

125. "Teacher Came to Class in Sikh Garb; Firing Upheld," *Los Angeles Times*, (August 2, 1986, http://articles.latimes.com/1986-08-02/local/me-1073_1_religious-garb.

126. *Cooper v. Eugene School District*, No. 4J, 301 Ore. 358 (Or. 1986).

127. Ibid.

128. Ibid.

129. Sikh Coalition Interfaith Letter to Oregon Senate President Peter Courtney and House Speaker Dave Hunt, February 4, 2010, http://www.sikhcoalition.org/documents/pdf/2–4-10-Coalition%20Letter%20to%20Oregon%20Legislature%20(Final)-1.pdf.

130. Ibid.

131. William McCall, Associated Press, "Teachers Still Can't Wear" (see n. 118).

132. U.S. Department of Justice, "Fulfilling the Promise," *The Justice Blog*, May 20, 2010, http://blogs.justice.gov/main/archives/805.

133. Oregon Legislative Assembly, House Bill 3686 (2010), http://www.sikhcoalition.org/documents/pdf/hb3686.en.pdf.

134. *Statement of the Sikh Coalition in Support of Equal Opportunity* (New York: Sikh Coalition, February 2010), http://www.sikhcoalition.org/documents/pdf/Sikh%20Coalition%20Fact%20Sheet%20on%20Equal%20pportunity%20in%20regon.pdf.

135. Sikh Coalition Letter to Oregon Governor Ted Kulongoski, March 8, 2010, http://www.sikhcoalition.org/documents/pdf/10–0308_Sikh%20Coalition%20Letter%20to%20regon%20Governor%20Kulongoski.pdf.

136. Ajeet Singh, "Out of Many, One," February 5, 2010, http://www.sikhcoalition.org/documents/pdf/10–0205%20-%20Ajeet%20Singh%20Testimony%20%28Final%29.pdf.

137. Ibid.

138. Ibid.

139. Ibid.

140. Measure History, 2009–2010 Oregon Legislative Session, https://olis.leg.state.or.us/liz/2010S1/Measures/Overview/HB3686.

141. Betsy Hammond, "Governor Signs Repeal on Teachers' Religious Dress; Ban Will Lift In July 2011," *The Oregonian*, April 1, 2010, http://www.oregonlive.com/education/index.ssf/2010/04/governor_signs_repeal_on_teach.html.

142. Chidanand Rajghatta, "In Historic Landmark, Sikh Caucus Formed in US Congress," *Times of India*, April 26, 2013, http://timesofindia.indiatimes.com/nri/us-canada-news/In-historic-landmark-Sikh-caucus-formed-in-US-Congress/articleshow/19732669.cms 143. Available at http://www.usccr.gov/pubs/Letter_Sikh-Military-Service.pdf.

143. Available at http://www.usccr.gov/pubs/Letter_Sikh-Military-Service.pdf.

144. Available at http://crowley.house.gov/sites/crowley.house.gov/files/Letter%20to%20Secretary%20Hagel%20re%20Sikh%20American%20Service%2003-10-2014.pdf.

145. Available at https://salsa.wiredforchange.com/o/1607/images/14.04.24%20Accommodation%20of%20Religious%20Practices%20Within%20the%20Military%20Letter.pdf.

146. Available at http://www.dvidshub.net/video/334102/vaisakhi-celebration.

9   American Muslims, American Islam, and the American Constitutional Heritage

Asma T. Uddin

Islam in America is not a monolith. Muslims in the United States come from more than seventy different countries and a range of Islamic traditions. American Muslims are the most highly educated community of Muslims in the world. A young community with a relatively high socioeconomic status, Muslims in America have started using their resources to create vibrant expressions of their faith in the fertile soil of the American civic and religious culture.

Estimates regarding the size of the American Muslim population must be drawn from independent sources, since the U.S. Census Bureau is prohibited from collecting data on religious affiliation.[1] The latest estimate puts the population between 2.6 and 2.8 million.[2] Although about 90 percent of American Muslims are Sunni, as is the case in most of the world, a diverse range of traditions is represented in the United States, including Shia, Sufi, and Ahmadi.[3]

Islam in the United States is a young, ethnically diverse, and predominantly immigrant faith. In 2011, approximately two-thirds of Muslims were first-generation immigrants (foreign-born).[4] A 2009 Gallup study found that American Muslims are the most racially diverse religious group in the United States.[5] South Asians and Arabs each account for one-third; African Americans one-fourth; and, collectively, sub-Saharan Africans, Europeans, Iranians, Caribbean, Southeast Asians, Latinos, Turks, and White Americans constitute the remaining 19 percent of the American Muslim population. Ethnic groups that have immigrated to the United States in significant numbers recently include Iranians, West Africans, Somalis, and Bosnians.[6] Approximately three-fourths of the American Muslim population is between the ages of eighteen and forty-nine, with almost half between thirty and forty-nine.[7] Muslims are the second most highly educated group in the United States, with 40 percent achieving a college degree or higher.[8] A diverse religious group in a diverse nation, American Muslims welcome religious pluralism and, despite images to the contrary, are among the more integrated faith groups in the United States.[9]

American Muslims have become increasingly active both civically and politically. Domestic and foreign policies formed in the aftermath of the September 11 terrorist attacks on the World Trade Center have fueled discontent, but rather than diminish democratic participation, these policies have increased it. Indeed, many Muslims have found that the American civic culture and value for religious freedom helps them not only practice but also better understand their faith. American Muslims do not see their religious identity as incongruous with their American identity; in fact, they report identifying with their faith and with the United States equally.[10]

The Islamic Society of North America (ISNA), the Council on American-Islamic Relations (CAIR), the Muslim Public Affairs Council (MPAC), the Universal Muslim Association of America (UMAA), and the Al-Khoei Foundation are among the prominent organizations involved in the American civic and political landscape. ISNA is the largest Muslim organization in America. ISNA and UMAA seek to unify the American Muslim community, and each hosts an annual convention. UMAA focuses particularly on the American Shia community. MPAC focuses on interfaith and government relations and advocates for the civil rights of American Muslims. CAIR advocates for the civil liberties of Muslims through media relations, lobbying, and education. The Al-Khoei Foundation works to build peaceful communities and is the fourth Muslim organization, and only Shia group, to hold consultative status with the U.N. Economic and Social Council, through which it promotes development, human rights, and minority rights.

Among these and other American Muslim groups there is, at times, tremendous debate and difference. Perhaps best illustrating this friction is the opposition of CAIR and MPAC to the appointment of Zuhdi Jasser to the U.S. Commission on International Religious Freedom. Jasser, who is the president of the American

Islamic Forum for Democracy, frequently criticizes CAIR and MPAC, claiming that they espouse an Islamist ideology linked to the Muslim Brotherhood. Leaders of CAIR and MPAC, in turn, charge that Jasser is unfit to protect religious freedom because, in their view, he regularly works against the religious freedom of Muslims. For example, they point out Jasser's support for the anti-sharia laws discussed later in this chapter, as well as his opposition to the accommodation of certain Muslim religious practices in the military.[11] Because of Jasser's political positions and alleged alliances with anti-Muslim advocates, CAIR argues that he "serve[s] as the de facto Muslim for anti-Muslim political leaders while he paints a small group of radical Muslim extremists as mainstream."[12] Jasser in turn has charged his critics with attempting to "bully" him into silence.[13]

American Muslims are also increasingly active in democratic politics. A majority of Muslim citizens are registered to vote and report their intentions to vote. Many have written to politicians or signed petitions. A good number also report supporting political candidates or attending rallies. During the 2006 congressional elections, Muslim organizations helped to secure the Democrats' control of both houses through intense electoral mobilization. They conducted voter registration drives, endorsed Democrat candidates, and "employed classic get-out-the-vote techniques" in several pivotal close races.[14] That same year, Muslims were able to celebrate another victory: the election of the first Muslim to Congress, Keith Ellison of Minnesota.

Taking full advantage of the freedoms afforded by the Constitution and the American civic culture, American Muslims have created a variety of initiatives to think critically about their faith. Discussed in more detail below, these initiatives range from leadership development programs that help cultivate intra-community leaders, to social service organizations that serve the broader American community, to media platforms that give American Muslims a space to tell and shape their own story.

Though American Muslims have flourished, they continue to face challenges in the United States. One challenge to political mobilization as a faith group is that there is no national American Muslim organization that represents a large percentage of Muslims.[15] One of the foremost challenges is Islamophobia, an exaggerated fear and hatred of and hostility toward Muslims that is fueled by negative stereotypes and based on the assumption that Islam is a violent religion and an ideological threat to the West.[16] This prejudice leads to the marginalization and exclusion of Muslims from American culture and society: 49 percent of Americans hold an unfavorable view of Islam and Muslims, and one in two Muslims report personally experiencing prejudice within the last year.[17]

The community also struggles with "homegrown terrorism." For a variety of political or religious reasons, some disaffected Muslims, such as the Boston Marathon bombers, have turned to violence.[18] Others have traveled abroad to join groups waging self-conscious "jihad" against the West or allied Muslim governments. These militant expressions of Islamist ideology, some contend, have been fueled in part by Wahhabi literature and foreign imams financed by Saudi Arabia, which has come under increasing scrutiny.[19]

In spite of these challenges, American Muslims are practicing their faith and engaging dynamically with American society and culture. An emerging American Muslim civic identity is taking shape through a variety of initiatives which both create and critically examine the culture and identity of American Muslims. The constitutionally protected rights to freedom of religion and expression allow—in fact, encourage—Muslims in America to explore and deepen their attachment to their faith.

AMERICAN MUSLIMS AND THE U.S. CONSTITUTIONAL HERITAGE

American Muslims have long drawn upon the U.S. constitutional heritage both to protect their rights in the face of opposition, and to use those rights to live and express their faith in myriad ways. Broad religious freedom protections, rooted in the U.S. constitution and various federal and state statutes, provide the legal framework for Muslim civil rights struggles. Where the law keeps the government from interfering, it has provided a social model that encourages both Muslim and non-Muslim private actors to fight back against anti-Muslim sentiment.

Together, these legal and social elements of the U.S. constitutional system have allowed American Muslims to think critically about intrareligious questions, challenge assumptions previously unchallenged elsewhere in the global Muslim community, and ultimately create a vibrant and authentic American Muslim culture.

PROTECTING THEIR RIGHTS: AMERICAN MUSLIMS IN COURT

A particularly frequent venue for religious liberty claims has been land use cases. When local governments oppose a plan to build a mosque by invoking zoning laws in a discriminatory or arbitrary manner, mosques have invoked the Religious Land Use and Institutionalized Persons Act (RLUIPA), a federal statute that prevents local governments from placing a greater burden on religious uses than on nonreligious uses, or from placing a substantial burden on religion without a compelling government interest.[20] In egregious cases, the community has also argued that the zoning code violates its right to free exercise of religion or, where discrimination is clear, that it has been denied equal protection.

These arguments have largely been successful. In *Islamic Center of Mississippi, Inc. v. City of Starkville*,[21] the Fifth Circuit held that the city's denial of a zoning exception for a mosque, when all nine prior applications for exceptions made by churches were granted, was an unconstitutional burden on the center's free exercise of religion. In *Islamic Society of Westchester & Rockland, Inc. v. Foley*,[22] a zoning board had rigidly applied the local zoning ordinance without making any attempt to help the organization comply with it. The trial court ordered, and the appellate court agreed, that the zoning board grant a variance on the property—one subject to reasonable conditions—to protect the rights of neighbors. A more recent case, *Albanian Associated Fund v. Township of Wayne*,[23] involved a town seeking to take a parcel land intended for a mosque by claiming eminent domain. The town cited the need to preserve open space; however, out of the 102 properties identified for preservation, only the mosque's was subject to condemnation. In a decision based on both RLUIPA and the First Amendment, the court denied the town's request for summary judgment.[24]

In Tennessee, the Islamic Center of Murfreesboro (ICM) was able to go ahead with its expansion plans despite intense local opposition.[25] Having been around for more than a decade, a burgeoning of the local Muslim population compelled the ICM to ask the county's permission to build various community resource facilities on a fifteen-acre plot. After the county approved the expansion plans, controversy and protest erupted. Some protests drew hundreds of people, and the new site was subject to both arson and vandalism. Tennessee's lieutenant governor, who endorsed the opposition while running for governor, went so far as to state, "You could even argue whether being a Muslim is actually a religion, or is it a nationality, way of life, a cult, whatever you want to call it."[26]

When the county granted the necessary permit, some citizens sued on the grounds that the citizenry had not been properly informed of the planning commission's meeting. They also argued that Islam is political (not religious) in nature and thus undeserving of First Amendment protection.[27] The U.S. Department of Justice filed a brief with the Chancery Court in support of the county's approval, in particular rebutting the suggestion that the United States does not recognize Islam as a valid religion.[28] The Chancery Court agreed with the Department of Justice, and despite continued opposition, the mosque broke ground in late September 2011.[29]

American Muslims have also fought for their religious liberty rights in a broad array of other legal situations. Although a significant portion of these cases have ended at preliminary stages or been resolved on procedural grounds rather than substantive religious liberty doctrines, these decisions still underscore the breadth of religious freedom protections available to religious communities. For example, *Potter v. Dist. of Columbia*[30] involved a firefighter-grooming policy that forbade male firefighters from growing a beard. The rationale for the policy was that facial hair would impede the effectiveness of protective respiratory equipment.[31] Muslim firefighters who sought to wear a beard in accordance with religious injunctions challenged the policy. Citing the Religious Freedom Restoration Act (RFRA), the firefighters argued that the policy did not meet the "least restrictive means" test—that is, it was an overly broad restriction, since the protective equipment had been shown to work correctly even when facial hair was present.[32] The court sided with the firefighters, stating that the city had failed to demonstrate that facial hair actually reduced the equipment's effectiveness.[33]

Fraternal Order of Police Newark Lodge No. 12 v. City of Newark also involved a grooming policy, this time a police department's requirement that officers be clean-shaven. In this case, the police department recognized medical exemptions but refused to provide religious exemptions.[34] The court struck down the policy, holding that providing exemptions for medical reasons and not religious reasons reflected a biased, rather than neutral, stance toward religion.[35]

In *Salahuddin v. Goord*, a Muslim prisoner claimed that prison officials violated his free exercise rights under the First Amendment and RLUIPA because they "forced Shi'ite and Sunni Muslims to conduct Ramadan services jointly, denied him Islamic holiday meals and the ability to attend Islamic worship services [while placed in disciplinary keep lock], and refused to provide him with a Muslim chaplain or a free Qur'an," while the facility provided Catholic inmates with a chaplain and a free Bible.[36] The Second Circuit Court of Appeals upheld the inmate's rights. The court annulled the district court's determination that "denial of one religious meal is . . . a de minimis burden on [the inmate's] religious exercise"[37] and explained that the proper determination was whether the denied meal was central or important to *his* practice of his faith.[38]

In *EEOC v. Sunbelt Rentals, Inc.*, the Fourth Circuit Court held that persistent harassment by derogatory comments directed at a Muslim employee after the September 11, 2001, attacks created a question of fact about whether a hostile work environment existed.[39] The Muslim employee was verbally derided in ways related to his physical appearance and religious belief, including being called "Taliban" and a "fake Muslim," and being asked whether he was on "our side" or "the Taliban's side."[40] The court determined that verbal attacks do not need to be "accompanied by physical threat or force" in order to create an actionable hostile work environment.[41]

More recently, Muslims have had to fight for their right to interpret their wills and order their personal lives according to sharia precepts. Ten years after September 11, 2001, the American Muslim community continues to be surrounded by a climate of fear and distrust—popularly termed "Islamophobia"—largely created and promoted by a small group of anti-Muslim organizations and individuals who, while small in number, are highly influential in shaping the national and international perception of Muslims.[42]

Primarily five key individuals and their organizations lead the Islamophobia campaign: Frank Gaffney of the Center for Security Policy; Daniel Pipes at the Middle East Forum; David Yerushalmi at the Society of Americans for National Existence; Robert Spencer of Jihad Watch and Stop Islamization of America; and Steven Emerson of the Investigative Project on Terrorism. These misinformation experts are advancing a notion of Islam as an intrinsically violent ideology, the goal of which is to achieve dominance over the United States and over all non-Muslims worldwide. These individuals seek to define sharia as a "totalitarian ideology" and "legal-political-military doctrine" committed to annihilating Western civilization as we know it today.[43]

The influential reach of Islamophobia's proponents into the legal and policy sphere can be seen in their campaign against what they allege to be a threat of the infiltration of sharia into American law. The movement against sharia had its first seeds planted in January of 2006 when an attorney started a group called the Society of Americans for National Existence. On the group's website, he "proposed a law that would make observing Sharia, which he [compared] to sedition, a felony punishable by 20 years in prison." In the summer of 2009, the Society's founder "began writing 'American Laws for American Courts,' a model statute that would [prohibit] state judges from considering foreign laws or rulings that violate constitutional rights in the United States."[44] Since then, his "model legislation" banning sharia law has been virtually "cut and pasted" into bills passed in Tennessee, Louisiana, Arizona, Arkansas, and Oklahoma, and versions of it have passed in North Carolina, Alabama, and Missouri.[45]

To date, "approximately sixteen states have either proposed or passed legislation aimed at banning sharia, or in a less direct fashion, 'foreign law.'"[46] Oklahoma's State Representative authored State Question 755, a constitutional amendment that appeared on the Oklahoma ballot in November 2, 2010, and was passed by Oklahoma voters.[47] The bill required that courts look only to federal and state laws to decide cases, explicitly prohibiting the use of international and sharia law. The Oklahoma law has so far been the only anti-sharia initiative challenged in court. Muneer Awad, the executive director of the Oklahoma chapter of the Council on American Islamic Relations, and an Oklahoma City resident, filed suit against members of the State Board of Elections to prevent them from certifying the election results for that question.[48]

In his case against what was called the "Save Our State Amendment" (SOS Amendment), Mr. Awad argued that the SOS Amendment violated his rights under both the Establishment Clause and the Free Exercise Clause.[49] He argued that the SOS Amendment labeled him a political and social outsider because of his Islamic practice and belief; characterized his Islamic religious beliefs as a threat from which Oklahoma must be saved; and conveyed "the unmistakable message that [his Muslim] faith is officially disfavored by the State generally, and the judicial system, in particular."[50]

In addition, under the Free Exercise Clause, Awad argued that the SOS Amendment interfered with the operation of his last will and testament. Because his will "refers to and incorporates his Islamic religious beliefs," the amendment would "render those will provisions unenforceable." Even though it is not possible to know, before his will is probated, how a court will handle the portions of the will that incorporate these religious beliefs, the presence of the amendment created a "cloud of uncertainty over the will's full enforceability because of its religious references."[51] The district court held in Awad's favor on both claims, and the Tenth Circuit Court of Appeals affirmed.[52]

CIVIL SOCIETY RESPONSES TO ANTI-MUSLIM SPEECH

While recognizing that the legal fight for civil liberties is key to their success, the American Muslim community has also sought to fill the gap where the law does not provide the answer. Such gaps encourage social, not legal, responses to anti-Muslim sentiment. The social response model holds that a vibrant civil society—which includes, among other things, religious institutions, civil rights and advocacy groups, political leaders, and various other influential voices—can step in and exert social pressure that pushes back against the mainstreaming of speech designed to denigrate.[53]

The case of Florida pastor Terry Jones provides a good example. Jones was a little-known pastor who led a very small church congregation of about fifty people. With the tenth anniversary of the September 11, 2001, attacks on the World Trade Center approaching, Jones declared that Islam was a "false religion" and "of the devil" and decided to burn copies of the Qur'an in front of his church.

In Jones's case, although his speech was legal, individual Christian and Jewish leaders, media personalities, and high-level government officials (including the president of the United States, the secretary of state, the secretary of defense, and others) publicly denounced his actions as unrepresentative of the American people. This public response made Jones a social pariah. Groups of citizens also created several internet videos that used humor to denounce Jones's message. For example, the video "Dude, You Have No Quran" depicts local news coverage of a copycat pastor who was also threatening to burn a copy of the Quran, but was apparently foiled when a local resident snatched away the copy before he was able to burn it. The local's humorous quote, "Dude, you have no Quran," quickly became a part of popular culture, featured in a video that rapidly collected over a million views on YouTube.[54]

The national controversy over the proposed Muslim community center Park51 is also illustrative. New York City Muslims had been praying at this location for some years and had purchased the building in the hopes of one day building a community center that would include a mosque, art and culture facilities, and recreational facilities that would serve both Muslims and the broader New York City community. The initiative was a long way from being completed and was still in its conceptual stages when Pamela Geller, a seasoned anti-Muslim campaigner, learned of the plans. She went on to create a wide public campaign against the center, dubbing the center the "ground zero mosque" and claiming that it would signify the "second wave of the 9/11 attacks" because of its proximity to the site of the World Trade Center.[55]

Geller's efforts quickly snowballed into a nationwide anti-mosque campaign that was "rife with vitriol toward all of Islam."[56] Nationally syndicated voices such as Newt Gingrich and Rush Limbaugh loudly drew parallels to "a Ku Klux Klan memorial at Gettysburg," a "Japanese cultural center at Pearl Harbor," or a "Nazi sign next to the Holocaust Museum," with each made-up scenario equating Muslims with the great villains of American history. Signs declaring that "Islam Kills" and "Islam Is Terrorism" were common sights at anti-Park51 rallies, occasionally spelling Islam with a double "S" scripted like the Nazi SS logo. Former vice-presidential nominee Sarah Palin equated the idea of a "Ground Zero Mosque" with a "stab . . . in the heart" for Americans.[57]

The Park51 incident led to a national conversation about the mosque specifically and religious freedom more broadly. Although many opposed Park51, many political leaders supported the American Muslim community and those building the center. In a speech delivered against the backdrop of the Statue of Liberty, Mayor Michael Bloomberg of New York City made clear that "Muslims are as much a part of our city and our country as the people of any faith. And they are as welcome to worship in lower Manhattan as any other group. . . . Political controversies come and go, but our values and our traditions endure, and there is no neighborhood in this city that is off-limits to God's love and mercy, as the religious leaders here with us can attest."[58]

Following in Bloomberg's footsteps, national political leaders came to the support of the American Muslim community.[59] Public support also came from those most affected by the 9/11 attacks. Numerous relatives of victims spoke out in favor of the project, including former Bush administration Solicitor General Ted Olson, whose wife had died in the attacks. Speaking on MSNBC, Olson said, "We don't want to turn an act of hate against us by extremists into an act of intolerance for people of religious faith."[60] These statements were echoed by the group September 11 Families for Peaceful Tomorrows, which welcomed Park51 as "consistent with fundamental American values of freedom and justice for all."[61]

In a development that showed the power of interfaith dialogue, Americans of various faith backgrounds formed a national coalition called Shoulder-to-Shoulder. Shoulder-to-Shoulder hosted a national press conference, and raised money to host programs and events countering anti-Muslim bigotry and promoting the acceptance of the Muslim community into the fabric of America's pluralist society.[62]

In the absence of legal restrictions on speech designed to create hatred of Muslims, it was the collective of private social actions mobilized against hate and vitriol that challenged those inclined to engage in such speech. Instead of being forced by the government to "get along," individual citizens and civil society organizations were able to grow toward the solution out of personal conviction. While the fight for broad-based social acceptance of the American Muslim community is by no means over, active participation by Muslims and non-Muslims alike in countering bad speech with good speech has put American society on a path toward progress.

CULTURAL EXPRESSIONS OF AMERICAN MUSLIM IDENTITY

Muslims in America are in the process of establishing unique cultural identities that blend their American identity with an understanding of their religion. A prominent American Muslim scholar, Dr. Umar Faruq Abd-Allah, argues that this "development of a sound Muslim American cultural identity must be resolutely undertaken as a conscious pursuit." Creating authentic expressions of American Muslim culture does not happen by accident, but rather must be deliberately endeavored. It is crucial because culture provides "an operative identity, produces social cohesion, and gives its members knowledge and social skills that empower them to meet their individual and social requirements effectively."[63] In short, an authentic American

Muslim culture is necessary so that American Muslims can lead successful and meaningful lives in America, where they are engaged with the world around them rather than existing in isolation.

American Muslims have taken this obligation seriously. A number of initiatives have sprung up that express various American Muslim identities and demonstrate a range from the more traditional to the progressive. American Muslims have entertainment gurus, "rock star" imams, community leaders, public intellectuals, and civic leaders, and they have created a plethora of media platforms. All of these efforts draw from the American constitutional heritage of religious freedom—a heritage that encourages deep and critical engagement with theology, spirituality, and the intersection of religion and lived realities.

Programs like the American Society for Muslim Advancement's (ASMA's) Muslim Leaders of Tomorrow Conference and the American Muslim Civic Leadership Institute (AMCLI) cultivate American Muslim civic leaders. ASMA is guided by the belief that "American Muslim youth need to be empowered with a faith that is tolerant, forward-thinking, and develops a distinct American Muslim identity," and dedicates itself to fostering an environment where Muslims can flourish and express themselves authentically.[64] AMCLI believes that the United States is stronger when all of its citizens, including Muslims, "participate in shaping [its] democracy."[65] There is also the American Islamic Congress (AIC), which combats negative stereotypes about Muslims in the United States through "interfaith and interethnic events," and also supports civil rights initiatives in Muslim-majority countries abroad.[66]

Part of this active engagement with Islam is realizing the obligations it places on believers to serve those outside the religious community. The Cordoba Initiative advances the qualities its namesake, the highly advanced medieval Spanish city ruled by Muslims, was famous for—pluralism and religious tolerance. Its co-founder, Daisy Khan, believes that the freedom of expression that Muslims enjoy in America comes with a responsibility to share creative thinking on religion, peace, and conflict, and build intercultural understanding.[67]

Muslim students founded service organizations like the Inner-City Muslim Action Network (IMAN) and the University Muslim Medical Association (UMMA) Clinic to improve the lives of the underprivileged and the underserved. IMAN seeks to create a dynamic and vibrant space for American Muslims in urban areas and to work alongside people of all religious, cultural, and ethnic backgrounds towards social justice and a cultivation of the arts. It also offers a free health clinic, career development initiative, and youth services, and advocates for healthier and more peaceful communities.[68] The UMMA Clinic is a community-based health organization that serves a diverse and underprivileged population.

America's constitutional heritage is perhaps best known for its encouragement of self-expression. Numerous American Muslim media initiatives have taken advantage of this freedom for Muslims to not only learn more about themselves as religious believers and a religious community, but also shape their own narratives. For example, founded in 2003, *Muslim WakeUp!* was a website that promoted progressive ideas in Islam; its mission was to celebrate religious, cultural, and spiritual diversity. Now inactive, the website for several years ignited controversy from across the spectrum and was criticized for its brashness, lack of foundation in traditional Islamic scholarship, sexual content, and intolerance towards Muslims who disagreed with it.[69] In contrast, *Qibla.com*, an online Islamic institute that provides courses and degrees in Islamic Studies and Arabic, focuses on traditional Islam, as does the conservative-leaning *MuslimMatters.org*, a group-blogging platform that engages "in discourses that touch our lives as citizens of the West, while maintaining our individual Islamic identities," and provides social commentary on a range of issues.[70] The author of this chapter, believing strongly in creating a space for authentic expressions of American Muslim identity and importance of gender as a lens for that identity, launched *AltMuslimah.com* in 2009; *AltMuslimah.com* is devoted to the intersection of gender and Islam.[71] These initiatives all wrestle with tough questions about Islam and the Muslim community. Thus, American freedoms have led to discussions more honest and vibrant among Muslims than perhaps anywhere else in the world.

That discussion happens in multiple forms. In the American Muslim entertainment sector, well-known artists include comedian Azhar Usman and independent filmmaker, Musa Syeed. Azhar Usman has gained global recognition as one of the top American-Muslim standup comedians. Usman is one of the co-founders of Allah Made Me Funny, the longest-running artistic collective of Muslim comic performers. The group wrote and starred in the concert film, *Allah Made Me Funny: Live in Concert*.[72] Fellow American Muslim comedian Dave Chappelle served as an executive producer of the film.[73] Musa Syeed's work has been featured in the Sundance and Tribeca Film Festivals, and he has created documentaries for PBS.[74]

"Rock star" imams—that is, imams with huge and hugely devout followings—like Khalid Latif, Suhaib Webb, and Hamza Yusuf, are doing essential work in creating an authentic American Islam—one that is fully Islamic and fully American. In so doing, these religious leaders are drawing from the American constitutional heritage and broad rights to religious freedom. They are reconceptualizing Islam and Islamic practice in the framework of American freedoms, and, even more importantly, are able to do so free from state control.

Imam Khalid Latif is the Muslim chaplain for New York University (NYU), Executive Director of the Islamic Center at NYU, and the Muslim chaplain for the New York Police Department. Inspired by the American cultural heritage of religious diversity and freedom, he has dedicated himself to intra- and interfaith work, fostering a strong Muslim community that values inclusiveness and understanding of others, and promoting greater dialogue and mutual education among people of other faiths. One of his most important accomplishments has been cultivating the Islamic Center at NYU as a space "for young American Muslims to celebrate their unique identity and have their voices heard in the larger public sphere."[75] Reflecting his wide appeal, Latif was invited to appear on the popular satirical news show *The Colbert Report*, in a segment called "Fear for All."[76]

Suhaib Webb is a contemporary American-Muslim educator, activist, and lecturer, and the current Imam of the Islamic Society of Boston Cultural Center (ISBCC), the largest Islamic center in New England. "His work bridges classical and contemporary Islamic thought, addressing issues of cultural, social and political relevance to Muslims in the West."[77] He advocates for an American Muslim identity that reflects the true nature of Islam and the Qur'an, as well as the customs and culture of the United States. Webb hopes to establish one of the first Muslim seminaries in order to nurture a new generation of Islamic scholars and leaders, who are "orthodox, but culturally conversant and civically involved."[78]

Webb follows in the footsteps of Sheikh Hamza Yusuf, a leading American Islamic scholar and co-founder and current president of Zaytuna College, the first four-year Muslim liberal arts college in the United States. Yusuf is one of the leading advocates for classical learning in Islam, and promotes the study of Islamic sciences and classical teaching methods around the world.[79] Zaytuna combines the liberal arts with an education in traditional Islamic disciplines, providing an education that places Islam in the context of American culture and offering its students principles for balancing American and Muslim culture in their lives:[80]

"The college's very existence in America repudiates notions of Islam as an exclusively Eastern ideology. Its presence instead indicates that Islam and Muslims can be authentically American, and can contribute to the nation's sociological, political and cultural advancement."[81]

Alongside the Sunni figures discussed above are prominent public figures and scholars from the Shia and Ahmadiyya communities, including Eboo Patel, Dr. Abdulaziz Sachedina, Professor Omid Safi, and Qasim Rashid. Dr. Ebrahim 'Eboo' Patel is the founder and president of Interfaith Youth Core (IFYC), an international nonprofit organization that models a service learning methodology that engages young people from various faith communities in interfaith community service projects, fostering cooperation and developing an understanding about how to live peacefully with one another. His work is woven with values common to both Islam and American civic culture: "public service, religious freedom, and pluralism."[82] Inspired by his multiple identities from his Islamic faith, Indian heritage, and American citizenship, Patel believes that religion is a bridge, rather than a barrier, to cooperation.[83]

Others in the Shia and Ahmadiyya community have not only drawn from the U.S. constitutional heritage, they explicitly advocate for it to the broader Muslim community. Dr. Abdulaziz Sachedina has been at the forefront of religious freedom advocacy; he "affirms freedom of conscience and religion through an inclusive theology grounded in universal moral guidance."[84] His reinterpretations of Shi'a doctrinal positions have, however, proved controversial. In 1998, Ayatollah Sistani criticized Sachedina's scholarship as tainted by "the influence of Western orientalis[m]."[85]

Qasim Rashid, an outspoken leader in the Ahmadi community, has conducted a grassroots campaign in Wisconsin to educate Americans about Islam as a peaceful religion.[86] He cites Prophet Muhammad's example when it comes to issues regarding religious freedom, and exhorts American Muslims to recognize the privilege of freedom of expression they take for granted in the United States and to educate themselves on those principles and America's foreign policy.[87]

In the pursuit of authentic expressions of American Muslim identity, several interpretations and fusions have emerged, among them an Islamic Punk style exemplified by Michael Muhammad Knight. Knight's novel, *The Taqwacores*, inspired "Taqwacore, a sub-genre of punk music dealing with Islam, its culture, and interpretation":

> The name is a portmanteau of hardcore and the Arabic word Taqwa, which is usually translated as "piety" or the quality of being "God-fearing," and thus roughly denotes fear and love of the divine. The scene is composed mainly of young Muslim artists living in the US and other western countries, many of whom openly reject traditionalist interpretations of Islam, and thus live their own lifestyle within the religion or without.[88]

Another fusion identity formed from subcultures blended with Islam is Mipsterz. Fusing "Muslim" and "Hipster," Mipsterz is an identity that is attuned to the avant-garde and obscure in culture. In 2013, the Mipsterz culture was suddenly thrust into the spotlight when the video "Somewhere in America" went viral. Set to hip-hop artist Jay-Z's song "Somewhere in America," the video depicts a group of young, hipster, Muslim women who wear *hijab* "posing artistically around an urban landscape" and having fun.[89] The video sparked a firestorm of controversy on the Internet among American Muslims. As one critic pointed out,

> In the name of fighting stereotypes it seems we're keen to adopt—especially for Muslim women who wear headscarves—tools and images that objectify us (either as sexualized or desexualized; as depoliticized or politicized) rather than support us where we need that support. We're so incredibly obsessed with appearing "normal" or "American" or "Western" by way of what we do and what we wear that we undercut the actual abnormality of our communities [*sic*] and push essentialist definitions of "normal," "American" and "Western." In that process of searching for the space of normalcy, we *create* "normal" and through that a "good" Muslim. And in all of this, we might just lose that which makes us unique: our substance.[90]

The debates around the Mipsterz video questioned what it meant to be Muslim and what it meant to be American/Western. An idea that emerged was that the cultural clash is not with westernization, but with "westoxification," a term used by Professor Ahmed Fardid from the University of Tehran "to describe the wholesale imitation of modern, capitalist, post-religious Western values and culture at the expense of other worldviews."[91] Indeed, the American constitutional heritage has given American Muslims the tools not just create to an authentic American Islam, but also to realize the limits of such a project, to the extent "Americanization" means giving up values (like modesty) that are considered central to Islam.

CONCLUSION

Drawing from the U.S. constitutional heritage, American Muslims have accomplished tremendous things—and learned a great deal about their faith. Their success is rooted in a sense of ownership: American Muslims have embraced their American identity to create an authentic American Islam. And while America has given Muslims the tools to understand various interpretations of their faith, Muslims, too, have been important contributors to America's social and religious diversity.

This success has far-reaching implications. Using their own experiences as evidence of how broad freedoms can lead to spiritual flourishing and a more authentic relationship with one's faith, American Muslims are well positioned to serve as ambassadors to the rest of the world, especially Muslim-majority countries where their co-religionists are not afforded similar rights. Contrary to common fears in these countries, the American Muslim experience demonstrates that religious freedom does not lead to a dilution of faith but, often, a renewed vibrancy.

NOTES

The author would like to thank Firdaus Arastu for her assistance with this chapter.

1. Yvonne Yasbeck Haddad, *Not Quite American? The Shaping of Arab and Muslim Identity in the United States* (Waco, TX: Baylor University Press, 2007).

2. Pew Research Center/Forum on Religion and Public Life, *The Future of the Global Muslim Population: Projections for 2010–2030* (Washington, DC: Pew Research Center, 2011), http://www.pewforum.org/files/2011/01/FutureGlobal MuslimPopulation-WebPDF-Feb10.pdf; Ihsan Bagby, *The American Mosque 2011: Basic Characteristics of the American Mosque; Attitudes of Mosque Leaders,*

Report Number 1 from the U.S. Mosque Study, 2011 (Washington, DC: Council on American-Islamic Relations, January 2011).

3. The Pew Forum on Religion and Public Life report, *Mapping the Global Muslim Population: A Report on the Size and Distribution of the World's Muslim Population* (Washington, DC: Pew Research Center, 2009); Allen D. Hertzke, "The United States of America: American Muslim Exceptionalism," in *The Borders of Islam: Exploring Huntington's Faultlines, from Al-Andalus to the Virtual Ummah.* ed. Stig Jarle Hansen, Atle Mesoy, and Tuncay Kardas (London: Hurst, 2009), 271–287.

4. Hertzke, "The United States," 271–287 (see n. 3).

5. The Muslim West Facts Project, *Muslim Americans: A National Portrait: An In-depth Analysis of America's Most Diverse Religious Community* (The Gallup Center for Muslim Studies, 2009).

6. Bagby, *The American Mosque 2011* (see n. 2).

7. The Pew Forum on Religion and Public Life, "Portrait of Muslims—Demographics," in *U.S. Religious Landscape Survey* (Washington, DC: Pew Research Center, 2008), http://religions.pewforum.org/pdf/report-religious-landscape-study-full.pdf.

8. The Muslim West Facts Project, *Muslim Americans* (see n. 5).

9. Abu Dhabi Gallup Center report, *Muslim Americans: Faith, Freedom, and the Future* (Gallup, 2011), file:///C:/Users/Rosanne/Desktop/MAR_Report_ADGC_en-US_071911_sa_LR_web.pdf.

10. Ibid.

11. "Zuhdi Jasser does not belong on USCIRF," *Muslim Public Affairs Council,* http://www.mpac.org/programs/government-relations/dc-news-and-views/zuhdi-jasser-does-not-belong-on-uscirf.php#.UwJyHZi7ZyM; "'Religious Freedom' Rep says No to Muslims' Rights in Military," *Muslim News Magazine,* http://muslimnewsmagazine.tv/muslim%20military%20rights.html.

12. Aseal Tineh, "Why the American Muslim Community Should Be Concerned about Zuhdi Jasser," *CAIR-Chicago,* http://www.cairchicago.org/2012/07/24/why-the-american-muslim-community-should-be-concerned-about-zuhdi-jasser/#sthash.mhdBDhPJ.dpuf.

13. "CAIR's Attack on Dr. Zuhdi Jasser Resembles a Desperate Schoolyard Bully," *American Islamic Forum for Democracy,* http://aifdemocracy.org/january-30-2014-national-muslim-organization-tries-to-silence-opposition-cairs-attack-on-dr-zuhdi-jasser-resembles-a-desperate-schoolyard-bully/.

14. Hertzke, "The United States ," 271–87 (see n. 3).

15. Abu Dhabi Gallup Center report, *Muslim Americans* (see n. 9).

16. Wajahat Ali, Eli Clifton, Matthew Duss, Lee Fang, Scott Keyes, and Faiz Shakir, *Fear, Inc.: The Roots of the Islamophobia Network in America* (Center for American Progress report, August 2011).

17. Ibid.; Abu Dhabi Gallup Center report, *Muslim Americans* (see n. 9).

18. Greg Myre, "Boston Bombings Point to Growing Threat of Home-grown Terrorism," The Two-Way, *National Public Radio*, http://www.npr.org/blogs/thetwo-way/2013/04/20/177958045/boston-bombings-point-to-growing-threat-of-homegrown-terrorism.

19. Center for Religious Freedom, *Saudi Publications on Hate Ideology Fill American Mosques* (Washington, DC: Freedom House, 2005), http://www.freedomhouse.org/sites/default/files/inline_images/Saudi%20Publications%20on%20Hate%20Ideology%20Invade%20American%20Mosques.pdf.

20. 42 U.S.C. § 2000cc-1 *et seq.* The statutory text provides, in part:

No government shall impose or implement a land use regulation in a manner that imposes a substantial burden on the religious exercise of a person, including a religious assembly or institution, unless the government demonstrates that imposition of the burden on that person, assembly, or institution—(A) is in furtherance of a compelling governmental interest; and (B) is the least restrictive means of furthering that compelling governmental interest. . . .

No government shall impose or implement a land use regulation in a manner that treats a religious assembly or institution on less than equal terms with a nonreligious assembly or institution. . . .

No government shall impose or implement a land use regulation that discriminates against any assembly or institution on the basis of religion or religious denomination.

21. 840 F.2d 293 (5th Cir. 1988).

22. 96 A.D.2d 536 (N.Y. App. Div. 1983)

23. CIV.A. 06-CV-3217PGS, 2007 WL 2904194 (D.N.J. Oct. 1, 2007)

24. Summary judgment is a procedural term of law used by a court to decide a case without having a complete trial. "Summary judgment" is granted if there are no material facts in dispute that would cause the judge or jury in the trial to rule against the party asking for such a judgment.

25. Lucas L. Johnson II, "Order to Hault Murfreesboro Mosque Denied," *Knoxville News Sentinel*, November 18, 2010, http://www.knoxnews.com/news/2010/nov/18/order-to-halt-murfreesboro-mosque-denied/.

26. "Justice Department Stands Behind Controversial Tennessee Mosque," *CNN U.S.*, October 18, 2010, http://www.cnn.com/2010/US/10/18/tennessee.mosque/.

27. Mark Bellinger. "Justice Department Enters Murfreesboro Mosque Controversy," *News Channel 5*, October 18, 2010, *http://www.newschannel5.com/story/13343278/feds-file-legal-brief-in-support-of-murfreesboro-mosque*.

28. Ibid.

29. "Murfreesboro Mosque Breaks Ground," *CNN*, September 29, 2011, http://religion.blogs.cnn.com/2011/09/29/murfreesboro-mosque-breaks-ground/.

30. 558 F.3d 542, 551 (D.C. Cir. 2009). Neither the term "Muslim" nor "Islam" exists in the court's opinion; only peripheral research reveals the firefighter's religious persuasion.

31. Ibid., 544.

32. Ibid., 546.

33. Ibid., 551. The court did, however, hint that had the District been less clumsy in presenting evidence, they would have defeated summary judgment. Ibid., 552 (Williams, J. concurring).

34. 170 F.3d 359 (3d Cir. 1999).

35. Ibid., 366.

36. Salahuddin v. Goord, 467 F.3d 263, 269 (2nd Cir. 2006).

37. Ibid., 584.

38. Ibid., 593–94.

39. 521 F.3d 306 (4th Cir. 2008).

40. Ibid., 316.

41. Ibid., 318.

42. The author's discussion of anti-sharia laws has been taken from the author's previous work, Asma T. Uddin and Dave Pantzer, "A First Amendment Analysis of Anti-Sharia Laws," *First Amendment Law Review* 10 (Winter 2012).

43. Ibid., 27–28.

44. Ibid.

45. Ali et al., *supra* note 1, at vi.

46. Anver Emon, "Banning Shari'a," Religion & American Politics, *The Immanent Frame*, http://blogs.ssrc.org/tif/2011/09/06/banning-shari%E2%80%98a/.

47. H.R. 1056, 52d Leg., 2d Reg. Sess. (Okla. 2010), https://www.sos.ok.gov/documents/questions/755.pdf. The final text of the State Question that appeared on the ballot read as follows:

STATE QUESTION NO. 755

LEGISLATIVE REFERENDUM NO. 355

This measure amends the State Constitution. It changes a section that deals with the courts of this state. It would amend Article 7, Section 1. It makes courts rely on federal and state law when deciding cases. It forbids courts from considering or using international law. It forbids courts from considering or using Sharia Law.

International law is also known as the law of nations. It deals with the conduct of international organizations and independent nations, such as countries, states and tribes. It deals with their relationship with each other. It also deals with some of their relationships with persons.

The law of nations is formed by the general assent of civilized nations. Sources of international law also include international agreements, as well as treaties.

Sharia Law is Islamic law. It is based on two principal sources, the Koran and the teaching of Mohammed.

SHALL THE PROPOSAL BE APPROVED?

FOR THE PROPOSAL—YES

AGAINST THE PROPOSAL—NO

48. Complaint Seeking a Temporary Restraining Order and Preliminary Injunction at 1, *Awad v. Ziriax*, 754 F. Supp.2d 1298 (W.D. Okla. 2010) (No. CIV–10–1186–M), *aff'd*, No. 10–6273, 2012 WL 50636 (10th Cir. Jan. 10, 2012).

49. Ibid.

50. Brief for Plaintiff, *supra* note 143, at 44.

51. Ibid., 22–23.

52. *Awad v. Ziriax*, 754 F. Supp.2d 1298 (W.D. Okla. 2010) (No. CIV–10–1186–M), *aff'd*, No. 10–6273, 2012 WL 50636 (10th Cir. Jan. 10, 2012); Awad v. Ziriax, 670 F.3d 1111, 1119 (10th Cir. 2012).

53. The author's discussion of civil society responses has been taken from the author's previous work, Asma t. Uddin and Haris Tarin, "*Rethinking the "Red Line": The Intersection of Free Speech, Religious Freedom, and Social Change*" (Washington, DC: Brookings Institution Publications, November 2013, U.S.-Islamic World Forum working group paper).

54. See Heidi Ewing and Rachel Grady, "The Public Square," *The New York Times*, December 16, 2012, http://www.nytimes.com/2012/12/17/opinion/the-public-square.html?_r=0; "Dude, you have no Quran!" *YouTube* video, posted by "01dh4k," September 13, 2010, http://www.youtube.com/watch?v=U2-KgBhslBQ; "Dude, you have no Quran!" *Know Your Meme* video, http://knowyourmeme.com/memes/dude-you-have-no-quran; BartBaKer, "Dude You Have No Quran AUTOTUNE REMIX," *YouTube* video, September 15, 2010, retrieved May 30, 2013, from http://www.youtube.com/watch?v=4HX5-ulcdXc.

55. Justin Elliott, "How the 'Ground Zero Mosque' Fear Mongering Began," *Salon*, August 16, 2010, http://www.salon.com/2010/08/16/ground_zero_mosque_origins/; Pamela Geller, (Director), "The Ground Zero Mosque: The Second Wave of the 9/11 Attacks," *YouTube* video, https://www.youtube.com/watch?v=6IkbW17AAyw; See also Tanya Somander, "Pam Geller: Park51 Is 'The Second Wave Of The 9/11 Attack,'" *ThinkProgress*, November 24, 2010, http://thinkprogress.org/politics/2010/11/24/131936/pam-geller-park51/.

56. Cathy Young, "Fear of a Muslim America," *Reason Foundation*, July 18, 2011, retrieved May 30, 2013, from http://reason.org/news/show/1011931.html.

57. Joe Tacopino, "Newt Gingrich comes out against planned Cordoba House mosque near Ground Zero," *Daily News*, July 22, 2010, retrieved May 30, 2013, from http://www.nydailynews.com/new-york/newt-gingrich-planned-cordoba-house-mosque-ground-zero-article-1.200446; Rush Limbaugh, "Why This Mosque on This Spot?" *The Rush Limbaugh Show*, August 17, 2010, retrieved May 30, 2013, from http://www.rushlimbaugh.com/daily/2010/08/17/why

this_mosque_on_this_spot; Joel Siegel, "Sarah Palin 'Refudiates' Ground Zero Mosque," *ABC News*, July 19, 2010, retrieved May 30, 2013, from http://abcnews.go.com/US/sarah-palin-takes-twitter-oppose-ground-mosque/story?id=11194148#.UaeHKUCsiSo.

58. "Mosque Plan Clears Hurdle in New York," *New York Times*, August 4, 2010, http://www.nytimes.com/2010/08/04/nyregion/04mosque.html?pagewanted=all&_r=0.

59. Following strong support of the project by Mayor Bloomberg, national leaders such as President Obama, former President Bill Clinton, Senator Orrin Hatch (R-UT), and many local New York officials also expressed support for the project based on religious freedom grounds.

60. Nick Wing, "Ted Olson, Former Bush Solicitor General and Husband of 9/11 Victim, Backs Obama on 'Ground Zero Mosque,'" *The Huffington Post*, August 18, 2010, http://www.huffingtonpost.com/2010/08/18/liz-cheneys-keep-america-_n_686697.html.

61. Stephanie Ebbert, "Patrick Backs NYC Mosque Plan," *The Boston Globe*, August 5, 2010.

62. Shoulder-to-Shoulder, http://shouldertoshouldercampaign.org/.

63. Umar Faruq Abd-Allah, "Islam and the Cultural Imperative," *Islam and Civilisational Renewal* 1, no. 1 (Special Issue: Islam and Pluralism, 2009):10–26.

64. Qamar-ul Huda, "The Diversity of Muslims in the United States: Views as Americans," Special Report 159, *United States Institute of Peace*, February 2006, http://www.usip.org/sites/default/files/sr159.pdf.

65. "About," *American Muslim Civic Leadership Institute*, http://crcc.usc.edu/initiatives/amcli/about.html.

66. "AIC's Story," *American Islamic Congress*, http://www.aicongress.org/aicstory/.

67. "About Us," *Cordoba Initiative*, http://www.cordobainitiative.org/about-us/; Huda, "The Diversity of Muslims" (see n. 64).

68. "About Us," *Inner-City Muslim Action Network*, http://www.imancentral.org/about/.

69. Muqtedar Khan, "Is Muslimwakeup.com Undermining the Progressive Muslim Movement?" *Ijtihad*, May 2, 2009, http://www.ijtihad.org/Muslimwakeup.htm.

70. "About," *Muslim Matters*, http://muslimmatters.org/about/; Qibla, https://qibla.com/

71. "Introducing AltMuslimah: Exploring Both Sides of the Gender Divide," *AltMuslimah*, http://www.altmuslimah.com/b/a_mission; Sally Steenland, "Exploring Gender and Islam: An Interview with Asma Uddin," Young Muslim American Voices series, *Center for American Progress*, October 5, 2010, http://www.americanprogress.org/issues/religion/news/2010/10/05/8463/exploring-gender-and-islam/.

72. "About," *Allah Made Me Funny*, http://www.allahmademefunny.com/about/index.html.

73. "'Allah Made Me Funny—The Official Muslim Comedy Tour' to Be Made into Feature-Length Concert Film," *Market Wired*, July 24, 2007, http://www.marketwired.com/press-release/Allah-Made-Me-Funny-The-Official-Muslim-Comedy-Tour-Be-Made-Into-Feature-Length-754294.htm; Elizabeth McQuern, "Dave Chappelle Produces Chicago's Azhar Usman in 'Allah Made Me Funny,'" *The Apiary*, August 24, 2007, http://www.theapiary.org/thebastion/2007/8/24/dave-chappelle-produces-chicagos-azhar-usman-in-allah-made-m.html.

74. "Bio," *Musa Syeed*, http://musasyeed.com/.

75. "Khalif Latif (imam)," *Wikipedia*, http://en.wikipedia.org/wiki/Khalid_Latif_(imam).

76. "Fear for All Pt. 1" and "Fear for All Pt. 2," *The Colbert Report*, Episode 789, October 28, 2010, http://www.colbertnation.com/the-colbert-report-videos/363665/october-28–2010/fear-for-all-pt—1 and http://www.colbert-nation.com/the-colbert-report-videos/363666/october-28–2010/fear-for-all-pt—2.

77. *Suhaib Webb.com*, http://www.suhaibwebb.com/.

78. Lisa Wangness, "In Life And Words, Muslim Leader Bridges Cultures," *The Boston Globe*, May 12, 2013, http://www.bostonglobe.com/metro/2013/05/11/imam-william-suhaib-webb-emerges-face-boston-muslim-community-time-crisis/Kd8v0O48vkHSZAnOpYCqOI/story.html.

79. "About: Hamza Yusuf," *Sandala*, https://sandala.org/About-Hamza-Yusuf.

80. Lonny Shavelson, "America's First Muslim College Opens This Fall," *Voice of America*, August 2, 2010, http://www.voanews.com/content/americas-first-muslim-college-opens-this-fall-99831529/162074.html; "Why Zaytuna College," *Zaytuna College*, http://www.zaytunacollege.org/about/.81; Shazia Kamal, "Zaytuna College: A Sign of Hope for Islam. *OnFaith*, September 29, 2010, http://www.faithstreet.com/onfaith/2010/09/29/zaytuna-college-a-sign-of-hope-for-islam/4031.

82. Fellows: Eboo Patel, *Ashoka*. http://usa.ashoka.org/fellow/eboo-patel.

83. "About IFYC: Eboo Patel," *IFYC* (Interfaith Youth Core), http://www.ifyc.org/about-us/eboo-patel.

84. John Musselman, "American Muslims: A (New) Islamic Discourse On Religious Freedom," *The Review of Faith & International Affairs* 9, no. 2 (2011): 17–24.

85. Abdulaziz Sachedina, "What Happened in Najaf?" http://islam.uga.edu/sachedina_silencing.html.

86. Samuel Freedman, "Persecuted Muslim Sect Uses Brochure Campaign to Push for Peace," *New York Times*, August 6, 2010, http://www.nytimes.com/2010/08/07/us/07religion.html

87. "Archive for the 'Publications' Category," The Official Website of Qasin Rashid, http://qasimrashid.com/category/publications/; Qasim Rashid, "Why Muslims Hate America," *OnFaith*, September 21, 2012, http://www.faithstreet.com/onfaith/2012/09/21/why-muslims-hate-america/11762.

88. "Taqwacore," *Wikipedia*, http://en.wikipedia.org/wiki/Taqwacore.

89. Aicha Lasfar, "Somewhere in America, Muslim Women are Being Judged," *Muslim Link*, December 5, 2013, http://www.muslimlink.ca/editorial/opinions/somewhere-in-america-muslim-women-are-being-judged.

90. Sana Saeed, "Somewhere in America, Muslim Women are 'Cool,'" *Islamic Monthly*, December 2, 2013, http://www.theislamicmonthly.com/somewhere-in-america-muslim-women-are-cool/

91. Brendan Behrmann, "The 'Mipsterz' Video Debacle: Westernization vs Westoxification," *AltMuslimah*, December 10, 2013, http://www.altmuslimah.com/b/spa/4873.

Contributors

Roger Finke is Professor of Sociology and Religious Studies at the Pennsylvania State University and Director of The Association of Religion Data Archives (www.theARDA.com). He is the past president of three major professional associations and has served as a member of multiple national and international councils and boards.

Finke has coauthored two award-winning books with Rodney Stark: *Acts of Faith: Explaining the Human Side of Religion* (University of California Press, 2000) and *The Churching of America, 1776–2005* (Rutgers University Press, 1992; 2005). His two most recent books are *The Price of Freedom Denied: Religious Persecution and Violence* with Brian Grim (Cambridge University Press, 2011) and *Places of Faith: A Road Trip Across America's Religious Landscape* with Christopher P. Scheitle (Oxford University Press, 2012). Dr. Finke established an online religion archive in 1998: *theARDA.com.* The archive was named one of the 30 Best Free Reference Websites in 2010 by a division of the American Library Association.

Steven K. Green is Fred H. Paulus Professor of Law and Director, Center for Religion, Law & Democracy, at Willamette University. Professor Green joined the Willamette faculty in August 2001, after serving for ten years as legal director and special counsel for Americans United for Separation of Church and State, a Washington, D.C., public interest organization that concentrates on First Amendment issues.

Professor Green has extensive litigation and appellate experience in First Amendment law involving issues such as school prayer, public funding of religious institutions, public religious displays, religious discrimination, religious free exercise, and freedom of speech. He has participated in several cases before the U.S. Supreme Court, including *Zelman v. Simmons-Harris* (2002), the Cleveland school vouchers case; *Mitchell v. Helms* (2000), authorizing state-paid computers and educational equipment to religious schools; and *Santa Fe Independent School District v. Doe* (2000), striking prayer at public school football games. He regularly submits *amicus curiae* (friend-of-the-court) briefs at the U.S. Supreme Court. In addition, Professor Green has significant legislative experience, having testified before Congress and several state legislatures. He helped draft federal and state laws affecting religious liberty interests, including the Religious Freedom Restoration Act (1993), the Religious Land-Use and Institutionalized Persons Protection Act (2000), and the Oregon Workplace Religious Freedom Act (2009).

Professor Green is a widely sought speaker at national conferences and a prolific author whose writings have been cited by the U.S. Supreme Court and lower courts. He is the author of *The Bible, the School, and the Constitution: The Clash that Shaped Modern Church–State Doctrine* (Oxford University Press, 2012) and *The Second Disestablishment: Church and State in Nineteenth Century America* (Oxford, 2010); coauthor of *Religious Freedom and the Supreme Court* (Baylor University Press, 2008); and a contributor to the *Encyclopedia of American Civil Liberties* and the *Yale Biographical Dictionary of American Law*. He is currently writing a new book on religion and the nation's founding.

Professor Green holds a PhD in American constitutional history and an MA in American religious history from the University of North Carolina, a JD from the University of Texas, and a BA in history and political science, Phi Beta Kappa, from Texas Christian University. He also took postgraduate study at Duke Law and Divinity Schools.

Professor Green serves on the public policy board of Ecumenical Ministries of Oregon and the board of directors of the American Constitution Society, Oregon chapter. He also serves on the editorial council of the *Journal of Church and State* and the legal advisory committee of the National Center for Science Education. He previously served on the religious liberty committee of the National

Council of Churches and as recorder for the Oregon Law Commission's study of the faith-based initiative in Oregon.

Professor Green teaches constitutional law, first amendment law, legal history, the lawmaking process, administrative law, and criminal law. In 2006, Professor Green received the Robert L. Misner Award for Excellence in Scholarship, which was established in memory of former College of Law Dean and Professor Robert L. Misner. Professor Green also received the 2003 Professor of the Year Award for Teaching. Dr. Green's email is sgreen@willamette.edu.

Kyle Harper is Senior Vice President and Provost, Director of the Institute for the American Constitutional Heritage, and Professor in Classics and Letters at the University of Oklahoma (OU).

A historian of the classical world, Harper graduated summa cum laude with a degree in letters from OU and then received his PhD in history from Harvard University in 2007. A revised version of his dissertation was published by Cambridge University Press as *Slavery in the Late Roman World, AD 275–425*. The book was awarded the James Henry Breasted Prize by the American Historical Association and the Outstanding Publication Award from the Classical Association of the Middle West and South. His second book, *From Shame to Sin: The Christian Transformation of Sexual Morality*, was published by Harvard University Press in 2013. Dr. Harper's research has focused on the social and economic history of the period spanning the Roman Empire and the early Middle Ages. His current work on the environmental and population history of the first millennium explores the impact of climate change and disease on the history of civilization.

In 2009 Dr. Harper was appointed founding director of the Institute for the American Constitutional Heritage, an interdisciplinary center for the study of constitutionalism. The Institute has rapidly grown into a center for teaching, research, and public engagement. In 2013 Dr. Harper was named OU's Senior Vice Provost, in which capacity he plays a crucial role in maintaining excellence in OU's curriculum and advancing OU's mission in a digital world. He recently created and introduced *Freedom.ou.edu*, an OU website featuring a weekly series of short lectures on constitutional law and constitutional history, making civic education available to anyone at any time.

Dr. Harper teaches a range of courses on Greek and Roman history, early Christianity, late antiquity, and ancient law. His email is kyleharper@ou.edu.

Charles C. Haynes is director of the Religious Freedom Center of the Newseum Institute in Washington, D.C. He writes and speaks extensively on religious liberty and religion in American public life.

Dr. Haynes is best known for his efforts to find common ground on First Amendment conflicts in public schools. Over the past two decades, he has been the principal organizer and drafter of consensus guidelines on religious liberty in schools, endorsed by a broad range of religious, civil liberties, and educational organizations. He is author or coauthor of six books, including *First Freedoms: A Documentary History of First Amendment Rights in America* (Oxford University Press, 2006) and *Finding Common Ground: A First Amendment Guide to Religion and Public Schools* (First Amendment Center, 2002). His column, Inside the First Amendment, appears in more than 200 newspapers nationwide.

Dr. Haynes is currently Chairman of the Character Education Partnership Board of Directors, serves on the Steering Committee of the Campaign for the Civic Mission of Schools, and chairs the Committee on Religious Liberty. He is U.S. Advisor for Face to Faith, a program of the Tony Blair Faith Foundation.

Dr. Haynes is the recipient of numerous honors, including the Emory University Medal in 2005, the First Freedom Award from the Council for America's First Freedom in 2008, and the Religious Liberty Award from the North American Religious Liberty Association in 2013. He holds a BA from Emory University, a master's degree from Harvard Divinity School, and a doctorate from Emory University. His email is chaynes@newseum.org.

Allen Hertzke is David Ross Boyd Professor of Political Science at the University of Oklahoma (OU) and Faculty Fellow in Religious Freedom for OU's Institute for the American Constitutional Heritage.

Dr. Hertzke is a Distinguished Senior Fellow for the Institute for Studies of Religion at Baylor University and Senior Scholar for Georgetown University's Religious Freedom project. He is author of *Representing God in Washington*, an award-winning analysis of religious lobbies, which has been issued in a Chinese language translation;

Echoes of Discontent, an account of church-rooted populist movements; and *Freeing God's Children: The Unlikely Alliance for Global Human Rights;* he is coauthor of *Religion and Politics in America,* a comprehensive text now in its fourth edition. He is editor of *The Future of Religious Freedom: Global Challenges* (Oxford University Press, 2013).

A frequent news commentator, Dr. Hertzke has been featured in such outlets as the *New York Times, Washington Post, Wall Street Journal, London Times, Time Magazine, New Republic, USA Today, Christian Science Monitor, Los Angeles Times, San Francisco Chronicle, Weekly Standard, BBC World Service, Sveriges Radio* (Swedish public radio), *PBS,* and *National Public Radio.* He has held positions in Washington, D.C., as visiting scholar at the Brookings Institution, and Senior Fellow at the Pew Forum on Religion & Public Life, where he directed the study "Lobbying for the Faithful: Religious Advocacy Groups in Washington, D.C." Between 2008 and 2010 he served as lead consultant, first for the Pew Charitable Trusts and then the John Templeton Foundation, to develop strategic recommendations for advancing religious freedom around the globe.

A winner of numerous teaching awards, Dr. Hertzke has lectured at the National Press Club, the U.S. Holocaust Memorial Museum, the Council on Foreign Relations, the Carnegie Council on Ethics and International Affairs, Harvard University, Princeton University, Georgetown University, the University of Notre Dame, the University of California–Berkeley, Calvin College, Wheaton College, and Baylor University, and before numerous audiences in China. He serves on the editorial boards of the *Oxford Journal of Law and Religion* and *The Review of Faith & International Affairs,* for which he served as guest editor for a special edition (Fall 2012) on strategies of advocacy for religious freedom. In May of 2012 he was selected to the Pontifical Academy of Social Sciences. From 2008 to 2009, he was a visiting senior research fellow at the Pew Research Center's Forum on Religion & Public Life, where he served as the primary researcher for the Pew Forum's November 2011 report *Lobbying for the Faithful: Religious Advocacy Groups in Washington, DC.*

Hertzke holds a BA from Colorado State University, an MS from Cornell University, and a PhD from the University of Wisconsin–Madison. His email is ahertzke@ou.edu.

254 CONTRIBUTORS

Thomas S. Kidd is Professor of History at Baylor University and Senior Fellow at Baylor's Institute for Studies of Religion.

Dr. Kidd's most recent book is *George Whitefield: America's Spiritual Founding Father* (Yale University Press, 2014). He is also the author of *Patrick Henry: First Among Patriots* (Basic Books, 2011) and *God of Liberty: A Religious History of the American Revolution* (Basic Books, 2010). His first book, *The Protestant Interest: New England after Puritanism*, was published by Yale University Press in 2004. *The Great Awakening: The Roots of Evangelical Christianity in Colonial America* was published by Yale in late 2007; he won a 2006–2007 National Endowment for the Humanities Fellowship to support *The Great Awakening*. His document reader *The Great Awakening: A Brief History with Documents* was published by Bedford Books in 2007. *American Christians and Islam* (Princeton University Press) was published in 2008. Dr. Kidd has published articles in *The William and Mary Quarterly*, *The New England Quarterly*, *Church History*, and *Religion and American Culture*. He writes for the Anxious Bench blog at *Patheos.com*. He also regularly contributes for outlets such as *The Gospel Coalition*, *WORLD Magazine*, and *USA Today*.

Dr. Kidd won a 2010 Baylor University Outstanding Professor Award, was selected for the 2004–2005 Young Scholars in American Religion program, and won a 2004 National Endowment for the Humanities Summer Stipend. Dr. Kidd received a BA and an MA at Clemson University. He came to Baylor University in 2002 after completing a PhD in history at the University of Notre Dame, where he worked with George Marsden. He teaches courses on colonial America, the American Revolution, and American religious history. Find him on Facebook at www.facebook.com/thomas.kidd and on Twitter @ThomasSKidd. His email is Thomas_Kidd@baylor.edu.

Robert Martin is an Assistant Professor of Sociology at Southeastern Louisiana University.

Dr. Martin received his PhD in sociology in 2013 from The Pennsylvania State University and was a research associate at The Association of Religion Data Archives from 2009 to 2013. His dissertation, "Faith in the Balance? An Evaluation of the Outcomes of Religious Free Exercise Claims in the State Appellate Courts, 1997–2011," explores the legal and social bases of disparities in outcomes of free exercise cases in state courts.

Vincent Phillip Muñoz is the Tocqueville Associate Professor of Political Science and Concurrent Associate Professor of Law at the University of Notre Dame. He serves as Director of Notre Dame's undergraduate minor in Constitutional Studies and Notre Dame's Tocqueville Program for Inquiry into Religion and Public Life.

Dr. Muñoz writes and teaches across the fields of constitutional law, American politics, and political philosophy with a focus on religious liberty and the American founding. His first book, *God and the Founders: Madison, Washington, and Jefferson* (Cambridge University Press, 2009) won the Hubert Morken Award from the American Political Science Association for the best publication on religion and politics in 2009 and 2010. His First Amendment church–state case reader, *Religious Liberty and the American Supreme Court: The Essential Cases and Documents* (Rowman & Littlefield, 2013) is being used at Notre Dame and other leading universities. His email is vmunoz@nd.edu.

Rajdeep Singh joined the Sikh Coalition in December 2009 and serves as its Director of Law and Policy, in which position he focuses on developing and promoting policy solutions for civil rights issues through an interdisciplinary combination of government affairs, media relations, and interfaith coalition building. In this capacity, he has substantively engaged with the U.S. Congress, the White House, and several federal agencies, including the Department of Justice, Department of Homeland Security, and Department of State; appeared on numerous television and radio programs; delivered dozens of presentations at government agencies, law schools, and universities; and designed an advocacy training program for grassroots community volunteers.

In recent years, Rajdeep has spearheaded and managed successful campaigns to expand federal hate crime tracking; repeal an 87-year-old Oregon law that prohibited public school teachers from wearing religious dress; and pass historic equal employment opportunity legislation in California that protects religious observers from workplace segregation.

Rajdeep has a background in bank regulation and is the author of *The Application of the Religious Freedom Restoration Act to Appearance Regulations that Presumptively Prohibit Observant Sikh Lawyers from Joining the U.S. Army Judge Advocate General Corps*, published by the *Chapman Law Review* in 2007, and *How State Photo Identification Standards Can Be Used to Undermine Religious Freedom*, published by the *Asian American Law Journal* at the University of California–Berkeley Law School in 2012. He received his law degree in 2006 at the College of William & Mary and his undergraduate degree in philosophy in 2003 at the University of Miami. Rajdeep is a member of the Florida Bar.

Harry F. Tepker, Jr., is Floyd and Irma Calvert Chair in Law and Liberty and Professor of Law at the University of Oklahoma (OU) College of Law.

Professor Tepker is the first member of the OU law faculty to appear, argue, and win a case before the U.S. Supreme Court. In 1987, the Court appointed Tepker as counsel for petitioner, an indigent juvenile sentenced to death, in *Thompson v. Oklahoma, 487 U.S. 815* (1988). It was the first case in which an American court overturned a death sentence on constitutional grounds because the condemned was too young at the time of the crime.

Professor Tepker has had a wide range of university and professional service, including chair of the university Faculty Senate; two-time chair of the campus Tenure Committee; secretary for the American Bar Association Section on Labor and Employment Law; historian of the Tenth Circuit Historical Society; and professor-in-residence for the U.S. Equal Employment Opportunity Commission (EEOC). During his tenure with the EEOC, he represented the agency in U.S. Supreme Court cases concerning university academic freedom in Title VII cases (*University of Pennsylvania v. EEOC, 493 U.S. 182* [1990]) and pension benefit plans under the federal age discrimination statute (*Public Employee Retirement System v. Betts, 492 U.S. 158* [1989]).

Tepker is the author of many law review articles and has earned numerous university teaching awards, including the University of Oklahoma Regents Award for Superior Teaching and the Merrick Foundation Award. In September 1998, the Regents of the University of Oklahoma named Professor Tepker as the first Calvert Chair of Law and Liberty. He teaches courses in the areas of constitutional law, employment law, and equal employment opportunity. Professor Tepker is a 1973 graduate of Claremont Men's College. He earned his law degree in 1976 from Duke University. He is a member of the

Order of the Coif, Phi Beta Kappa, and the American Bar Association. Before joining the OU faculty, he practiced law for five years, specializing in labor and employment issues, as an associate with the Los Angeles firm of Gibson, Dunn & Crutcher. His email is rtepker@ou.edu.

Asma T. Uddin is Counsel for the Becket Fund for Religious Liberty, Washington, D.C., and Founder and Editor-in-Chief of *AltMuslimah.com*, a web magazine dedicated to issues on gender and Islam. A 2005 graduate of the University of Chicago Law School, she was a member of the *University of Chicago Law Review*.

As the primary attorney for Becket's Legal Training Institute, Uddin works with local partners around the world to train advocates, lawyers, judges, religious leaders, journalists, and students in religious freedom law and principles. She has also traveled throughout Europe and to various countries in the Middle East, North Africa, and Southeast Asia to research regional issues and provide critical training for minority faith communities as well as politicians, journalists, and human rights organizations. As Legal Counsel, she has defending religious liberty in the United States through several prominent cases at The Becket Fund. Her work at *AltMuslimah* has earned wide recognition. The *Huffington Post*'s Senior Religion Editor, Paul Brandeis Raushenbush, noted, "*AltMuslimah.com* is important because it gives a specific platform to the intersections between gender, belief and well-being in Islam—all with superior levels of intellect and writing. The internet would be the poorer without *AltMuslimah* as a destination and font of knowledge for seekers of all religious backgrounds." Uddin also helped edit the book *A Muslim in Victorian America*, which was published in 2007 by Oxford University Press. She also served as an Associate Editor and legal columnist for *Islamica Magazine*. Uddin was an expert panelist for the former *Washington Post* religion blog, *On Faith*, and is currently a contributor to *Huffpost Religion*, CNN's *Belief Blog*, *Comment Is Free* at the *Guardian*, *Al Jazerra*, and *Common Ground News*. She speaks widely on issues of gender and faith, and national and international religious freedom. Her work has been published in the *Rutgers Journal of Law and Religion*, *The Review of Faith & International Affairs*, *St. Thomas University Law Journal*, the *Chicago-Kent Law Review*, and the *First Amendment Law Review*, and by Ashgate Publishers and several prominent university presses. Asma is currently co-editing a book of personal essays on women and religious experience, and guest-editing a special issue of *The Review of Faith & International Affairs*.

Robin Fretwell Wilson is the Roger and Stephany Joslin Professor of Law and Director of the Program in Family Law and Policy at the University of Illinois College of Law.

Professor Wilson joined the University of Illinois in the fall of 2013 from Washington & Lee School of Law, where she was the Class of 1958 Law Alumni Professor of Law and the Law Alumni Faculty Fellow for 2011–2012. A graduate of the University of Virginia School of Law, she served on the Editorial Board of the Virginia Law Review. After law school, Professor Wilson clerked for the United States Court of Appeals for the Fifth Circuit and prac-ticed at Fulbright & Jaworski, LLP, and Mayor, Day, Caldwell & Keeton, LLP, prior to teaching.

A specialist in Family Law and Health Law, Professor Wilson's research and teaching interests also include Insurance and Biomedi-cal Ethics. Professor Wilson is the editor or author of seven books, including *Same-Sex Marriage and Religious Liberty: Emerging Conflicts* (Rowman & Littlefield Publishers, Inc., 2008, with Douglas Laycock and Anthony A. Picarello); *Reconceiving the Family: Critique on the American Law Institute's Principles of the Law of Family Dissolution* (Cambridge University Press, 2006); and *Health Law and Bioethics: Cases in Context* (with Sandra Johnson, Joan Krause, and Richard Savor, 2009). Her articles have appeared in the *Cornell Law Review*, *Emory Law Journal*, *North Carolina Law Review*, *San Diego Law Review*, and *Washington and Lee Law Review*, as well as in numerous peer-reviewed journals. Named Professor of the Year by the W&L Women Law Student Organization in 2008, Professor Wilson is a member of the American Law Institute. In 2010, she was ranked in the Top 10 Family Law Scholars in the United States in Scholarly Impact. Professor Wilson's work has been featured in the *New York Times, Wall Street Journal*, National Public Radio's *All Things Consid-ered, Washington Post, Los Angeles Times, U.S. News & World Report, ABA Journal, Chronicle of Higher Education, Chicago Tribune, CNN Headline News, Good Morning America, ABC News, CBS News, Philadelphia Inquirer*, and *Essence Magazine*, among others.

Professor Wilson is the past chair of the Section on Family and Juvenile Law of the Association of American Law Schools (AALS) and of the AALS's Section on Law, Medicine and Health Care. Professor Wilson has also worked extensively on behalf of state law reform efforts. In 2007, she received the Citizen's Legislative Award for her work on changing Virginia's informed consent law. She may be reached at wils@illinois.edu.

Index

Equal Protection Clause, 177, 179,
183; as applied to same-sex
unions, 180, 182
Ervin, Sam, 69–70
Establishment Clause, 54, 55, 65,
123, 210; Clarence Thomas's view
of, 170–72, 176–77; "secular
purpose" rule for, 60
Evangelicals, and deists, 34–35
Everson v. Board of Education, 54,
55, 65

Face to Faith, 124–25
Fardid, Ahmed, 239–40
Farr, Thomas, 6
Finke, Roger, 16, 107
First Amendment, 9, 10, 11, 17, 18,
40, 65, 69, 175, 189–90n62, 190n64;
and public education, 117–30.
See also free exercise of religious
freedom; religious freedom
First Amendment Center, 128, 129
Fitzgerald, Tami, 198n65
Flag Salute cases, 11
FlyRights (mobile phone app), 203
Focus on the Family, 127
Forbes, J. Randy, 193
Fourteenth Amendment, 15, 69, 171,
177, 178, 186n45
Fox, Jonathan, 93, 112
France: and tensions with the U.S.,
48. *See also* French Revolution
Frankfurter, Felix, 14
Franklin, Benjamin, 72
*Fraternal Order of Police Newark Lodge
No. 12 v. City of Newark*, 229
Free Exercise Clause, 53, 55, 97,
171–72, 182, 231–32
free exercise of religious freedom:
cases involving, 16–17, 91–93,
97–102, 103–11, 156–57; com-
pelling interest test as applied to,
16–17, 18, 55, 92, 98–99,

100–102, 109–10; consequences
of rulings on, 93–97, 111–12;
debates over, 8–9; for religious
minorities, 103–7; in state
constitutions, 101–2; state courts'
handling of cases, 107–11, 115n52;
strict scrutiny as applied to,
13–19, 92, 111
French Revolution: American
response to, 46; anti-Christian
aspects of, 43–44

Gaffney, Frank, 230
Galston, William, 11
Gay, Lesbian & Straight Education
Network (GLSEN), 127
gay marriage. *See* same-sex marriage
Geary Act (1892), 196
*George v. International Society for
Krishna Consciousness*, 111–12
Gill, Anthony J., 112
Gingrich, Newt, 233
*Gonzales v. O Centro Espirita
Beneficente Uniao do Vegetal*, 100
Graham, Billy, 69
Green, David, 18–19
Green, Steven K., 7
Griffin, Leslie, 5–6, 17
Griswold v. Connecticut, 187n56
Guinness, Os, 118

Hall, Mark David, 72
Hamburger, Philip, 17, 72, 73
Hamowy, Ronald, 174
Hare Krishnas, 111–12
Harrington, Kevin, 204
Harris, William T., 83–84
Hastert, Dennis, 197
Hastings, Selina (Countess of
Huntingdon), 41–42
Haynes, Charles, 10
Helsinki Accords, 24
Henry, Betsey, 43–44